ORGANIZING FOR POWER AND EMPOWERMENT

Empowering the Powerless: A Social Work Series
Alex Gitterman, Series Editor

*The Empowerment Tradition in American
Social Work: A History*
Barbra Levy Simon

Empowering the Powerless: A Social Work Series
Alex Gitterman, Series Editor

ORGANIZING FOR POWER AND EMPOWERMENT

Jacqueline B. Mondros

Scott M. Wilson

Columbia University Press
New York

Columbia University Press
New York   *Chichester, West Sussex*

Copyright © 1994 Columbia University Press

Library of Congress Cataloging-in-Publication Data

Mondros, Jacqueline B.
Organizing for empowerment / Jacqueline B. Mondros, Scott M. Wilson.
p.   cm.—(Empowering the powerless)
Includes bibliographical references and index.
ISBN 0-231-06718-6—ISBN 0-231-06719-4 (pbk.)
1. Community organization—United States.   2. Social action—United States.
3. Social service—United States.   I. Wilson, Scott M.   II. Title.   III. Series.
HN65.M58   1994
361.2'0973—dc20   93-31676
CIP

⊗
Casebound editions of Columbia University Press books are
printed on permanent and durable acid-free paper.

Printed in the United States of America
c 10 9 8 7 6 5 4 3 2 1

For

Betty and Allen Mondros

Jacob and Neil McGuffin

Betty and Harry Wilson

and Lucy Wilson

CONTENTS

EDITOR'S NOTE

Organizing for Power and Empowerment is the second book in Columbia University Press's new social work series, Empowering the
Powerless. The conventional and perhaps tired wisdom is that power
corrupts and absolute power corrupts absolutely. Social workers struggling to provide services to vulnerable and oppressed populations have
come to know and understand that powerlessness also corrupts and
absolute powerlessness corrupts absolutely. It corrupts because oppressed people who must cope with the psychological and social states
of powerlessness often turn their rage against themselves, or against
their families and neighbors. Many respond with chronic apathy and
despair. As public and private human service budgets are slashed, and
caseloads increased to unmanageable levels, staff, like clients, become
overwhelmed and feel powerless because of the magnitude of needs
and the limited resources to meet them. Such powerlessness leads to
hopelessness and despair, often called burnout, and may cause staff to
turn on each other and/or their clients.

In these social and organizational contexts the limited attention in
social work education to community organizing is a distressing reality.
Many social work schools have abandoned community organizing
content, replacing it with increased emphasis on person change content, and have, in doing so, become part of the problem. Much of this
mournful state of affairs has been attributed to conservative political
times. It is hardly mitigated by the fact that many of us have profes-

sionally "grown up" to be uncomfortable with community organizing content. When I was a social work student I recall my own considerable discomfort with community organizing literature. Its tendency to use successful change outcomes to justify manipulative membership recruitment and motivational processes was bothersome.

What makes this book unique is the authors' equal attention to the *processes* as well as the *outcomes* of community organizing. Mondros and Wilson discerningly emphasize that when community members are honestly and fully involved in organizing processes, they will be better able to pursue and even successfully attain power. The authors elucidate this basic premise step by step in a brilliant exposition of organizing concepts and vivid case materials showing how to involve constituencies in experiencing the subjective state of feeling empowered and, simultaneously, how to organize members to gain actual power to bring about change in policies and programs.

For social worker administrators, practitioners, and educators committed to an empowerment philosophy, this is indeed a timely book. It provides knowledge and methods to help people to attain and accrue power. Social work education should include and systematically present this vital content. I recommend this book for adoption in generalist, foundation, clinical, and fields of practice courses. I am pleased as well as proud to present the book, and confident that it will make a significant contribution to the profession's literature.

Alex Gitterman
Series Editor

PREFACE

This is a book about social action organizations, and the way ordinary citizens build organizations in an attempt to gain power and bring about some change in policies and programs. It is also about the way people's involvement in social action organizations influences their views of themselves and their ability to make change.

American social action organizations have a long history, and indeed are one of the distinctive features of our polity. In 1832 de Tocqueville described the general tendency of democracy as a mindless and peaceful process by which citizens isolate themselves from all others, willingly leaving society at large to its own resources. As de Tocqueville (1969) saw it, individualism "at first saps the virtues of public life; but in the long run . . . is at length absorbed in downright egotism" (507). Although he viewed this process to be intrinsic to democracy, aristocracy, and despotism, he found it absent in America. The Americans, de Tocqueville observed, only avoided this consequence because of their free institutions and tradition of active citizenship, defined as a public virtue born of enlightened self-interest. de Tocqueville wrote,

> The free institutions of the United States, and the political rights they enjoy there provide a thousand continual reminders to every citizen that he lives in society. At every moment they bring his mind back to this idea, that it is the duty as well as the interest of men to be useful to their fellows. Having no particular reason to hate oth-

ers, since he is neither their slave or their master, the American's heart easily inclines toward benevolence. At first it is of necessity that men attend to the public interest, afterward by choice. What had been calculation becomes instinct. By dint of working for the good of his fellow citizens, he in the end acquires a habit and a taste for serving them. (512–513)

Indeed, American history is replete with examples of such free institutions that promote "active citizenship," people pursuing change through the organization and institutionalization of power. These groups include labor unions, civil rights organizations, farmers' groups, antiwar and antiimperialism groups, women's rights organizations, welfare mothers' associations, pro-choice and pro-life groups. These groups have grappled with, and had influence on, major issues of American life, and they have kept the democratic argument vital. Tocquevillians argue that these groups have performed a socially corrective function that has enabled this country to avoid potential decadence.

Following in the Tocquevillian tradition, the recent work of Bellah, Madsen, Sullivan, Swidler, and Tipton (1985, 1991) reexamines Americans values and instincts related to these free institutions. In *Habits of the Heart* (1985) Bellah and his colleagues observe that Americans no longer join such collectives. They assert that the value of individualism has superseded regard for collectivity. In *The Good Society* (1991) the authors attribute this trend to Americans' fundamental ambivalence toward social institutions and the concern they have about the limitations such entities place upon their autonomy. Yet, in both works, the authors note that the people they interviewed consistently articulate that something is missing in their individually pursued lives.

One indeed might observe that progressive social action organizing has greatly diminished since the sixties, when public funding ran out and public sentiment turned inward. Media attention points to active organizing now being done on the right of the political spectrum. With economic, political, and social supports in decline, with increased apathy and hopelessness, with the move to mobility through individualism, today's progressive social action organizing is viewed by some as little more than an anachronism. Such pessimism would support the views of Bellah et al.

Other recent writers on organizing, however, have noted a rise in organized social activism (Boyte 1989, Mott 1986, Weisner 1983, Wenocur and Reisch 1986). In fact, the daily media carries many stories about small organizing efforts. Evening television frequently reports some local effort to save a supermarket or stop a toxic waste dump or resist an effort to use a port as a base for missiles. Politicians and theorists alike lament how difficult it is to enact legislation given the proliferation of organized single issue interest groups. National pro-choice advocacy groups are again getting a great deal of media attention. A number of organizing efforts have emerged in response to the AIDS epidemic. Perhaps most innovative are new organizations with international agendas that attempt to influence international diplomatic or economic relations. The best examples of this innovation are the various organizations that have worked to condemn apartheid, pressure the United States to change its political agenda and South Africa to change its economic and social system. These recent examples of people organizing around an issue in pursuit of rearranging power and causing change suggest the persistence of de Tocqueville's vision of America and Americans.

Social action organizations remain a persistent part of the American scene even at a time when funding and positive public sentiment for progressive causes seem to be diminished. If, as Bellah et al. argue, contemporary Americans articulate the need for such associations while simultaneously rejecting them, it behooves us to understand people's ambivalence. Then we may know how such organizations can fulfill people's search for collectivity, how they can counter people's ambivalence and engage them in a way that allows them to use such institutions in pursuit of a common good. Finally, if such organizations do, in fact, counter a trend to the decay of active social and political involvement of citizens, then we should understand how to enhance them and use them to stimulate the debate about our collective future. These are the questions and preoccupations that animated this book.

The fact that so little is known about these organizations, their organizers, and members, led us to do an exploratory study. Beginning in 1984 we selected forty-two East Coast community organizations, analyzing for variations among them and discovering common themes. A discussion of the methods used in the study is offered in the appendix. The findings of this study underlie the description of social action organizing presented in this book.

Design of the Book

A basic struggle we faced was how to tell the reader about social action organizations. We found that merely reporting the findings of our study failed to convey the rich practice wisdom and insights we uncovered. Yet we did not want to restrict ourselves to a few examples or "war stories" because we wanted to demonstrate the variety of experiences confronting these organizations and the breadth of choices available to them. We wanted to show how principles of organizing could be employed in similar organizations that wish to effect change. Hence, we have chosen to let the various organizers and leaders we interviewed speak for themselves, and we have used their quotes, experiences, and stories to elucidate the practice principles. We have also included practice illustrations from our own work and that of others. Consequently, the reader is exposed not only to us and to our thinking but to forty-two organizers and forty-two leaders as well.

Our second problem was the currency of examples we have chosen to include. The issues of local organizing efforts, such as tenant rights and health problems, transcend time. They endure and remain relevant. But the issues of national and statewide organizations are often generated out of national events, and quickly seem dated. Yet these issues often spurred important organizing, and are excellent examples of organizing principles. Therefore, we use current examples as much as possible (recognizing that they too will soon seem dated) and explain more fully the older examples we felt it was important to include.

Our third dilemma was how best to order these insights on social action organizations. Most texts describe organizing in developmental terms, and we agree that to a certain extent organizing can be viewed as a developmental process. Brager and Specht (1973), for example, describe the developmental process of building an organization, noting that there are both expressive and technical tasks at each developmental stage. By focusing on the developmental process, however, they are constrained from addressing the technical and expressive tasks in detail, a discussion we deem necessary. Staples (1984) attempts to solve this problem by first describing the steps involved in building a new social action organization and later discussing certain organizing tasks in greater depth. This arrangement, however, does not treat these important tasks in the context of an organizing process.

A developmental approach is particularly applicable to the establishment of a new organization. When the organizer creates the organization, is the "pioneer" with whom people first have contact, and is the initial person to unearth, discern, and identify possible issues, the organizing process may be somewhat predictable. Yet a developmental process doesn't tell the whole story of these organizations. The nature of the work depends very much on the organization the organizer enters, the current state of its membership, leadership, and issues, and the social and political events surrounding the organizer's arrival. Even in a new organization organizers must determine whether there is an urgent and compelling issue that must be addressed or whether a process of issue identification is needed. They must also determine whether to involve more people before identifying issues or begin with the small group at hand.

The process is even more complicated when the organizer enters an established organization. In these cases the well-being of the organization, the existence and skills of established leaders and members, current issues and workloads, and the social context must be considered. Does an organizer in this situation begin by developing leadership, identifying and/or addressing a new issue, or continuing a campaign? These are complex decisions, and ones not attended to in a standard organizing process.

We organized the book in a way that we felt would best deliver a message about how social action organizations pursue and apply power, accurately representing the dynamic interchange of organizers, leaders, and organizations, and allowing us to examine the technical and expressive tasks in detail. While the book follows a standard developmental process of organizing best applied to new organizations, whenever appropriate we refer to what might be different in established organizations and at times direct the reader to a related topic discussed elsewhere in the book.

Consequently, in the initial chapter we set forward the assumptions and definitions that shape our view of organizing as exercising power. This chapter serves to orient each of the other chapters as they further detail the work of organizing.

In chapter 2 we examine the organizers as principal actors in the organization, tackle some of the technical issues they face, then address how they work with members and leaders. Much of this book is devoted to what we learned about organizers in investigating these issues: their backgrounds, their training, their beliefs, and their motivation to organize. We describe the way they perceive themselves, their ideologies and styles, and the way they are viewed by their leaders. We look at similarities and differences between their job descriptions, daily activities, and their professed skills. We address questions of stress, burn-out, and support systems.

We next examine (in chapters 3 and 4) the members and leaders who constitute social action organizations—their interests, values, knowledge, skill, and socioeconomic characteristics. We describe their relationships with the organizer and the organization, and how members perceive organizational processes and tasks. We consider who becomes active in social action organizations and why, addressing such issues as what would motivate a person to join a group to fight for low-income housing when its construction could just as likely benefit nonparticipants (O'Brien 1975, Olsen 1965).

We look at how organizational structure affects the recruitment of members. We also examine why people stay involved in social action organizations, how organizers try to retain members' activism, how roles and tasks are assigned, how leaders are developed, and how an esprit de corps emerges. We explore how the organizer builds consensus and mitigates dissension, builds a sense of common fate, develops commitment to the organization, and protects it against internal destruction. We show how these processes are influenced by members, and how the members themselves view them.

We then address the process of organizing itself—moving through issues, strategy and tactics, action implementation, and victories. In chapter 5 we deal with the question of how issues are generated, how they are selected, and how priorities are set. We go on to describe ways in which issues are developed by research—how they are linked to one another or to larger issues—and examine values about tackling new issues and multiple issues simultaneously. Viewing organizational strategy and tactics as the way in which an organization pursues its issues—in effect, the way in which they pursue power—we describe the general change strategies employed by social action organizations, the genesis of strategies and tactics, how they are chosen, and the criteria used to select them. We also consider how targets are identified and pursued and the ways in which organizations set and review goals.

In chapters 6 and 7 we examine how strategy is developed and then implemented and describe the various roles organizers, leaders, and members assume during the action phase. This separation into two chapters underlines the importance of separating the planning of strategy and tactics from actual action and its meaning for organizers and other participants.

In an attempt to expand on a generally little-examined area we discuss, in chapter 8, how social action organizations define, evaluate, and communicate their successes both to members and to the general public. We consider the importance of victory in social action organizations, how success is defined and measured, and address arguments made on means versus ends in organizing.

Next, in chapter 9, we discuss the decisions organizers face about the structure, composition, staffing, and funding of their organizations. We examine the organizations themselves, including such areas as the age of the organization, the geographic domain of the organizing (local through national), the size, composition, and structure of membership, organizational goals, the size and composition of staff, and funding patterns. Here we also address the role played by ideology in these organizations, their goals for change, their definition of change agent (i.e., what actors or forces can effect change), the stimulus for action, and finally the type and amount of opposition they face and how opposition affects the organizing.

Finally, in chapter 10, we discuss current approaches to organizing. We summarize how power building is conceptualized and implemented in various models. In closing, we make what we hope are helpful suggestions for future practice as organizers struggle to find new answers in a different and challenging political climate.

There is nothing sacrosanct about the organization of the book, and we hope our readers will not feel bound by it. Therefore readers may want to read those chapters that are of pressing concern to them and their organization. For example, readers who are currently involved in a campaign may want to read the strategy chapters first. If the organization is experiencing trouble recruiting new supporters, the chapters on members and leaders may be of initial interest.

While clearly our intention is to be helpful to organizers, we hope that the book will be useful to other professionals and activists as well. Organizing is essentially a means of recruiting and engaging people in a process of generating or supporting a plan or a proposal for change. As such the principles of organizing can be useful to those who find themselves involved in task groups, coalitions, political campaigns, or those simply trying to make change within a social service agency or a corporation. Agency administrators and employees struggling with budget cuts can use the ideas here either to attempt to influence funding sources or to engage the staff in making the decisions about what and where the cuts should be made. Further, these ideas can often be employed in clinical settings. For example, a clinician who works with a group of homeless mothers used these techniques to help them organize for repairs and police protection in a park where they frequently took their children. She saw this work as a natural extension of her clinical work with her group. Our hope is that our work will encourage and enhance such innovative practice.

ACKNOWLEDGMENTS

The words, hopes, and wisdom of many organizers and leaders of social action organizations are represented in this book. Our heartfelt thanks goes out to those who took hours of their precious time to share their knowledge and ideas with us. They include, in Albany, Fred Greisbach and Kim Hopper of Coalition on the Homeless, New York State Office; Carol Reichert and Esther Lewis of Family Planning Advocates of New York State; and Laurie Nichols and Mary Young of the Student Association of the State University; Mary Jean DeSandes and Joan Ross of Community of Neighborhood Organizations in Allentown, Pennsylvania; Evelyn Slaght and Paul Pittman of Maryland Committee for Children in Baltimore; in Boston, Tony Palumbo and Sheila Walsh of Boston Mobilization for Survival; Mary Quinn and Dottie Stevens of Coalition for Basic Human Needs; Chris Leonard and Angie Wilkerson of Massachusetts A.C.O.R.N.; and Jennifer Jackman and Ellen Kassimer of National Organization for Women, Massachusetts chapter; Stephanie Joyce and Helen Kaufman of Suffolk Action Coalition in Long Island, New York; Dennis Hanratty and Joe Ruffin of Mount Vernon United Tenants in Mt. Vernon, New York; Jim Lanard and Bill Goldfarb of New Jersey Environmental Lobby in New Brunswick; Steve Weingarten and Al Boyer of Coalition for People in New Haven; Lynn Ide and Marian McLaughlin of Connecticut Citizen Action Group in Hartford; Mercedes Gallagher and Terry Gabriel of Del-AWARE in New Hope, Pennsylvania; in New

York City, Ron Hanft and Charlie Blanc of the American Friends Service Committee/New York Metropolitan Region; Ken Grossinger of Human Serve; Chris Graber and Lucy Santiago of Interfaith Community Concerns of the Lower East Side; Mike McGee of the New York State Neighbors and Tenants Coalition; Gene Russianoff and Helmut Lesold of New York Public Interest Research Group, Inc.; Roger Hayes, Jim Buckley, and Ann Deveney of Northwest Bronx Community-Clergy Coalition; Felice Jurgens and Adam Veneski of People's Fire House; David Schilling and Marjorie Horton of Riverside Disarmament Group; Angel Garcia and Carmen Silva of South Bronx People for Change; and Ed Heveman and Susan Davidoff of War Resister's League; Ellen Ziff and Maria Perry of United Passaic Organization in Passaic, New Jersey; Ira Resnick and Hector Rivera of Patterson Interfaith Communities Organization of Patterson, New Jersey; in Philadelphia, Bob Wendelgass and John Boyle of Action Alliance for Senior Citizens; Chris Sprowal and Leona Smith of the Committee for Dignity and Fairness for the Homeless; Mike Casey and Ben Stahl of Farm Labor Organizing Committee; Debbie Fischetti and Elsie Mariani of Kensington Action Now; John Dodds and Cardell Johnson of Philadelphia Unemployment Project; Belinda Mayo and Jean Finkelstein of Tenant Action Group; and Robin Robinowitz and Ronnie McPhearson of Women's Alliance for Job Equity; Mark Friedman and Steve Dorsey of Speaking for Ourselves, Inc. in Plymouth Meeting, Pennsylvania; Sandy Johnson and Harvey Flad of Hudson River Sloop Clearwater, Inc. in Poughkeepsie, New York; Denise Smith and John Scunzio of Injured Workers of Rhode Island in Providence; in Washington, D.C., Paul Marchand and Elizabeth Boggs of the Association for Retarded Citizens; Mary Ann Buckley and Van Gosse of the Committee in Solidarity with the People of El Salvador; Enid Kassner and Virginia Beverly of National Anti-Hunger Coalition/Food Research and Action Center; Sue Hyde and Frances Hanckel of National Gay and Lesbian Task Force; Debra Ness and Carol Werner of National Abortion Rights Action League; Monica McFadden and Kathy Wilson of National Women's Political Caucus; and Jim Dickson and Al Raby of Project Vote.

When you write a book about organizing, you can make many enemies. To them, our thanks for providing some of the recent examples included herein.

When it takes ten years to write a book you also accumulate debts to many friends who have provided help and support. Columbia University Press kept faith with the project. Drew Akason, George Brager,

Steve Holloway, and Neil McGuffin offered many insightful comments about organizing practice that have found their way into and richly enhanced our manuscript. Alex Gitterman urged specificity and practice examples and Irving Miller patiently gave sound advice on organization and language. Their contributions advanced the literacy and accessibility of the book. Finally, we could not have endured ten years writing without the loyalty, support, patience, and gentle prodding of our families; we are deeply beholden to Neil and Jacob McGuffin and Lucy Wilson. We promise to immediately start taking out the trash and cooking dinner.

ORGANIZING FOR POWER AND EMPOWERMENT

CHAPTER ONE

Social Action Organizations and Power

The groups people organize to attain power we call social action organizations. Such an organization we define as a self-generated (as opposed to legally mandated) association of people organized to wrest power resources from established individuals and institutions and create change. This goal of transferring power from the "establishment" to themselves distinguishes these groups from those who wish only to transfer functions or tasks, to improve morale, or to plan (Grosser and Mondros 1985). These organizations purport to be more than friendship or mutual aid networks. They seek to achieve consistency, i.e., that members feel empowered, that the organization and members pursue concrete activities to achieve power, and that the organization, ultimately, has power.

Our principal assumption, therefore, is that the accumulation and wielding of power is the primary goal of social action organizations, whether they define themselves by common geography or shared culture and issues (Effrat 1974). The goal of amassing power may be explicit or implicit; it may spur the organizing initially or come as a result of trying to make a change. For example, a neighborhood organization that attempts to get a stoplight on a busy corner or a national organization that attempts to influence nuclear testing policy begin working on a concrete issue. Subsequently, these organizations discover that they must amass power in order to realize their goals. Other organizations form with the explicit notion that in order to make change on any issue they must first accrue power. For example, a neighborhood organization may be organized to pursue influence so that it can change many aspects of community life and a group of welfare recipients will organize a strong association before it undertakes any issue related to welfare rights.

Before we offer our own analysis of power and its relationship to social action organizing, we think it is important to review the rich traditions of research and theory that inform the study of social action organizing.

Theoretical Traditions

For those who are interested in social action organizations and their pursuit of power, there is a rather wide and useful literature to study. The sociological, historical, and political science literature offers analyses that attempt to explain the roots of social protest or offer case studies of how influence is manifested in a city or around an issue in order to deduce theories about power. There is little in these bodies of analysis, however, directed to application, i.e., how one uses these theories to organize.

Social work literature provides typologies that describe various types of organizations and practice texts that give insightful advice to the organizing practitioner. The social work literature generally assumes the concept of power without placing it at the center of exposition and analysis. In our attempt to fuse an understanding of power and protest with an appreciation of organizing practice, we find both types of literature make important contributions.

The literature that informs social action organizing basically takes one of four distinct paths. First, there is the literature that comprises theoretical debate over the origins of societal discontent (McAdam, McCarthy, and Zald 1988, Rule 1988). Such theories attempt to explain the social context that generates social protest. Writers such as Smelser (1969) and Gurr (1970) argue the relative deprivation tradition of protest, i.e., people protest when times are relatively prosperous or when they are most desperate. Others support resource mobilization theory, which suggests that protest occurs when people have access to resources they can use to create change (McCarthy and Zald 1977, Walsh 1981, Wilson and Orum 1976). There are others who argue that protest emerges from either source, or from both simultaneously (Kerbo 1982).

There have also been some valuable attempts to apply theoretical notions of influence to decision making in the real world. The literature on community power, best exemplified by the work of Dahl (1961), Dahrendorf (1959), and, most recently, Crenson (1971), though choosing to focus on how power works in a municipality, does refer to community organization attempts at influence. This theoretical literature, while very valuable in its effort to suggest what motivates social action and what effects influence, is less suggestive of the process of acquiring influence and seldom proposes specific practical guidelines to would-be activists.

Second, there is a very small body of literature that seeks to classify and compare community organizations either by structure or style. Probably most notable in this group is Rothman's (1970) article, "Three Styles of Community Organization Practice," which classifies all organizations into social planning, locality development, or social action. Rothman sees building power as a goal of social action organizations, and attempts to define the characteristics of these organizations. Grosser and Mondros (1985) also define various types of community organizations, categorizing social action organizations as "power transfer organizations." Fisher (1984) also distinguishes between community organizing models. Gerlach and Hine's book *People, Power, Change* (1970) is important in that they offer several major variables (structure, commitment, and ideology) through which organizations pursue their objectives, which they test in two large social movements. While power plays a central, albeit sometimes implicit, role in all these topologies, the organization and its operations—how it handles its task of power building—are not explored in detail. Consequently, this literature does not offer explicit help to organizers.

Third, there is a literature that describes organizational campaigns and social protest movements. Piven and Cloward's *Poor People's Movements* (1977), Goodwyn's *The Populist Moment* (1978), Fisher's *Let the People Decide* (1984), Sale's *SDS* (1974), and Garrow's *Bearing the Cross* (1986) all fit in this category. We also place here such works as Susser's *Norman Street* (1982), Wellstone's *How the Rural Poor Got Power* (1978), Hertz's *The Welfare Mothers Movement* (1981), and Ecklein's *Community Organizers* (1984) that are among the strongest accounts of recent organizing efforts. Even some biographies may be included here, most notably Alinsky's biography of John L. Lewis (1949) and two biographies of Saul Alinsky (Fink 1984, Horwitt 1989). Acquiring power is a central theme in all these works; it acts as a backdrop concept for all organizational activities and work. In almost every case, however, the concept of power is only a background element, not explicated or explored. Conclusions are not drawn about what these organizations can teach us about power and power building, nor is there any attempt to generalize from these organizations to others that would attempt to make change. Readers are left to draw their own inferences about how these organizations pursued power, and practicing organizers must deduce how the lessons learned might help them in their day-to-day work.

The final category consists of a fairly extensive literature, gleaned from practice wisdom, that describes organizing skills. Social work has contributed such texts as Grosser's *New Directions in Community Organization* (1976), Brager and Specht's *Community Organizing* (1973), Spiegel and Mittenthal's *Neighborhood Power and Control* (1968), Burghardt's *The Other Side of Organizing* (1982b), and Rubin and Rubin's *Community Organization and Development* (1986). Following in the tradition of Alinsky (1972, 1974), organizers Si Kahn (1992) and Lee Staples (1984) have written texts on skills for organizers and leaders. A myriad of pamphlets about how to offer passive resistance, how to organize a demonstration, how to operate a subscription campaign have been published and sold by organizations themselves. These are, of course, written for the practitioner and so are, despite the absence of generalizability, enormously helpful to organizers.

These books also assume that community organizations are essentially efforts at empowerment. Many texts propose this explicitly; however, they do not make clear how each skill, each knowledge area, and each assumed value is connected to this fundamental premise about empowerment. The skill apparently may be learned and practiced apart from any theoretical construct about power, suggesting that the organizer's baggage has no unifying purpose. As "practice wisdom," this literature is very important, but it cannot be construed to be more than that.

In even such a cursory review of the literature it is apparent that the theoretical and conceptual literature and the practical literature do not intersect or cohere. For the most part, the former does not apply theories of power and protest to practice and the latter is mostly reticent on the subject of organizing as applied power. In idiosyncratic case studies and texts of insightful practice wisdom the issue of power is not placed at the center of exposition and analysis. Consequently, skill and action are only weakly linked to practice theory or more fundamental conceptions of power and influence, and the lessons learned are not generalized to other organizing efforts. Knowledge about social action organizing could be greatly advanced by a union of the conceptual and practical literatures.

As in any work of this type, we have had to make some theoretical and definitional choices in order to pursue our task. These decisions necessarily suggest certain assumptions and biases about social action organizations, organizing, organizers, and leaders and members, and we need to say directly what these assumptions are.

Assumptions and Definitions

An understanding of organizing requires probing and scrutinizing its practice by inquiring what organizers and members of social action organizations actually do to acquire and wield power.

As the concept of power is central to our work, it is necessary to define what we mean by it. We accept Weber's definition of power as "the ability to recognize one's will even against the resistance of others" (Gerth and Mills 1946:180). Weber's definition makes two points. First, power does not necessarily come from formal sanctions granted by authority; it can spring from many other sources such as wealth, knowledge, cultural norms, coercion, and numbers (Rossi 1969). Second, Weber's definition clearly implies that power is an outcome measured by the extent to which another's activities conforms to one's preferences. Some theorists use the term influence to describe the process of accruing, gaining, and exercising power to distinguish between outcomes and process (Holloway and Brager 1989). Other authors have used the term empowerment to suggest this process (Mondros, in press). Unfortunately, the term *empowerment* has become common parlance in the rhetoric of academicians and politicians, and applied hopefully—but not always critically—in attempts to characterize widely diverse behaviors. Such usage undermines a clear sense of the term. Its clear definition is necessary in any work that uses power as a central construct.

To us, *power* connotes both a process by which it is attained (i.e., the concrete activities one pursues to exercise influence) and an outcome (i.e., actual power measured by the extent to which another's activities conform to one's preferences). We think it is important to make a distinction between actual power and the feeling of being powerful. Empowerment, we believe, refers to a psychological state—a sense of competence, control, and entitlement—that allows one to pursue concrete activities aimed at becoming powerful. Freire (1968, 1973) describes what we agree are the components of empowerment.

It is probably psychologically possible for one to pursue power and attain it without feeling empowered. Conversely, it is frequently the case that a person can feel empowered, i.e., competent, "in command," and entitled, without pursuing concrete activities to enhance one's power or without having power. Consistency is achieved when one feels powerful, works to attain influence, and enjoys a relative degree of actual power.

People, especially middle-class and professional people, frequently feel empowered, and their rank, status, and resources may allow them to have episodic influence in limited spheres. If they discover that they don't have sufficient influence to affect change in the larger social context on broad issues of social concern, they may form groups to generate sufficient power to make a change (Holloway and Brager 1989). On the other hand, poor people who lack status and resources frequently feel powerless and are incapable of exerting even episodic influence. Consequently, they must form groups to gain even sporadic and limited spheres of influence. In these examples, it is the numbers of people who support a social action organization that is the organization's source of power.

At some point, all social action organizations come to have notions about power, and their operations reflect this. As we will see, they may have very different views about who has power and how difficult it is to get, how it is obtained, and how it is pursued. They have different understandings about potential resources, such as numbers of people or expertise that can be brought to bear, and have different ideas about the ways in which the social, political, and economic environment affect the timeliness of their efforts. Despite their other differences, they share an important aim—to become powerful enough to effect certain changes in the larger environment. In seeking change they simultaneously seek power itself.

Because the field of action we looked at is so vast, and still quite uncharted, we had to organize and focus our investigation. We drew on studies of organizing and our own thinking to develop a comprehensive framework that we felt would capture the essential elements of the organizing process. The boundary dimensions were 1. the organizer, 2. the leaders and members of the organization, 3. the organizing process, and 4. the organization. Each of these dimensions includes elements of the larger economic, social, and political context that influence these internal dimensions of organizing.

These, we believe, are the critical dimensions by which organizing should be viewed. Taken together, these four interrelated dimensions focus on the dynamics of actors and activities and influence the nature of the social action organizing that is pursued.

Organizers

We call the salaried staff of social action organizations *organizers*. The fact that they are employed and remunerated gives them special status within the organization and holds them accountable in special ways. In our view, organizers are potent actors in their organizations. Their degree of power varies among organizations. Some organizers truly control almost all major decisions and activities. In other organizations, members are charged with decision making, but the organizers frequently exert influence on decisions and directions. Although these organizers work closely with members and leaders, they still are often "first among equals" (Schwartz 1961).

Although there are differences, organizers have common tasks. While their daily responsibilities and titles may vary, organizers' primary tasks are to enhance the organization's pursuit of its goals. Consequently, their tasks involve helping people to feel and become empowered, helping their organizations pursue concrete activities directed at gaining influence, and enhancing their organizations' actual power. As we shall see, organizers employ various methods of going about these tasks and emphasize different tasks.

We view the organizer as the actor who attempts to make all other aspects of the organization cohere. We see this person as assuming responsibility for the maintenance of organizational structure and goals, membership and leadership, and work processes. Within that responsibility the organizer thinks and acts in concert with the goal of achieving power for the organization, and inculcates that goal in membership and leadership. Organizers adhere to certain values, particularly about power and change, and these values inform specific tasks like recruiting leaders or choosing strategies.

Organizers' knowledge about how to amass power is used to inform the work of the organization. Consequently, interpersonal skills used to recruit people to the organization, help them work at organizational tasks, and build their enthusiasm so that the organization's issues will be directed at power building. We propose that certain affective elements animate organizers, enable them to attend to many things at once, and maintain an objectivity about the organization and a subjectivity about the people. In sum, we argue that the knowledge, skills, values, and affect of the organizer are put to work in the organization. Therefore, we examine how the organizer's values, knowledge, skill, and affect influence the organization, its participants, and the organizing process.

Constituents, Members, and Leaders

Both in the literature and in practice, those who support the organization are variously called the organization's "constituency," "membership," and "leadership." Such inexactness in terms, however, is likely more than semantic. Rather, it suggests differing views about the people connected to the organization, the intensity of their interaction in it, and expectations held of them. We use the term constituency to mean those the organization speaks on behalf of. Constituents are not members of the organization but, it is argued, they would benefit from the organization's activities and influence. Members are those who actually affiliate with the organization. That is, they join the group by paying dues or putting their name on a mailing list. Finally, leaders are members who accept responsibility in the organization, shaping the organization and its endeavors and exuding a sense of organizational "ownership." In our view, an organization will likely have constituents, members, and leaders, and their degree of participation and activity can be expected to vary.

We explore several issues related to our assumptions about the organizations' members. We assume that organizers, acting alone, have little potential power; they must recruit and bring together people who share a vision. If it is the members who are the major resource of the organization—the numbers or "people power" that offers potency—then recruiting and maintaining a cadre of people to direct these organizations is an important concern. We conjecture that these people, too, hold certain attributes that inform their decision to join an organization and to promote certain issues and strategies over others. They bring various types and levels of interest, willingness, values, knowledge, and skills. If they differ among themselves demographically—older or younger; white, black, or Hispanic; poor, working-class, middle-class, or professional—we assume these differences must be considered within the organizational context and in the organizing process. If social action organizations are normative groups, members' compliance is likely gained through rewards and benefits rather than through remuneration or coercion (Etzioni 1961).

The Organizing Process

We ask questions about the organizing process itself. These questions are based on several assumptions. In our view, the organizer, members, and organization form a unique constellation of factors, the interactions of which are made manifest in the work of the organization. We assume that the dynamic interactions of members, organizers, and the organization would affect how the organization pursues its goal of power building. We identify two specific processes through which power is pursued and accumulated: 1. the selection of organizational issues and 2. the selection, pursuit, and evaluation of organizational targets, strategies, and tactics. These areas we consider to be the technology of organizing. The issues on which the organization works establish the boundaries of the power struggle. They are the battleground for increased power, and concern for the issues creates the need for power.

As social action organizations seek power, they invariably select someone or something to try to influence. The people or systems social action organizations seek to influence we call *targets*. As we shall see, these organizations hold various beliefs about their targets as a consequence of their views of power. Many organizations identify only those external to the organization (e.g., a landlord, a legislator) as targets, while some say that potential members can also be considered people they would like to influence. Some believe that the target must be an individual, while others believe that a system or institution is the appropriate target, and others hold that both individuals and systems may be targets. Some organizations believe that targets are amenable to change, while others see them as intractable opponents. The definition of the target, and the perception of its degree of intransigence is frequently an important factor in strategy development.

We recognize that the organizers' values, knowledge, and skills are not self-contained; their imprimatur can be found in every aspect of the organizations' work. Therefore, every step in an organizing process from issue selection to developing leadership provides a means for examining the way the organizer perceives and pursues each task.

Social Action Organizations

The final set of questions we examine are related to assumptions about social action organizations as entities. Essentially, we assume that the way in which these organizations choose to structure themselves to achieve goals (i.e., staffing patterns, the manner by which decisions are made and roles and tasks distributed, formalization, activities, and issues of external resources) are central to building the power of an organization. We propose that these organizational structures and processes are primarily an outgrowth of the organizer's and members' visions. Consequently, in every chapter we look at how these organizational factors influence the organizing process.

With these dimensions in mind, we offer an understanding of current social action organizations, their organizers, members, native leadership, and organizing processes.

CHAPTER TWO

The Organizers

According to most students of organizing, the organizer is the driving force in a social action organization (Alinsky 1971, Biklen 1983, Rothman 1969). Alinsky viewed organizers as the "highly imaginative and creative architects and engineers" of community organizations, the "bringers of a vision of change and its real possibility, not tied to a given geographic base or constituency" (Alinsky 1971:65). Critics have pointed out the potential for control and demagoguery implicit in that definition and suggested its possible negative implications (Aronovitz 1964). Both perspectives, however, accept organizers as potent actors in their organizations and as worthy subjects of investigation.

While other chapters look at aspects of the organizer's work, this chapter has the unique job of examining organizers themselves. We discuss aspects of organizers' backgrounds, experience, motivations, day-to-day duties, and influence on the organization.

Development of an Organizer

People move into and remain in organizing roles despite the generally low pay, long hours, and pressures to achieve with limited resources. Why? When talking of how and why they got into organizing, organizers describe a combination of intentional factors and happenstance. Certain developmental factors can almost be "predictors" of the choice to make organizing a career. Unintentional or serendipitous factors influence different people at different stages in their development and assume varying degrees of importance in the choice to organize. We track these scenarios developmentally.

Some organizers ascribe their career choice to having family members who were socially and politically active. Their family backgrounds educated them about social conditions and legitimated their activism. They develop a worldview (a set of values and beliefs about people and society) early on, and this view continues to influence their subsequent decisions. Their families initially expose these organizers to social concerns, and such exposure can apparently be powerful where it occurs, but is not in itself sufficient to result in a career choice to organize. Other experiences typically follow that build on early family experiences.

Some organizers date their interest in organizing to a personal experience of volunteering or activism in high school or earlier. Organizers describe early volunteering in social welfare organizations or political campaigns, involvement in service clubs, and beginning work on social issue campaigns that lead to the desire to "do something about it." By this stage a few organizers may see themselves as experienced campaigners and may comfortably describe themselves as "doing organizing," but most still lack clear-cut identities.

College provides exposure to course materials and readings that can generate greater social and political consciousness and/or offer opportunities for campus activism. Organizers may experience college as the "cradle" of the development of their organizer's consciousness.

Some organizers are moved toward organizing out of a negative, frustrating, yet consciousness-raising experience in another type of work. Dissatisfaction with a previous job or career can be a route into organizing. The dissatisfaction appears to follow a common process: the individual develops or strengthens a political analysis or goal, experiences mounting frustration at the initial job's poor compatibility with the analysis or goal, and finally comes to appreciate organizing as a better way to influence issues of concern. Examples we have encountered include the journalist who got tired of reporting events rather than influencing them, an organizer who saw that her work in a Community Action Program didn't confront the causes of poverty, and the environmental lawyer who was increasingly frustrated by the limitations of legal action in countering powerful corporate actors.

Whether organizers brought a political consciousness to their initial job or whether an awareness evolved during their tenure, they feel the need to move into organizing because of its potential to promote broader change.

Personally experiencing repression or deprivation is another motivation to organize. Some organizers have been personally victimized, overcome negative conditions, and experienced personal empowerment, and then feel an impetus to help other victims gain similar experiences. For example, a young welfare mother came to a tenants' rights group for help in getting the heat turned on in her apartment. She got involved in a demonstration and felt so empowered when the tenants' group won their point that she stayed on to eventually become a paid organizer.

Some organizers experienced the transition from powerless victim to self-confident salaried activist in the same organization. Such organizers are "success stories" in leadership development and self-empowerment. The fact that these individuals have remained with work that replicates their own experiences affirms the leadership development possibilities for others.

The factors noted previously, either alone or in combination, consciously influence organizers in their career choices. While their decisions were not necessarily calculated at the time, organizers, in retrospect, describe a clear progression of events and experiences leading them to their careers. For them an evolving consciousness directs them into organizing.

There can be, however, a markedly greater degree of serendipity leading to the choice of an organizing career. Some organizers express something like surprise at having become organizers. Essentially we view this group as organizing before they have any commitment to it per se or before they have formed a consciousness that defines such work as appropriate for them.

The organizer's initial commitment may be to issues or to an organization working on them rather than to a career in organizing. Organizers commonly describe being urged by other people to consider using their skills as organizers or being offered a job to move from volunteer work to salaried staff. In these cases they perform organizing tasks before having a real understanding of the politics and perspectives that underlie social action organizing.

Serendipity appears most obvious as people get their initial organizing job or move for the first time—even as a volunteer—into an organization. They repeat the refrain: being lucky to have seen an advertisement for an organizing job, which they applied for and got despite their lack of similar paid experience; stumbling onto an organization through college work-study or a friend, becoming active, and the activity evolving into a job without their applying for it.

Summing up, there are several dimensions of the process of entering the field of organizing:

- Entry into the field is through diverse paths. No single event or experience seems both necessary and sufficient to bring people into organizing.
- Some experiences have what researchers call "sharpness of effect." Those experiencing them are strongly affected, and the effect is lasting. A strong family background in activism or a personal experience of overcoming oppression are two examples in our findings. These are primary formative events, in our view, because of their powerful influence.
- There is no clear boundary or entry to the field of organizing. There are no qualifying examinations, no firm career ladders, no developmental steps all new entrants must take in order to be "vetted" as organizers. The line between active volunteer and professional organizer is diffuse, and some people cross the line in terms of tasks they accomplish before they realize they have "become organizers."

Motivation to Organize

While we have examined the career paths of organizers, we now examine their motivation to continue organizing. As Cloward and Piven comment in their introduction to Delgado's analysis of ACORN organizing, "We need to know more about the young men and women who dedicated themselves to the vocation of organizing when others dropped out to return to schools and careers, or to make sandals" (Delgado 1986:xiii). What motivates people to continue to organize? Motivation begins with what we call *conscious contrarianism*—a process whereby the organizer rejects dominant ideology and replaces it with an alternative worldview. Motivation to continue to organize is then reinforced by job and career satisfaction.

Saul Alinsky (1971) and Steve Burghardt (1982a, b) describe organizers as having serious concerns with society's values and view the choice of organizing itself as an effort to fulfill a personal need to promote social change. What they describe is the same as what we call conscious contrarianism, which has three components: a worldview, a power analysis, and the selection of organizing as the career that best justifies the organizer's views.

The Worldview Organizers are characterized by a strong sense of what is "just" in and for the world (Lippman 1937). This perspective reflects democratic political values and Judeo-Christian values by no means unique to organizers. These values adhere to biblical and democratic traditions that include justice and fairness to individuals, a sense of collective societal responsibility for the welfare of individuals, and a sense of altruism that accepts personal responsibility for solving problems (Walton 1969).

The organizer understands that society has certain responsibilities to care for and about the vulnerable, that individuals have valued roles in promoting and maintaining the ideal, and that building sufficient power to act is the way to exercise responsibility. The impulse to organize arises from one's acceptance of individual responsibility to work actively with people to effect change in the direction of ideals, as opposed to those who only visualize utopias. In some cases the move from altruism to political opposition begins with a religious worldview. This is particularly true for people who come from religious backgrounds or are members of the clergy.

The worldview aspect of conscious contrarianism reflects values held by many socially concerned people who do not organize; the impulse and ability to picture a more perfect world is shared by utopians, futurologists, civic and church groups, among others. Thus, it is a necessary but not sufficient explanation for "Why organize?"

Power Analysis Becoming an organizer often involves analyzing what is wrong with others' thinking and behaviors—why things occur in society. Mainstream definitions of who benefits in society and why are questioned along class, racial, ethnic, gender, and other lines. Mainstream methods of promoting change, i.e., "going through channels," are countered with tactics that challenge power holders (Tropman 1985). This active rejection of many popular values and traditions begins to mark organizers as different from others sharing a view of a better world. The thrust of their analysis becomes essentially adversarial, suggesting that those in power make the rules. As one organizer says, "People [who] come into community organizations quickly learn to talk about it in terms of power, in terms of good/bad." The rejection of values can come through personal problems. For example, one woman had been a housewife whose husband was injured at work. She describes herself adhering to the work ethic and institutional values until employment and benefits were stripped away. She needed to protect her family, and became frustrated dealing with doctors, lawyers, and insurance companies. At that point she rejected the *system*'s values, which protected powerful interests but not an injured worker and his family. She volunteered at a local worker's rights group and, within a year, became the group's organizer.

Organizers also contrast faith in the ameliorative powers of the current social welfare system with an understanding of problems in terms of power differences. Social services are depicted as "band-aid" work, not directed at the root causes of poverty, and not proposing broader solutions.

Anger is often involved as organizers reject dominant ideology. They find injustice unacceptable, and are angered by the patent unfairness they see. The rejection process is not just intellectualized but very deeply and sometimes personally felt. Organizers who go through this rejection process essentially define themselves outside the mainstream of their own society, opting for a marginal status, potentially isolated from friends, neighbors, and family.

The Deliberate Selection of Organizing Work At this point organizers have rejected mainstream values, understanding them to be the result of power relationships. They have replaced dominant ideology with alternative visions of what might be and have developed a personal sense of responsibility for change. These ideas generate the initial motivation to organize.

Need theories of motivation (Maslow 1970) may suggest what happens next. According to theory, behavior is motivated by a desire to fulfill needs. We have suggested above that a key element of the motivation to organize reflects a desire to fulfill personal values and change goals. This motivation is followed by expectancy theories (Vroom 1964) that suggest decisions (i.e., career choices) are made on the basis of the likelihood of meeting predetermined expectations. Organizers anticipate organizing will have the highest probability of allowing them to produce change and thereby fulfill their change goals. They look for work that involves social change, and organizing becomes the most likely vehicle.

In this third part of the conscious contrarian process, organizers seek out jobs that at least appear to contain the possibility to promote change. As people who are almost constantly engaged in adversarial activities, organizers profess a marginal status in society. They are not in the mainstream; indeed, they attack it. They want to reshape the mainstream rather than pull away from it. Yet in order to build a large organization, organizers are constantly involved with others. These people are frequently not, at least not initially, of like mind. This paradox of societal isolation versus the need to maintain close relationships with the organization's members is a theme that will surface often in these chapters.

The organizers, however, seldom describe feeling alone and alienated. Indeed, they frequently mention the benefits they accrue from the work. They have said that it's fun to meet a lot of people—to see changes in people and situations over a fairly short period of time—because they like to teach and there's a lot of teaching and training in organizing, and because they take satisfaction in developing things and seeing them grow and get to use skills they have developed in new and different ways.

As organizers move into this field and identify themselves with specific organizations or movements or issues, they bring diverse experiences and motivations to the work. There are personal elements reflecting social awareness and personal career desires; there is a political awareness and a concomitant position of "opposition" that is formed prior to organizing, or shortly thereafter.

The Working Organizer: Ideal Characteristics

Once people begin to organize their goals and views should be in harmony with the organization's. The organizer's views are now placed in the context of actual opportunities, constraints, relationships, failures, and successes, and these test the initial motivation and analysis of the organizer. We propose that organizers are sustained in their work as long as the job is sufficiently congruent with the organizer's needs and expectations. Given this we analyze what organizers and members describe as ideal organizer characteristics and trace how the awareness and expectations organizers bring interact with others' expectations and contributions.

Despite Alinsky there is no "bible" of ideal traits for organizers. There is an appreciation of multiple, sometimes dichotomous skills existing side by side. Organizers' attributes reflect changing situational demands and the interests and capacities of the people with whom organizers work. The portrait being drawn is far from chameleonlike, though. There is much substance to the "ideal organizer."

The sum reflects an appreciation of the organizer as a well-rounded individual.

Diversity in Definition

Organizers and leaders suggest an array of ideal characteristics for organizers. This description, by an organizer who has done both grassroots and mobilizing work, captures the complexity and richness of such an ideal:

> I think an organizer needs a strong ego as opposed to a big ego. I think organizers have to have a fairly strong sense of their own worth and ability because it's not reinforced a lot [by others] in organizing. [I have found] this particularly true since coming here and seeing that what an organizer can do is not culturally rewarded. I think there has to be a sense of humor, a real person who likes meeting new people, likes people (and not just people who think like he or she does), an openness to people. An organizer has to have some good smarts, be able to think through consequences constantly, be able to anticipate. I think, too, just in terms of politics, that you should have a fairly strong commitment but not too rigid an ideology, a belief that the system does not work for a lot of people and that you really want to try to change that.

Brager and Specht (1973) describe organizers as having technical and expressive skills. We can see these in the preceding quote. Technical content embraces "good smarts," an ability to think things through, and an ability to anticipate. Expressive content incorporates "a sense of humor," "a real person that likes meeting new people," and "an openness to people." Less clear is the appropriate allocation between these two categories of such content as "a strong ego but not a big ego," "a fairly strong sense of their own ability," or "a belief that the system does not work for a lot of people and that you really want to change that." The two categories are too few and too rigid to encompass all the content included in the previous description, let alone what a larger number of respondents draw as a rich mosaic of organizer characteristics.

There is a need for a more complex depiction of desirable organizer skills and characteristics. We first suggest three major categories, and then describe each in greater depth.

Change Vision Attributes How organizers view the world in political terms, their goals for change, and their notions about power justify all other technical and interactional skills organizers employ. Indeed, technical and interactional skills are selected and exercised *in the service of* the organizer's individual vision of change. While we discuss later in this chapter the most common orientations to change, we describe here how adherence to a change vision dictates that organizers acquire certain personal characteristics, such as persistence and dedication, that allow them to pursue their goals for change.

Technical Skills The organizer employs two types of technical skills— those related to efficacy on issues and those related to organizational health and effectiveness. Technical skills involving issues include an ability to analyze issues, opponents, and power structures; a competency in the development and implementation of strategy and tactics; a proficiency in the assessment of the status of instrumental goal achievement; and an expertise in public relations tasks and communications with the media. Technical skills related to organizational effectiveness include an ability to formulate, build, and maintain effective structures for recruitment and involvement of members; a proficiency at forming and maintaining task groups (e.g., committees, boards, coalitions); and a competency in the skills of fund-raising and organizational management (such as budgeting, contract negotiation, supervision, resource allocation, planning, etc.). These technical skills are employed to reach the desired outcomes suggested by the organizer's change vision.

Interactional Skills Interactional or expressive skills include an ability to respond with empathy, a competency in purposefully assessing and intervening with individuals and groups, and a facility in identifying, developing, educating, and maintaining organizational members and leaders. Interactional skills grow out of those aspects of the organizer's change vision that suggests people are empowered and gain power through organizing.

Change vision, technical skills, and interactional skills overlap to some extent, but there is also sufficient difference to warrant discussing each in some detail.

Change Vision

Organizers have different understandings of how change is made. Despite these differences and no matter the orientation, their impulse to change seems to summon forth certain personal characteristics that enable them to single-mindedly pursue their change agendas despite their marginal status in society and the odds they face. An organizer's survival, first and foremost, depends on strong personal dedication or commitment. Dedication may be to organizing itself—in the context of a personal political philosophy—to the organization's philosophy, issues, or goals, to the organization's members or constituents, or to any or all of the above. Each of these reflect organizers' attempts to bring their personal worldview into the workplace.

Members often appreciate dedication indirectly. They marvel at the organizer's ability and willingness to work long hours at low pay. Organizers' willingness to work is taken as evidence of a motivation more selfless than that of material gain. Persistence and endurance in organizers are valued by leaders, but, in general, members seem not to know the sources of these qualities. Organizers, however, agree that the seeds of their commitment are their political views.

Organizers vary in how they react to the consequences of this commitment. For some commitment to work limits other parts of their lives. They recognize that commitment may mean being away from family and friends or staying single "as a virtual prerequisite for the long hours, out-of-control schedule, and passionate involvement." Other organizers counter the physical and emotional exhaustion such commitment can entail by compartmentalizing their lives, creating breathing spaces away from work with family or friends.

Organizers talk also of "survival skills" that buffer personal disappointment and stress in the work of organizing. Chief among these is a sense of humor, particularly given the serious nature of most issues social action organizations take on. This "gallows humor" is used to balance the unrelenting workload and difficulties that organizers face.

A second important survival skill is the ability to avoid personalizing events, attacks, slights, or tensions. It's important not to feel that people act as they do because they are out to "get the organizer."

Self-motivation and self-discipline are related traits that help organizers survive under pressure and without an abundance of positive resources or victories. They provide an underlying sense of purpose, which is acted out as self-direction.

The organizer's vision of change prescribes doggedness, dedication, and discipline. Such personal characteristics are the sine qua non of an organizer. Technical and interactional skills are developed and honed, but always in relation to this basic vision. As one organizer says,

> You have to be prepared to really push hard, because you are going to be dealing with a lot of resistance. And whether you do that cor-

rectly, or whether you just bulldoze people, which means that in the long run you alienate them and screw up, can be a very subtle distinction. You have to be able to make clear why it's important to do something, and that it needs to get done, and keep people on the point of doing it and how to get it done. And all of that takes a lot of fairly aggressive projecting. I'd say that being tenacious, persistent is very important. You can seem like a fairly shy person, you can be less than completely eloquent, but if you are tenacious that will make up for a lot of the other things. That's pretty evident in people who are organizers. They get things done because they don't give up, because they keep calling someone, because they keep trying, and they wear people down.

Technical Skills

Organizers see themselves as experts in technical areas. Technical skills fall into two areas: skills related to issues and skills related to maintenance of organizational health and effectiveness.

Skills Related to Issues Expertise in the processes of organizing—issue identification and strategy development and implementation—is one facet of an organizer's technical skills. It includes the knowledge of specific models of organizing and how to implement them—an ability to translate private problems into public issues; an ability to analyze, partialize, and redefine an issue so that it lends itself to action; an ability to focus on central rather than peripheral aspects of an issue; an ability to analyze an issue and the skills to research it thoroughly; an ability to change the organization's issue focus quickly; an ability to set outcome goals and plan action strategy, making adjustments when necessary; and an ability to think through organizational and issue consequences and to evaluate the effectiveness of organizational activity. The organizer must have substantive information on the issue itself, including policy, laws, programs, and research findings related to the issue the organization is pursuing. All this requires a mastery of detail, the retention of large amounts of information, and constant analysis. Organizers' work on issues is further elaborated in chapter 5.

Organizers not only must be aware of issues but must also have an in-depth understanding of the political environment in which they function and be able to intervene in it successfully. Organizers constantly update their analyses of power in areas that concern them, keeping abreast of who controls what, who relates to whom and why, individuals' and institutions' bases of power and vulnerabilities. An economic analysis of who owns what and who stands to gain and lose is basic to such power analyses. Also important is an analysis of key actors—individuals and groups who have amassed sufficient power to enable them to influence an issue—and how and why they are motivated to act or not to act.

Once equipped with the results of their power analyses, organizers need skill in shaping perceptions—of the public, of key actors, of opponents—on issues, on what's at stake, about the social action organization and its interests. These are public relations skills. They include a working knowledge of how the media operates and how to attract it to the organization's story, and, concomitantly, how to ensure that what appears in print or on television is slanted to the organization's viewpoint. Strategy skills are further elaborated in chapters 6, 7, and 8.

Members of social action organizations express great respect for the technical skills of their organizers. In some cases the respect borders on awe.

Skills Related to Organizational Health and Effectiveness Almost all organizers (with the rare exception of those in large organizations with separate administrative staffs) must develop technical skills used to maintain a viable and growing organization. These skills include the ability to design member training, to form effective task and decision-making structures such as committees and boards, to involve diverse people in common and enjoyable tasks, to supervise and direct organizing staff, to design fund-raising events and write funding proposals, to plan and promote multiple simultaneous projects, and to share power or accept direction from members.

Organizers and members often give scant attention to another important organization-building and maintenance skill—the ability to maintain accountability systems, particularly for funding sources. This includes basic bookkeeping, the ability to collect and maintain program and project information, report writing, and meeting and presentation skills.

Interactional Skills

If technical skills engage the mind of the organizer, the organizer's heart is captured by working with other people. Brager and Specht (1973) call these skills "expressive skills." People and the situations in which the organizer meets them call upon a wide variety of interaction and communication skills. Members in all types of organizations emphasize the importance of this skill area over technical skills; these are, after all, the skills most often experienced by members when they work closely with organizers. Even in national organizations, where interpersonal interactions are less frequent than in local organizations, members talk of the dynamic impact, for better or worse, that the organizer has on them during even infrequent visits or through written or telephone communications. Organizers, in general, stress communication skills directly in proportion to the amount and intensity of their interactions with members, constituents, or even targets. Organizers' interactional skills are treated more fully in chapters 3 and 4.

A useful way to capture these interactional skills is to group them under three subcategories: 1. the organizer as the sender of messages, 2. the organizer as the interpreter of messages, and 3. the organizer as the sharer of messages.

Message Sender Organizers and members talk of attitudes organizers must radiate to secure desired responses from members and leaders. These projecting skills are calculated to draw specific reactions from people. Here is the organizer as impresario, role model, and inspiration. Importantly, organizers must have "the ability to act with conviction." They are very conscious of serving as positive models for others, projecting an image they hope leaders and members will emulate. The purposeful use of these skills is to inspire others to action rather than enhance the organizer's own prominence:

> I guess you have to try to be a good news person. Not to be wrongly optimistic, but just say "let's check this out," when other people are yelling "oh, no." Like saying anything is possible, but also saying let's see what good we can get out of this thing. Galvanizing someone—making it clear to them how they themselves can act in order to get what they want.

The message sender role for an organizer requires a capacity to be liked and trusted. Accommodating their messages to each intended audience, organizers reach out to the special needs and interests of each new person. People must feel the organizer is really interested in their problems, that the organizer is able to communicate information so that people understand the consequences for them.

Organizers consciously present their behaviors, their attitudes, and their motivations to others as models they might emulate. Organizers present what is possible, what is doable, and what works in hopes that their attitudes are infectious, that others will take on aspects of these behaviors and attitudes.

Message Interpreter Another expressive or interactional skill involves the ability to analyze, understand, hear, and articulate the positions and motivations of people whom the organizer wishes to involve in the organization. Organizers use what they learn about how members think, their "sacred cows," the level and focus of their anger, and the degree and roots of their passivity to recruit them, to develop their sense of outrage and injustice, and to ally them with the organization's agenda. Using this skill, the organizer helps people understand that they are not alone with the problem, that they are not to blame for their difficulty, and that they, and others like them, have the right to be protected from injustice. Essentially the organizer takes the grievances people articulate as individual problems and transforms them into public issues that can be acted on by the organization. An organizer describes this process:

> What I do is create a vehicle for people to be able to act on their interests in a successful way. I will talk to someone who has just been denied a bank loan. They will see it as an embarrassment, something that happened to them because they're just a poor working-class slob. They're resigned to it. You have to be able to talk to them about the fact that they were turned down unfairly, that the banks loan to corporations and people who are much greater risks, and you have to explain to them, because they don't under-stand it, what exactly their rights are, and that it's OK to try to change that . . . they don't have to look over their shoulders and they don't have to accept what is patently unfair. I explain the injus-tice and I show them the research that backs it up. I explain issues so clearly even my mother could understand. Then they can tell someone else.

A part of the organizer's success in the role of message interpreter relies on an ability to receive others' messages, hear them, and use them to shape their own behavior and thinking. Important here is how well the organizer considers member opinions and supports members in their choices. Leaders appreciate the ability of their organizers to value and credit their ideas. Threatening, bullying, or blaming for not being involved don't work. Participants feel supported and valued when the organizer explains the benefit of involvement. They come because they might miss something if they're not there.

Further, organizers must communicate that people have to make their own decisions about what others—the organizer included—are saying. Part of the skill of interpreting messages is to help people to think and act for themselves, to coach them in developing their own ideas rather than only listening to everybody else's.

Message Sharer The ability of the organizer to create and maintain close personal relationships with members is what we call message sharing. This skill mitigates the powerful and distancing role of the organizer as technical expert by whom people are awed but with whom they may not feel comfortable. Organizers reject the need for the "professional distance" that is sometimes argued by other helping professions. Rather, the organizer tries to create personal bonds among equals as human beings, as comrades-at-arms. In addition to having the capacity to lead, there is meaning in how an organizer greets someone. She or he needs to know people well enough to ask about their kids or their dog.

At the same time, the informal social relationships that organizers have with members must not become an obstacle to accomplishing goals. Organizers also have to promote shared expectations about roles, both their own and those they hold for members. Social action organizations are human systems, but they are also aimed at producing changes on issues; warm personal relationships and an insistence on people producing results require constant balancing. Organizers clarify these expectations in individual conversations, at meetings, and sometimes by holding training sessions. In these discussions the organizer's expectations about roles are articulated. It is important for organizers to communicate firmly that there is a job to be done and that they cannot do it by themselves.

Members appreciate the multiple, varied skills of their organizers. Both organizers and members emphasize that other actors are expected to be shaped more by the organizer than vice versa, an important confirmation of the centrality of the organizer in the organization. Yet this central role is performed well only if other members are central in the organizer's thoughts and actions.

It's part of being enthusiastic and people-oriented. Making sure that people do not feel they do the drone work, but that every bit of work is important. Without every single person who is doing it, we wouldn't be where we are. Appreciate what other people do because they always have to sacrifice some part of their personal life to do it. So I'll say to Mrs. Rivera, "Talking with the five people at your church is important for the success of our meeting with the mayor. Because if they come, we'll be stronger in the meeting. And I appreciate your taking time to do that because I know your kids have been sick. Your efforts will make that meeting a success."

It is clear that there are a multiplicity of attributes and capabilities and behaviors required of "ideal" organizers. Such diverse expectations create serious challenges for those who want to organize. It is unrealistic to expect flesh-and-blood organizers to act out ideal versions. At best organizers can use an idealized vision to assess their strengths and weaknesses and move to correct those weaker aspects of their work.

Multiple expectations may also cause problems for organizers whose members continue to expect far too many diverse talents in their organizers and wind up holding their staff hostage to unrealistic demands. These demands are particularly problematic because the skills are often contradictory.

We see a blithe tendency to rattle off a paradoxical list of organizer traits or tasks as all being vital. The gregariousness of a "people person," easily able to form and maintain warm relationships with diverse people, may not be found in the same person who has excellent research, grant-writing, or strategist skills. The expectation that the organizer build intimate relationships *and* simultaneously maintain objectivity and analytical distance suggests the presence of competing, if not impossible, demands.

A mobilizing organizer in a national organization, who had done grassroots work in the past, saw the contradictory demands, but "solved" the problem through working in an organization that demanded of him only his specialization. He perceived the intimate expressive skills as most necessary at local levels and the analytic and writing skills as more important at the national level. He saw his own career changes as moving toward the work he most liked and was best at—for him the analytical end of the spectrum—and pretty much accepted that he would not be as effective working at the local level any longer. Such specialization can work in large organizations where others can take on the unfilled roles, but this may not be an option for most organizers. Where the only certain resource to accomplish tasks is the paid organizer, the human tendency to move toward doing work you like is a danger in organizing if some tasks are simply left undone.

Beyond job diversity and paradoxical demands on organizers a third concern surfaces in organizers' discussions of their work—isolation. Many comments reflect what Alinsky (1971) described as the organizer as "inside outsider" and what Burghardt (1982a) speaks of as the organizer as marginal. Even while organizers view themselves as being intensely involved with others, they must also see themselves as isolated and alone. This isolation is expressed in several ways:

- The organizer has separate work to do—work that is incontestably his or her own—that others may not be capable of doing. The organizer must also help members to view their work as significant. In elevating the significance of member contributions, the contribution of the organizer is sometimes overlooked or diminished.
- The organizer is expected to be a high-energy person to survive in what is often an emotionally and physically exhausting job. Further, the organizer is asked to extend his or her energy to others in the organization, to inspire and energize them, and not to be discouraged by members' passivity or low morale.
- The organizer is to understand and appreciate other members' and constituents' limitations, norms, values, and goals, but not be limited by them. The organizer must also bring an objectivity free of members' biases to his or her analysis.

These stresses are an almost inalterable part of the work of organizers. Two critical concerns are the gap between an organizer's own visions of organizing and those of others in the organization, and the contrast between organizers' own visions of organizing and the realities they find on the job.

Compatibility Between the Job and the Ideals

We postulate that organizers are most likely to remain in their jobs if sufficient compatibility exists between 1. the organizers' initial goals and motivation to organize (needs), 2. the traits and skills organizers envision as needed for the job (expectations), and 3. the actual work they do (the job). In this section we look first at how organizers describe their current work, and then we look for compatibility among these three factors.

The Job The most common organizer job description contains components of administration, planning, policy decision making, program development and action implementation, public relations activities, and service activities.

We identify four categories of tasks: work related to goal attainment, leader development, public education, and organization building.

Work related to goal attainment is the most prevalent category of work for organizers; it is the sine qua non of organizing, in fact. Typical of these activities are: researching issues, developing strategy and tactics with groups of people around an issue, carrying out direct action campaign tactics, directing lobbying work, and training people as lobbyists.

Job tasks related to development of leadership among members and constituents include working with leaders—training them, developing their skills, building their confidence, encouraging relationships among leaders, fostering good membership and board relations, staffing committees, communicating with affiliates and members, and working with a decision-making policy board. Generally scant attention is given to recruitment activities, a subject we will examine in detail in a later chapter.

Typical public education tasks are media work, writing about issues, talking to community groups, and general education on issues.

The final category of tasks directly involves keeping the organization functioning: fund-raising and proposal writing, managing the office, accounting, holding staff meetings, working on organizational development, providing staff support, directing the organizer trainee program, and coordinating volunteers.

Compatibility We look for the degree of agreement between organizers' hopes for their jobs and their actual work by comparing their views of their change goals, their ideal work skills, and actual job tasks. Organizers' change goals can be categorized as: 1. substantive change, 2. leadership development, and 3. increased public awareness. Skills associated with each goal include interactional skills, technical skills, and public relations skills. Finally, the associated categories of job tasks are work related to goal attainment, leadership development, public education, and organization building.

In our discussions with organizers we find that their goals are mostly congruent with the skills they value. For example, organizers who hold goals for leadership development also value having the interactional skills associated with working with members and leaders, and spend a great deal of time doing just that. The strain occurs when organizers begin to carry out tasks on the job that are not sufficiently compatible with their expectations and that evolve from situational demands or the competing expectations of other actors in their organizations. In general the value organizers place on developing leaders is not borne out in the press of day-to-day issue and organizational maintenance work, and this is a strain for the organizer. Conversely, technical tasks are a part of every organizer's job, although the associated change goals and skills are not valued by all of them. The same is true for the public education area.

Still, only a small minority of all organizers describe their jobs as being seriously discordant with their hopes and expectations. The few who do leave organizing.

One might ask why most organizers—despite the degree of stress, competing demands, long hours, and low pay—seem to be quite satisfied with their jobs. In a seeming paradox, organizers were gratified with the specifics of their employment when the day-to-day tasks they carried out were essentially in line with their perception of *what ought to be done to create change*. That is, organizers who believed that the way to effect change was to develop strong leaders, and who held jobs that allowed them to work extensively and intensively with leaders, were gratified in their work. In contrast, the organizer who believed change would come from leadership development, yet found herself primarily planning programs, doing research, and writing grants, was preparing to leave the field. Essentially, the beliefs held by organizers about how to effect change and their ability to realize those beliefs on the job account for their satisfaction or dissatisfaction.

Orientations about change strongly influence not only how organizers see their jobs but also how they work with members and leaders, how they select issues, targets, and strategies, and how the organization itself is constructed and functions. Here we explore organizer's beliefs about change more fully in order to understand how their beliefs influence their work.

Change Orientation

Organizers hold a set of beliefs about how and why social change occurs, a "theory which relates cause and cure" (Brager and Specht 1973:83). These beliefs may be more or less articulated but nonetheless frame the way an organizer envisions an organization will have to work in order to achieve the desired goals. These beliefs are then available to shape the organizing process. Knowing the beliefs organizers hold about change is, therefore, crucial to understanding how organizations pursue social change.

Drawing on analyses of social action organizations (Fisher and Kling 1990, Gramsci 1971) and our own experience, we call these views of change the organizer's *change orientation*. These orientations depict a cause-and-effect scenario about how change is made. Change orientations include:

1. a definition of change or a change goal;
2. an identification of the target(s) of the change effort and a view of the general relationship between the target(s) and the organization (e.g., how cooperative or adversarial the target will be);
3. an understanding of resources that must be brought to bear to create the desired change;
4. a change strategy (e.g., how the resources are used to influence the target).

We identify four "change orientations": countervailing institutions, pluralist pressure, mass education for action, and charismatic vision.

Countervailing Institutions There are three related change goals implicit in this view. First, it proposes that most people see themselves as, and in fact are, powerless; so a goal of the organization is to help people to see themselves as and act more powerfully. A second goal is to accomplish substantive changes on issues. A third goal is to redistribute power by inducing power holders to bow to pressure on substantive issues. This orientation is closest to incorporating Gramsci's understanding of "subaltern groups" in whose consciousness exist beliefs about how societies are and should be organized (1971:52–55).

This orientation accepts power holders as public or private figures who enact formal authority or informal influence. These power holders are perceived as resistant to giving up power. An organization of people must contend for it and take it from those who currently possess it. Power holders are organizational targets who must be forced to cooperate.

The largest possible number of people brought together into a disciplined, permanent, formal organization is viewed as the major resource for change in the countervailing institution orientation. That is, the larger the organization's membership, acting in a unified manner, the greater its power. The social change strategy entails bringing people together in an organization; the organizer then helping them to see that by working collectively they *can* be powerful, and that a major means for doing so is through working toward attaining change on issues *they* define as concerns. By defining their own issues proactively they are exerting more power than they would by reacting to issues created and framed by others (Freire 1968). As the organization gains in numbers it succeeds in accomplishing concrete results, which help individual members to feel and be more powerful, wrests power from power holders, and redistributes it to the organization.

Pluralist Pressure The changes sought in this orientation are the enactment of laws, regulations, or policy actions related to specific issues (e.g., enactment of the proposed Equal Rights Amendment to the Constitution or enforcement of environmental protection statutes and standards). This change orientation accepts that government and the legal system are the legitimate mechanisms through which social change is negotiated and implemented. Analyses are carried out that assess government and political actors as either actual or potential collaborators, neutrals, or opponents on issues. Governmental actors are viewed as potentially malleable; they can be persuaded to be cooperative or at least remain neutral on issues. The influence of those who hold opposing interests are to be minimized.

The orientation suggests that concerned, reasonable people with a good deal of issue expertise can convince power holders of their views and are the major resource for making change. These people can either associate in an organization or act individually. The change strategy entails identifying an issue, collecting data to develop expertise, recruiting people to the viewpoint by providing public education programs that disseminate the findings, formulating solutions, and influencing governmental actors to accept the proposed changes.

Mass Education for Action This change orientation argues that combined economic, social, and political interests disenfranchise many Americans, dominate the social agenda, and create institutional injustices. The change goals are to express and include the needs and views of the disenfranchised in the polity, and to realize substantive changes that will improve their lives. Government—primarily at the federal level with its abundance of resources and centralized power—is the accepted change target. But those power holders who are political actors are viewed as highly resistant to the changes desired by disenfranchised people, and are therefore adversaries. This change orientation implies that change can be made only during certain historical periods, when economic, social, and political events reveal "windows of opportunity" (Piven and Cloward 1977).

The major resource for making change is "seizing the moment" by amassing large loosely associated groups of people to exert disruptive pressure on political decision makers. The change strategy reflects an understanding of change as cyclical, accepting that organizing is a process of taking two steps forward and, hopefully, only one step back. During conservative periods a few people (often called "activists") analyze political and economic factors and attempt through mass education and media events to maintain a level of public consciousness on issues. They hope to interest people who can be activated during the more opportune historical moments. When the economic, political, and social climate allows, these activists coalesce and recruit a large constituency to disrupt and put pressure on government. Government then defuses the disruption by acceding to some of the demands. As the climate for change recedes, regression occurs, and some changes are reversed. Activists once again try to interest and prepare people for the next auspicious moment.

Charismatic Vision This change orientation is based almost completely on moral values and visions of a just world. The change goal is that social and public policies and decisions reflect and promote values of justice and fairness. The change targets are government or corporate power holders who enact or implement policy that is considered immoral. These targets are seen as relatively resistant to changing their behavior and must be shamed or embarrassed into it.

The major resource for making change is moral indignation articulated by one or a few leaders and their followers, even though their overall number is small. The change strategy requires that the morally righteous constantly monitor public and corporate decisions for violations. Led or guided by charismatic leaders, people react quickly by bearing witness or testifying to acts or events they view as immoral, attempting to shame decision makers into reversing current policies. Actions are often strongly condemning and confrontational (e.g., civil disobedience).

Generally, organizers support a single change orientation, although a few adhere simultaneously to a combination of them, supporting aspects of each. Nevertheless, to organizers, these change orientations are not merely an abstract set of beliefs. Rather, the change orientation to which they subscribe provides the guidelines for what they wish to do with members, issues, and strategy, and dictates the kind of organization they wish to build or work within. In fact, in many ways that we will see throughout this book, the priorities organizers set, the work they choose to do (as well as the work they avoid), and the way in which they pursue their tasks are strongly influenced by the change vision to which they subscribe.

Organizers' principles for action are primarily derived from their change orientation. We call the principles for action suggested by a change orientation the organizers' *practice method*. If change orientation is the organizer's ideology, then practice method is their "ideology in action."

While change orientations are abstract views about the best ways to effect change, practice methods refer to operational ways of working. Practice method guides action and suggests what someone should do in a particular situation. In other fields practice methodologies are more fully conceptualized. Commonly, these practice methods prescribe a particular understanding of people's problems and their capacity for solving them and suggest preferred roles, processes, and desired outcomes.

We posit that in organizing a similar relationship exists between an abstract view of change and organizing method. Practice methods are not so fully developed in the organizing literature. Harry Boyte lists several current methodologies, with roots in the sixties and earlier, that "champion the interests of ordinary people against unresponsive government and corporate structures." His traditions include Alinsky's locality-based method of community organizing, public interest advocacy as pioneered by Ralph Nader, and constituency organizing, which brings together and mobilizes those concerned with specific issues and abuses (1980:7). We suggest the elements that constitute a practice method for organizing:

1. a delineation of roles for staff, leaders, and members,
2. a preferred process and criteria for selecting issues,
3. an understanding of the target,
4. a preference for a particular strategy, and
5. an understanding of the role of an organization.

From a review of the literature, talks with organizers, and our own experiences we have deduced three prominent practice methods of social action organizing; each method is associated with a particular change orientation.

Organizers who adhere to a countervailing institutional view of change most often employ a *grassroots practice method*. They attempt to organize a broad-based constituency of people in a geographic area who identify specific issues out of their own self-interest. The organizer works with a constituency to identify individual targets and to choose a strategy that is more than likely confrontational. The development of a highly structured, disciplined, and permanent "people's" organization is a primary task of the organizer.

Organizers who adhere to a pluralist pressure change orientation most often employ a *lobbying practice method*. Organizers who use this model attempt to organize a constituency around a specific issue for the purpose of changing or preserving conditions that are related to that issue. Issues are identified by monitoring the legislative process, and targets are generally governmental actors who must be influenced to enact legislation. The organization these organizers build is generally comprised of loosely associated members who pay dues and are asked to respond to issues.

The *mobilizing approach* is the third practice method, associated with both the change orientations of mass education for action and charismatic vision. Mobilizing organizers attempt to organize a constituency concerned with specific issues and abuses in the social, political, or economic system. Issues emerge from an analysis of the social, political, and economic events of the day. A strategic premise of these organizers is that only by mass collective and opportunistic defiance and protest can the dominant institutions be influenced to alter their agenda. Spontaneous disruption is valued over building an organization.

In subsequent chapters the reader will see that the organizers and leaders who constitute social action organizations make widely contrasting decisions during the organizing process. Issue and strategy selection is based on different criteria. Members are involved to various degrees, and organizers use different techniques to involve and engage them. Such wide variety must be accounted for.

We will argue that it is the organizer who brings these differences. It is the organizer who shapes and molds the organizing process, if not the organization. Contrary to other helping roles where workers are informed and shaped by organizational context, organizers often create the organizational context and its work. It is she or he who provides direction, ideas, guidelines, and expertise to the organizing. Organizers bring the vision of what the organization is to become. This vision is generated by the organizer's change orientation and practice method. These two factors have perhaps the most profound influence on how an organizer organizes, and they permeate the organizational decisions around members, leaders, issues, strategy, and structure. The influence of change orientation and practice method will become apparent throughout the book. In the final chapter we attempt to comprehensively describe each practice method, suggest each one's deficits and strengths, and make suggestions for their sustenance and growth.

There are many paths to becoming an organizer, and organizers don't appear to be discouraged by the long hours, stress, or isolation that they acknowledge exists. Instead, they are fueled by their beliefs, commitments, and visions for change. For the most part, organizers are satisfied with their jobs because they create the organization or the organizing program and their jobs along with it. Lacking that opportunity, they find employment in an organization where the day-to-day tasks are highly compatible with what they perceive they ought to do to create change.

There can be no question that the organizer is a central and powerful force in a social action organization. Both members and organizers understand and accept the organizer's influence and ascribe much of the organization's success to the organizer's work. Moreover, organizers bring to the organization beliefs about change (a change orientation) and associated principles for action (a practice method) that profoundly influence how the organizing and the organization will proceed.

CHAPTER THREE

Recruiting Participants

Much of this book is focused on the roles, tasks, and vision of the social action organizer. Indeed, we believe that such attention is warranted, given the pivotal role the organizer plays in building an organization powerful enough to make social change. As we have said, however, the power amassed by social action organizations invariably and inevitably comes from the people who are attracted to them. It is the participants who bring the public legitimation, financial resources, and active participation that allows the organization to continue to exist and flex its muscles. Consequently, organizers are a necessary but insufficient resource for a social action organization, and recruitment and member maintenance are important concerns (Piven and Cloward 1977). As one state-level organizer sees it,

> In the words of Bob Dylan, if you ain't busy being born you're busy dying. [It's about] power, and the ability to influence the political process to achieve our goals. Power comes mainly from either money or numbers. We're never going to have all the money we want; we need the numbers. We are a political organization. Those numbers speak louder than anything.

Despite the obvious validity of this organizer's words, many organizers face serious problems in both attracting and holding onto volunteer participants. This chapter and chapter 4 examine the critical aspects of recruitment and member maintenance.

Member Recruitment and Maintenance

The work organizers do to involve people is what Staples and others refer to as "building the base" (Brager and Specht 1973, Fisher 1984, Staples 1984). There are three aspects included in this process: 1. recruiting and engaging new people, 2. keeping current members motivated and involved, and 3. deepening member participation. Each represents an ongoing demand for organizers' attention. Burghardt emphasizes that organizers must get people to attend meetings, especially the first one, and must follow up and involve potential members, and that this outreach—like action on issues—must continue throughout the life of the organization (Burghardt 1982b). This work is important to the health of an organization and is frequently quite consuming for the organizer. For these reasons it is important to understand why it is necessary to have both new and continuing participants.

The Need for Member Participation

There are symbolic, strategic, and pragmatic arguments for member recruitment and maintenance. Large memberships make the organization seem powerful to power holders and the public, giving the organization a potency it in fact may not have. Brager and Specht note that for organizations, "the task, to begin with, is to *seem* to control the sentiments of large numbers" (1973:144) until that goal is actually achieved. Numbers of people allow organizers to use "smoke and mirrors"—at least for a time—so that the organization has the aura of power before it really has potency. Organizers may claim large numbers of adherents for public relations purposes (e.g., large mailing or membership lists), or, more vaguely, claim to represent "concerned citizens" or "the public" on an issue. Claims to a large constituency are especially powerful in legislative lobbying. One national-level organizer comments: "If we had no members we would be out of business. It's that simple. You not only lose your funding base, but you also lose strength. If I went to Congress and told them I represented ten members, I'd be in big trouble, as opposed to representing 160 thousand members. So membership recruitment is a constantly important aspect of our association."

The large membership is also a symbol of organizational vitality to current and potential members. The morale and confidence of members increases as they see that the organization is alive and growing with new members.

While appearing to represent a large number of people may work for a time, at some point an organization will be challenged and need to give evidence of its strength. Then numbers have strategic importance, allowing organizations to match their rhetoric with real "people in the streets." The ability to produce large numbers of active participants intensifies the pressure an organization is able to bring to bear upon issues. Tactics such as marches, demonstrations, boycotts, and letter writing campaigns rely on people to carry them out. They are not feasible without numbers. If threats to disrupt cannot be carried out, the array of pressure tools available to a group is limited, and the organization is likely to be taken less seriously by opponents. On the other hand, the ability to amass a large number of demonstrators on a fairly regular basis confers credibility such that the organization may only need to threaten the opponent with action in future confrontations.

Pragmatically, new members bring issues, ideas, experiences, skills, and their own networks of friends and contacts, all of which are important organizational resources. Members can also be an important source of finance by paying dues, using their contacts with funding sources, and running fund-raising events. A solid financial base coming from members reduces organizational uncertainty and dependency on other funding sources that may have strings attached.

Members may also reduce the workload of staff by taking on tasks staff would otherwise have to do (e.g., office work, producing newsletters, recruitment, casework). Frequently these are tasks that members, because of their relationships, can accomplish more readily than staff (e.g., local fund-raising, new member recruitment, outreach to other groups, media contacts), making the organization that much more effective.

Once on board, however, members are not necessarily permanent assets. Member attrition, even among those who have been very active, is a fact of life in most social action organizations. Sometimes the reasons are unavoidable—people move, work and family demands take precedence, or members experience illness or difficulties in getting to meetings. Member attrition in some social action organizations can reflect particular life circumstances. For example, organizations for the unemployed tend to experience natural attrition; when members get a job they tend to leave the organization, to return only if they are again unemployed. In student groups members graduate or leave the area over the summer.

People can also drop out after a period of activism because they are "burned out," because they are unhappy with the organization, or because their own problem has been addressed—reasons that frustrate an organizer who may have been investing in those people as long-term participants. For all these reasons it is necessary to recruit new members to replace those who are gone. Despite attrition, the constant renewal of membership keeps a social action organization vital.

Given the importance of recruitment, we would expect a good deal of such activity to take place in social action organizations. But we are concerned that the importance organizers and leaders attach to recruitment in theory is only questionably present in practice. Our analysis of how forty-two organizers actually allocate their time shows that less than 1 percent of their time, on average, is spent recruiting. While this is a rough estimate, many organizers we have talked to admit they don't perform the activities that add up to the "constant recruitment" they say is needed.

The most obvious explanation for this discrepancy is that recruiting is a lot of work. Unlike strategy development, which has obvious benchmarks and a clear resolution, recruitment is never good enough and never finished. There are always more people to interest and involve. Unlike working with current members whose interests and strengths are familiar, recruiting requires talking with strangers on their turf and their terms.

There can be a built-in tension between issue or campaign work and recruiting for organizers if they distinguish these activities and see little overlap between them. They tend to choose program work over recruiting, because of their own priorities and what they hear members want, with no one else picking up the recruiting work. Research and strategy require the skill and experience of an organizer. Frequently recruiting can be successfully performed by people with other skills. Since it can be argued that members are in the best position to recruit within their own networks, it is easy for organizers to believe that members *should* carry that load and to blame them when little recruiting is accomplished.

Another reason organizers may not recruit is because when people join they invariably and appropriately bring their own agendas, questions, and status needs. These create additional demands on organizers, and some organizers experience these as interference. Like some librarians who only grudgingly allow others to borrow "their" books, some organizers are frustrated by the people who comprise "their" organizations. Consequently, they question how much time and energy should be expended on recruiting and working with participants. Defensively, organizers and their long-term leadership may disparage recruits as less committed than those who seek out the group. Such an analysis would place the responsibility for joining in the recruit's hands and obviate any form of active outreach. Organizers wind up, like the proverbial preacher, attending to the "already converted."

Whatever the reasons, the constant and comprehensive recruiting some organizers and members talk about is probably rarely achieved. To the degree it is not, organizers should understand that their issue work and the health of their organizations may suffer. If recruitment is not consciously built into every activity of staff and volunteers, it may be easily overlooked. The burden is on the organizer to view recruitment and member maintenance as separate and important work and treat it as such. We will suggest both a way of conceptualizing participation and methods that can be purposefully employed to engage and sustain members.

High Access Social Action Organizations

Many students of organizing have stressed continued positive interactions between organizers and participants as critical to successful organizing (Delgado 1986, Fisher 1984, Gerlach and Hine 1970, Henderson and Thomas 1980, Mondros and Wilson 1986; O'Brien 1975). Most of these discussions focus on the interactional skills of the organizer. We think the actual dynamics in organizations are better captured by a transactional view of the relationships among members and between members and the organizer. Staff, existing members, and new members all contribute to the form, intensity, and growth of those relationships. An organization may or may not want to involve newcomers who have shown interest, and may or may not have ways of sustaining their interest. At the same time newcomers typically have ideas about the way in which they would like to participate in the organization. The organizer, current members, and newcomers, then, must negotiate their expectations. These relationships may also change over time, in response to the experiences of the participants.

If organizers are to involve people they need to understand that there are real environmental deterrents to participation. For example, it is difficult for people to travel to take part in national, regional, and statewide activities at remote headquarters. Local organizers, too, have seen a change in the participation patterns of their members (Mondros and McGuffin 1992). Changes in the economy, particularly the need to work or to work more, have already made people less available for community participation. Recognizing these real obstacles, organizers must ensure that their organizations are accessible, inviting, open, and "user friendly." Such organizations promote "high access" because they are consciously designed to make it easy for people to join, to find personal and social niches within the organization, to assume responsibility and maintain their allegiance, and to progress to higher levels of responsibility and leadership. Consequently, organizations that are purposefully accessible counter the problems social action organizations typically face in engaging and maintaining people.

Social action organizations use what we will call *bridges, barriers*, and *gates* to promote or limit access. Bridges are structures or processes that facilitate peoples' participation, such as outreach, orientations, training, buddy systems, and the availability of roles. Barriers are conscious or unconscious structures or procedures that impede entrée to or within an organization: insiders' jargon, narrowly controlled decisions, and one-way and limited communications are examples. Gates are structures or procedures that are used within organizations to allow mobility to some people while excluding others, such as use of predetermined criteria for access to leadership positions. While barriers block involvement arbitrarily, gates are often legitimate ways of ensuring a competent cadre of people is installed in key roles.

Figure 3.1 displays the continuum from high access to low access organizations. We develop these concepts further in this chapter and in chapter 4. They are used throughout the process of member recruitment and maintenance, and it is to these processes that we now turn.

FIGURE 3.1
Continuum of Member Access

HIGH MEMBER ACCESS	AMBIGUOUS ACCESS	LOW MEMBER ACCESS
No barriers erected; bridges help members in; few gates for leaders	Few bridges, gates, or barriers for members; staff and leader roles unclear	Few barriers or bridges for members; many gates for leaders

The Phases of Participation

We see member participation as a process composed of four phases, each with its own opportunities for the organization to use bridges and gates and avoid barriers.

Phase I: Identifying a Member Pool In this phase the organizer selects a group of people who appear likely to support an issue or organization. Selecting a responsive constituency or "membership pool" is the first hurdle, and one that some organizations never surmount. If an organizer selects an inadequate base, i.e., one with few people, one that cannot be built up over time with increasing numbers of people, or one that *should* be responsive but is not, he or she is reduced to being a "prophet in the wilderness," proclaiming a message to a deaf audience (Haley 1969). Identifying needed member characteristics and then correctly targeting a responsive population for recruitment creates a bridge to those who are likely to join while avoiding wasteful efforts with others. Failure here almost certainly ensures limited success in "building a base" (Brager and Specht 1973, Lippitt, Watson, Wesley 1958, Von Hoffman 1962).

Phase II: Creating and Communicating a Message In this phase the organizer creates a message that will pique the interest of the desired population. The message persuades people about either the importance of issues or the idea of working with the organization, and acts as a bridge to induce people into the organization. The messages must be broad enough to attract sufficient numbers of new people and delivered clearly, forcefully, and in ways the intended audience can hear to attract joiners from a population pool. Weak, intermittent, narrowly conceived messages or those crafted without the intended audience in mind act as barriers rather than bridges. Once the organization's message is heard and acted on by enough people, the next phase begins.

Phase III: Initial Engagement In this phase the organizer builds a bridge for people from what might be passing interest into participation in the work of the organization. The organizer reaches out in a meaningful way such that newcomers feel an initial attachment to the group. Barriers to participation are assiduously avoided. Taking advantage of whatever has brought someone into contact with the organization—curiosity, hope, need, or fear—the organizer assesses why he or she got involved and tries to enhance this motivation. New members' impressions of the organization are tested against the initial reality they experience; their idea of how to be involved is contrasted with the opportunities offered by the organization. If, however, newcomers perceive their participation is not wanted or needed, they may never return.

Phase IV: Sustaining and Deepening Participation In this phase the organizer attempts to sustain the interest and participation of members across time. The organizer continues to assess and enhance an individual member's personal interests and commitments, building bridges from mere membership to organizational activism. Increasingly, members are encouraged to become involved in more complex tasks, roles, and decisions. As their participation endures and duties expand, they can become "leaders," those who are responsible for the organization and its work. Gates are used to select out those who are invested enough to enter the inner circle of leaders who will make the most important decisions in the organization.

In this chapter we look closely at the first two phases of member involvement, paying particular attention to the interactional tasks of the organizer in each phase. Initial engagement and sustaining and deepening participation are the focus of the next chapter.

Phase I: Identifying a Member Pool

The major organizer task of this phase is to select a pool of potential members from which a large number of active members results. Organizers have to know how to identify a member pool; they generally use one or a combination of three major principles to select: networks, representativeness, or special individual attributes.

Networks Organizers often identify member pools by tapping into people's natural networks, which, if responsive, will produce more members more quickly. This approach is expedient. The organizer can contact one individual who will, in turn, contact others in a network or introduce the organizer to others. People are likely to be more responsive to the organization if they join with their friends. Gerlach and Hine (1970) discuss the importance of face-to-face recruitment by committed members along lines of preexisting, significant social relationships.

Further, the legitimacy of the organization is increased when people trust and respect someone in the primary group who speaks well of the organization. For example, the director of a senior center may designate an individual to represent the club at social action organization meetings. This concept is widely used in the parish ministry model, where churches and synagogues join as an institution. The rabbi, parish priest, or pastor sanctions the social action organization and encourages parishioners to join. The religious leader generally encour-

ages or designates a few congregants to represent the church or
synagogue as an affiliate of the social action organization. The following quote captures the potential importance of being recruited by
someone known and respected:

> I received a visit first in my house from the organizer, who was sent
> to talk to me by the pastor. He explained to me his concerns with
> things in the community. Obviously my pastor thought that I was a
> person that knew something about it or could help somehow. . . .
> The point that my pastor considered me a community leader in my
> own right was an energizing factor. That was highly important,
> more important than my own idea that I wanted to do it.

These leaders trust their clergy and are flattered to be singled out. Being chosen confers a special status in their congregation and the community that encourages their participation in the organization. Such
personal recruitment by someone respected and trusted by the individual suggests the importance of expressive rewards as motivation for
participation.

When organizations use a group membership structure (i.e., people
affiliate as members of a preexisting group), the entire membership of
the primary organizations is recruited. The organization then can
claim to represent all the members of their member groups. Again, the
parish ministry model or congregational organizing approach perhaps
makes best use of this principle. By working through local churches
and synagogues their organizers tap into a natural primary network,
have access to a large number of people at one place and time, can
claim to represent all the congregants, and additionally have identified
a group that, at least in theory, will be responsive to a message of social
justice. These organizers propose to build bridges from the congrega-
tions to the organization. They are really "networks of networks,"
with individuals recruiting their own friends and neighbors at the
house of worship. Another less personal form of networking occurs
when organizations purchase other groups' mailing lists and attempt
to attract those people into their organization. Environmental organizers, for example, make extensive use of this approach, reasoning that
an individual with demonstrated interest in environmental concerns is
more likely to respond to a message from their group. In some cases
the identification of a natural network may seem obvious. For example, a local organizer may simply contact all area churches, synagogues, civic groups, and block associations. A national women's
rights organizer may automatically look to member lists of other wom-

en's political and pro-choice groups as a "natural" member pool. Similarly, people who have experienced a problem (e.g., family and friends of victims of an illness, relatives of the physically or mentally challenged) are natural pools from which to draw activists on those issues. For example, Mothers Against Drunk Driving (MADD) automatically reaches out to the families of victims.

Sometimes the issues of an organization would logically suggest a network that is so infirm, impoverished, vulnerable, or overwhelmed that getting them to fully participate would be enormously difficult if not futile. Such is the case with children, students approaching graduation, caregivers of Alzheimer patients, and the mentally ill homeless. In such circumstances a professional network focused on these problems can be a possible member pool. Though the professionals may not experience the problem in the same way as the victims, they often have career interests that motivate them.

Organizers, however, must be careful not to restrict themselves to "obvious" member pools. It is easy to get locked into one or a few networks, ignore other potential ones, or even anger a competing network. For example, women in high school and college are a natural pool for organizations dealing with women's issues because they are beginning to experience discrimination personally, and have free time and few commitments. Yet they may be overlooked because they are members of sororities and school clubs rather than the political organizations women's groups frequently draw from.

It is also important not to exclude someone who wants to participate but doesn't have a network. This can easily happen when someone is new to the community and hasn't yet formed bonds. Parish ministry model organizations may unwittingly exclude the unaffiliated. Some people are not affiliated with a religious institution, but that should not preclude their participation.

Representativeness When a group's constituency is ethnically, racially, religiously, geographically, and socially diverse, it is more difficult for opponents and targets to dismiss the organization (Brager and Holloway 1978). For example, a senior citizens organization that draws members from senior clubs and centers is harder for politicians to ignore if the membership reflects the demographics of the seniors in the city. A statewide student organization ideally represents every campus. An organization promoting rights of and opportunities for working women will want to recruit union women, women working in male-dominated fields, and women from churches and clubs to secure a broad cross-section of legitimacy and influence. Strategic composition of a membership to reflect the constituency combined with sheer numbers of members is the ideal combination.

If some parts of the potential constituency are unrepresented or underrepresented, infusions of new demographic groups are needed to strengthen the organization's representativeness. Organizers often talk of the need to increase their representativeness by adding new groups of people—most often minorities, low income people, women, or people from various church denominations.

Yet while organizers want to attract a rainbow membership, the desired people may not be interested in the organization and its issues. These people may not define the organization's issues as a problem, especially one worthy of their time and commitment. For example, pro-choice organizers have sometimes had difficulty attracting young women because they have not had the experience of growing up in an era when abortion was illegal and have not personally suffered the tragedies of an earlier generation.

Many organizers say that effort alone won't result in a more diversified membership. Trying to sell new people on issues they don't respond to is essentially attempting to add them without altering the organization's agenda to reflect their concerns. The organizer can't just say, "I want Black students," and go out and get them. The organization must take on issues that concern its constituents, change the agenda or focus, and make the organization appealing to them on a substantive level.

An environmental organizer for an upstate, basically white middle-class New York organization uses another approach to encourage activism, one that capitalizes on the self-interest of a new group and allows them organizational autonomy: "If you are talking about Harlem, why in the world would they support our organizational goals? What we are doing there is focusing on people who are abusing the Harlem River and the waterfront. You find the people, and if they are interested you assist them so that their organization grows, and later it may have some affiliation with us." This organizer does not attempt to alter the membership pool of her own organization at all. Rather, she reaches out to a new pool of people of a different race and class basically as a consultant, and sets up a separate organization of those people in hopes that some organizational affiliation may occur between the two groups. The coalition, then, can claim to be more widely representative.

Special Personal Attributes It is common for organizers to have ideas about the individual characteristics that would make someone a valuable member. There is no agreement about what makes for an "ideal member," but organizers try to engage those who fit their own notions. "You're the fish I wanted to hook," says the union organizer in the film *Norma Rae* when the title character agrees to distribute leaflets. These special attributes are valued over demographics or how many others people are likely to bring along with them. People are valued first and foremost because they are responsive to the organization. Beyond this three categories are important: 1. personal stakes or self-interest in the organization's issues, 2. personal relationships people have already established or are in a position to establish (e.g., formal or informal positions of influence in the community), and 3. capacities to contribute directly through personal energy, experience gained through a history of activism, and expertise in one or more areas.

Many organizers feel that people will be more interested in joining, working in, and continuing to participate in an organization if they work on issues in which they have self-interest. They believe these self-interested people are empowered by their work and more willing to fight for what they want. Consequently, they identify potential member pools by identifying people who experience the problem the organization is pursuing. For example, an organizer working on pre- and perinatal issues visits clinics, laundromats, and toy stores looking for women who have recently given birth or are pregnant.

While self-interest is certainly a major motivation for an individual to join an organization, a member pool of self-interested individuals has its drawbacks. People's life circumstances may prevent active involvement, they may not bring the necessary organizational skills, and they may leave the organization as soon as their individual problem is resolved. The self-interest is evident in organizations composed of people with physical, mental, or economic limitations (e.g., developmentally challenged, workplace injured, welfare recipients, or the unemployed). Yet, organizers who have such overwhelmed and impaired constituencies may still need less burdened members to do the work of the organization.

Even in organizations of less disabled populations, a wholly self-interested membership will cause problems. Members often simply drop out when their individual problems are resolved. It is a frustrating irony—success often results in attrition. One leader describes three types of members—those who come to the organization because of their own problem and leave after it is solved; those whose problem is addressed but stick around to help others with similar problems; and those who learn of the organization's work and participate in it, even though they bring no problem of their own. In this approach member pools are not rigid. There are attempts to use self-interest to attract members, without the organization being strangled by the problems self-interest brings. The organizer defines self-interested people as her primary member pool, and builds the organization's agenda from their interests. In her organization new people create new demands that the group must be willing to accede to. She then finds a way of bridging their immediate self-interest to the broader organization through leadership development work. And there is still room for others who don't come to the organization out of their own needs.

A second attribute organizers often look for is people who have influence. These are often altruistic individuals who care about the organizations' causes and issues but are generally less needy. Often they bring skills and talents that are immediately useful to the organization. For these reasons many organizations' boards of directors are composed of well-known figures and politicians. Name recognition, ability to attract funding and media exposure, and entrée to power are major advantages of this member pool. Equally important are the skills these people bring.

Still, selecting a pool of altruistic people may present different sorts of problems. Recruitment is harder with members who lack the immediate experience of the problem and the compelling drive to resolve it. Such people are often overcommitted and have little time to give to the organization on a regular basis. Perhaps most important, members engaged purely out of altruism may lack the anger that is needed to keep members in a fight. They may reject the use of confrontational tactics, even when they are needed to make a change. Consequently, the organization's resources are limited. An organization can, however, protect itself from the limiting influence of these people by ensuring that they are not in the voting majority. Allowing such people to serve on an advisory board that consults but doesn't make organizational decisions, is another way of involving altruists without allowing them to control the direction of the organization.

Organizers often look for people with special skills, particularly a history of activism. People with a history of activism are familiar with the work, know what to expect, and can work most easily with staff. Expertise in the organization's issue areas, leadership qualities, anger, wanting to do something about a problem, and not stopping at complaining about a problem are other individual attributes organizers hope for in new members.

Once again identifying a member pool on the basis of such personal characteristics is problematic. First, it is often difficult to know where to go to find such people, and initially difficult to assess who has skill and who doesn't. Second, most people will not innately possess such skills. Work with the unemployed, welfare recipients, the homeless, the elderly, and students may get stalled at this juncture. Moreover, identifying people on the basis of skills may prematurely establish gates to member involvement, allowing only those with skills to enter. Too often organizers are tempted to focus their recruitment on the basis of skills rather than attempt to train current members. For example, an organizer may find someone who is angry about a problem and wants to organize around it, but who gets nervous when speaking in front of a group. It may be seductive to find a more articulate speaker rather than work on developing speaking skills with this new member.

Organizers often give too little thought to what the potential membership pool could be for their organizations. Identifying member pools should be a thoughtful assessment of who might become involved in the organization and why. We have described three principles for identifying member pools—the use of natural networks, representativeness, and member attributes—that can serve as guidelines. Knowing that each principle has its advantages and incipient problems, organizers can use them consciously. As much as possible organizers should look to combine the principles of networking, representativeness, and special attributes, using the advantages of one to offset the deficits of another. A good example of such a combination is used in a senior citizens organization. The member pool includes senior clubs located in various churches, settlement houses, and union halls. By involving the clubs the organizer taps the social networks of individual seniors, pulls in diverse people who reflect the city's aging population, and is able to identify people with self-interest on current issues. Professionals and altruists serve on an advisory board whose job it is to make recommendations, advise on legislation, and seek funding.

The concern with finding members raises the issue of excluding people—of creating clear barriers to participation. Organizer Saul Alinsky, for example, warned against the conflict of interest inherent in including politicians because their covert, personal motives may often be at odds with the organization's collective needs and interests (Alinsky 1971). While it stands to reason that organizers guard against subversion of the organization by an individual with self-serving interests, the social action organizers we interviewed showed little tendency to exclude anyone. They put their emphasis on *inclusion* over exclusion, and this appears warranted to the extent that their organizations are not targets for infiltration. It is easier to expel one or two unwanted members than to involve the necessary numbers of desired ones. Thus, the identification of member pools is essentially a process of building bridges from individuals to the organization rather than erecting barriers to limit participation.

Phase II: Creating and Communicating a Message

The second phase of enjoining participation is the creation of recruitment messages and defining the means of communication to get them to people in the membership pool. This phase is often called "outreach." We will use this term to include both the message given and the methods used to present them. We will also discuss how recruitment messages reflect peoples' reasons for joining.

What is it that the organizer and leaders want to say to prospective recruits? It is perhaps axiomatic to suggest that recruitment messages should be crafted with an audience in mind. Like any astute advertiser, the organizer should craft a message out of what he or she knows of the interests and motivations of potential members. Essentially, the message, something that people are likely to hear and respond to, forms a bridge from prospective members to the organization.

It is probably true that people join organizations for diverse reasons. Wilson proposes that "people join associations with a variety of motives, and that they are more or less rational about action taken on behalf of these reasons" (Wilson 1973:26–27.) Still, he notes that established organizations offer a "dominant character" or dominant reward that becomes the group's primary incentive to new members. The fervency of joining will depend on how highly this primary incentive is valued by an individual. Yet, "supplementary incentives" are also needed to augment the rewards for those not fully dedicated to the primary incentive. Wilson (1973), in agreement with others (O'Brien 1975), suggests that combined motives are likely, with people giving importance to different motives.

Therefore, soliciting and analyzing the interests and likely motivations of those in desired member pools is important as a form of marketing research. The resulting information is used to design "high-probability" recruitment messages. The content addresses the following questions: "What do we want to say in this message?" "What's in it for a joiner?" "What can the recruit contribute?" "What can I say the effort will produce?" The answers are ways to bridge individual interest to the work of the organization.

Primarily, an assessment of people's interests will yield enough information to be able to get them interested and involved. Knowing who joins and why tells you who is likely to join and how to present the group and its work to them by connecting with their values and perceptions. This initial assessment also allows organizers to learn something of the overall public image of the organization.

These assessments can be either formal or informal. Informally, organizers can learn why people join through casual discussions with members who have. As one grassroots organizer puts it, "We don't do it formally; we sit down after a meeting to have a beer and people tell you that without being asked."

Many organizations use meetings of members or constituents to present and discuss problems and issues. Such meetings are variously called community meetings, annual conventions, and national, state-wide, or regional conferences. While they are generally focused on issues, the agenda can include a discussion of what brought the people there and how they chose the organization.

More formally, some organizers complete intake forms or cards for all new recruits listing interests, concerns, and what attracted them to the organization. These are reviewed to see how people state problems and view issues (Mondros and Wilson 1982). Formal door-to-door surveys about community concerns can also ask how and why respondents might come to participate in the organization, as can the occasional mailed surveys placed in a group's newsletter.

Whatever the data collection approach, organizers can communicate more purposefully when they understand something of people's motives. Generally, people say they join social action organizations for one of three reasons: self-interest, concern for the issues, or an attraction to the organization itself. Correspondingly, three types of recruitment messages can be used to build a bridge from people's motives to the organization: 1. messages that focus on people's self-interest in the issues, explaining what instrumental outcomes people can get out of belonging to the organization, 2. messages that capture people's interest and concern, and 3. messages that project an image of the organization's style.

Self-Interest as a Bridge to Participation

Many members cite self-interest as a powerful motivation for joining. The mother of a mentally retarded child, a housewife concerned with a landfill in her neighborhood, residents of an old inner-city neighborhood experiencing withdrawal of city services, tenants, welfare recipients, lesbians, and the unemployed all sought help from an organization for conditions they faced. These leaders make clear that they sought out the organization because of a problem they could not solve for themselves. Consequently, many organizers' primary message is intended to appeal to people who directly experience a problem.

From de Tocqueville (1969) to Alinsky (1972), the potential of receiving benefits that are needed or personally advantageous has long been noted as a bridge to participation. The argument is that while disadvantaged people have interests in common, they are also self-interested individuals who rationally calculate what membership in an organization can do for them (O'Brien 1975, Olsen 1965). Individuals must receive "personal advantages" (i.e., instrumental results) from joining, and the inability to offer individual instrumental rewards will always limit participation. Consequently, social action organizations must offer individual benefits that *only* accrue to members. There are ways, however, of mitigating the power of this public-private dilemma. Examples include offering collective benefits, using a federated structure that builds on primary organizations that do offer individual benefits, or providing social incentives (viewed as less stable and as not competitive with the other rewards).

We also view self-interest as a strong motive for many members, and argue that it should at least be a part of all organizations' recruitment messages. Of course, self-interest is more easily assessed when organizers have easy access to people, but geography should not be used as an excuse for ignorance. On the other hand, self-interest should not be the sole message of an organization. First, prospective joiners are likely to have motivations other than self-interest. Second when self-interest is the only message, it is almost an invitation for people to leave the organization when their problem is resolved.

Consequently, while a message of self-interest may be used initially to recruit people, organizers must add other messages subsequently to build on the initial motive, broadening members' concerns beyond the most narrow definition. The organizer must build a bridge from the recruit's initial self-interest to other issues that are perhaps more abstract and not as personally threatening and finally to a broader concern for the health of the organization. In these messages organizers emphasize the potential power of a multi-issue people's organization and its ability to bring pressure to bear on a variety of issues that may be of interest to a recruit's fellow members. In the following practice illustration an organizer is shown working with new recruits. The organizer's initial work with the people in the meeting concerned repairs in their apartment building. The landlord agreed to make the repairs, and the organizer is now working to take the first small step of broadening their initial self-interest from their building to the neighborhood surrounding it.

ORGANIZER: How are the repairs going on the building?

MR. J: Real well. They fixed the elevators Monday, and they were working on the lights today.

MRS. G: I can't believe we finally got it done. I can't believe we did it. Nobody believed Old Man Manson would listen to us folks.

ORGANIZER: Yeah, well, it took a lot of work. But you folks were terrific. It's amazing what can be done when you work together. By the way, where is Mr. Cruz tonight?

MR. L: Said he couldn't come. Said he had other things to do. And anyway, we got the work done so he didn't know what there was to talk about.

ORGANIZER: I bet a lot of you thought that. How about it? Is there anything else you want to do about your neighborhood? (Here I consciously used the word neighborhood so we could get into a discussion of issues beyond their own building).

MRS. K: I don't really bother much with anything else. As long as my building is okay, I'm satisfied.

ORGANIZER: Do you really think so? What happens when you go out? Do you feel safe on the streets? Do your streets get cleaned and your garbage picked up? How do you feel about that vacant lot on the corner of the block? It's got a ton of garbage and I bet a lot of rats. (The example of the vacant lot was conscious. A few people had complained about it). Then, too, if the other buildings in the neighborhood go downhill, your landlord is not going to want to fix anything and you'll have the same problems again. (Here I wanted to point out the relationship between their building and the surrounding neighborhood).

MRS. N: That's true, you know. The landlord will follow what he sees around him. I have an aunt living on Euclid Avenue and they can't get their landlord to do anything either.

ORGANIZER: I bet you all know other people in the neighborhood with the same problems. And like you, they don't know what to do. I bet you could teach them how to organize their building like you did. (Here I was trying to engage their pride of accomplishment). And maybe together we could work on things like police protection or the vacant lot. Luis, do you think people in the building across the street might want to do something about the lot? (Luis had mentioned the lot to me before and I thought he might pick up on it).

MR. L: I think they might do something. Their building is bad and they live right next to that lot. I think Cruz has a friend in that building who asked about us.

ORGANIZER: Great. Luis, why don't you talk to Cruz and see if he'll talk to his friend. (Here was a chance to give Luis something to do and to reinvolve Cruz).

MRS. G: I'd like to see that. This used to be such a nice neighborhood, and I think we can make it better for everyone. If our block is nice, our building will be nice too. And we can show them how we did it. After all, they're our neighbors.

ORGANIZER: How about it then? Let's make a list of who we know who lives in these other building and who will contact them. Maybe we can form a committee which will work on housing in the neighborhood. (At the end of this discussion, I felt we had made the first move beyond the building to a neighborhood issue, and at least Luis and Mrs. G. were with me).

Issue Interest as a Bridge to Participation

Messages tailored around issues take into account that concern for an issue is a motivation for joining. Some volunteers in social action organization leadership positions typically report that they feel a need to do *something* on the issue, to contribute something toward its alleviation or solution, even if they don't directly suffer from the problem.

Some people come to the organization for the issue rather than out of need or attraction to the organization. Issue interest most reflects the literature's notion of shared goals or ideology; an individual's values are articulated in the issue and confirmed by acting on it (Gerlach and Hine 1970, Wilson 1973). To capture these people organizers craft recruitment messages that stress the issue or problem, the wider social justice goals being sought, and the danger of staying silent.

Using only issue messages has its limitations as well. If people join only because of the issues, they may feel no special connection to the organization. They can as easily work with another group with a similar agenda. Recognizing this, organizers appeal to other motives. As Gerlach and Hine (1970) suggest, the existence of a vehement opposition enhances people's interest in joining social action organizations. Organizers' use of military terms (e.g., *troops, target, action*) is purposeful—it is used to create a clear sense of friend and foe, of overt conflict, and of danger and high stakes. The need to declare "Which side are you on" enhances identity and commitment to the group. Values and interest are further enhanced by working alongside others of like mind. Messages that emphasize the existence of the opposition and the esprit de corps of the group can be used to enhance the initial motive and to build a bridge from issue interest to investment in the organization itself. The illustration below shows a national organizer for gay rights making use of opposition to build commitment to the organization. He speaks with a group of well-to-do gay men in New York.

MR. B: I don't see why we would want to spend the limited resources of this organization on the gay bashing issue. The AIDS issue is much more important.

MR. T: That's true. It just isn't as important as the AIDS work.

ORGANIZER: That's true when you only think about numbers. But when you think about how it hurts our people, I'm not so sure. We live comfortably here in New York, we're out of the closet, and most people are pretty supportive, or at least not hostile. But what of all the others who live places where it's not acceptable to be gay, where it's criminal? Would we want to live there? Could we even travel there? Our cocoon is pretty small when you think about it.

MR. R: That may be true but there just aren't enough incidents of it to warrant our spending a lot of staff time on it.

ORGANIZER: True, but you know gay bashing is on the rise, even here in New York. And there are people who would just love to see the trend continue. Homophobes use that to justify continuing discrimination laws—"the people don't like gays either, blah, blah, blah. They're different—it's okay to bash gays." If you ask me, this is just the tip of the iceberg. "Gay bashing is okay, and it's okay to ignore AIDS because it's just a gay disease, and it's okay to discriminate." We have to stop homophobia everywhere we find it. And if our organization doesn't take it on, who will?

MR. C: It's true. Nobody else gives a damn.

ORGANIZER: That's what this organization is for—to protect every one of us. And since we're in better shape in New York, we must be all the more committed to helping folks in the small towns. They have to live under those creeps, and we're more free to fight them.

Organizational Attraction as a Bridge to Participation

Many organizers believe that members join because of the attractiveness of the organization, its style, its work, and its successes. Several aspects of an organization spur member interest: the organization's "track record," the strategies used, the political stance taken, the degree of aggressiveness promoted, the way issues and goals are proposed, the composition of the membership, the opportunities for involvement and personal growth, and the skill of the staff are all mentioned as attractive elements.

Usually leaders report that a combination of factors drew them. They believe that members have some sense of the group before joining, and use that information to make their decision to join. Members may hear about social action groups through friends, neighbors, newspaper articles, or through other organizations in which they are members. Local organizations, in fact, may be quite familiar. Statewide and national organizations receive media exposure that perhaps makes people more receptive to a contact from the organization. Although it is hard to believe that recruits have anything more than impressions about the organization before joining, these early opinions may be enough to pique initial interest.

Consequently, organizers use messages that project an image of their organizations. It is hoped that people will be attracted to this organizational persona. The illustration below shows an organizer who works on homeless issues making a presentation about the organization to the Women's Auxiliary of a Presbyterian church.

ORGANIZER: Have any of you heard about Bradetown Emergency Action Team, or what we call B.E.A.T.?

MRS. S: I think I have. Weren't you the group that worked on getting the city to increase the numbers of beds for the homeless?

ORGANIZER: That was us. And we have done a lot of other things too. We got the city to place homeless families immediately, instead of keeping them overnight in welfare offices. We forced the Board of Elections to register homeless people who wanted to vote. We closed down the old Chelsea Hotel—which, as you know, was an awful place. We forced the city to build two new permanent residencies for the mentally ill homeless. We've only been around since '83, and you can see from the list I'm handing out how many things we've won. (Here I was trying to stress our track record of successes).

MRS. T: You're doing a lot for them, I know, but you know it's a problem for us too. All the homeless hanging out around the church has made this neighborhood a disgrace. We have all kinds of vandalism, the kids can't play outside, it's dangerous to walk home from church at night . . .

ORGANIZER: (Of course, I knew this would come up. People are bothered by the homeless, and I have to be careful to recognize that they have legitimate concerns. I wanted to now tell them how our organization understood their worries, and included them in our agenda. But I also wanted to reach to the fair-minded part of them, to their sense of justice.) I think that's what makes B.E.A.T. different from other organizations. We try to understand homelessness as a *community* problem. We understand that you don't wish the homeless ill, but you want to live decent lives too. So, for example, we push for small shelters all around the city, not just putting gigantic ones up in one neighborhood that already has a lot of shelters. And we work for permanent residences where the homeless get the help they need and are not out there bothering the neighbors. And we work together—homeless people, professionals who work with them, and neighborhood people—to find the best solution for that particular neighborhood. We don't work against you. We work with you. Your concerns and ideas are part of our work.

There are many advantages in communicating the style of the organization. Since these organizations are often in competition with other groups working on the same issues, organizers craft messages so their group will stand out in the eyes of prospective recruits who could as easily go elsewhere. Further, by projecting a "style," organizers are more certain to attract people who not only agree with their issues but with their strategies and structures as well.

Communicating only the organization's style, however, also has its limitations, basically because it relies on first impressions and what the organizer believes will be attractive rather than knowing what actually is appealing. It is understandable why organizers believe that the style of the organization is an important drawing card for new recruits. Because organizers themselves bring the change orientation and practice method that are major components of organizational style, they may be projecting onto recruits the ideas, images, and beliefs they would like new members to have rather than those that might come from an actual assessment of others' interests and beliefs.

Too, an audience can be as easily turned off to an organizational style as enticed by it. Frequently people need to work within the organization—to experience the people in it and the way it works—in order to appreciate its usefulness. This is especially true if the group is aggressive. As one organizer explains,

> People are afraid of conflict. They're afraid of confrontation. If I say we're going to go to the mayor and demand such and such, I'll gain some people, but I'll lose a lot too. As people work on an issue, however, they often begin to truly experience the odds they're up against. They see things for what they are, and they get frustrated. Then, they're ready to do battle. I don't sell our aggressive style. I let people experience the need for it for themselves.

Messages that speak to self interest, issue interest, and organization style all have strengths and drawbacks. It is important for organizers to know which ones work best for their particular organization and which are most attractive to the member pools they would like to reach. It is generally a good idea to transmit a combination of messages, designed to cover all kinds of motives.

Recruitment Methods and Cost-Benefit Calculations

Organizers use a variety of recruitment methods, and, as McLuhan (1964) suggests, there can be a good deal riding on the ones selected. In addition to the content of the messages, the methods used also project the image of the social action organization. Personal contacts, house meetings, telephone calls are all personalized ways of meeting and "selling" new people, and can communicate personal concern. Mailed solicitations, on the other hand, can suggest a more impersonal, distant organization. Rather than recruit on "automatic pilot"—using methods traditional to the organization or those most amenable to the staff—organizers can think through alternative methods by examining the costs and benefits of each approach.

Organizers view recruitment methods at least implicitly in cost-benefit terms. The costs of time and resources, and necessary loss of attention to other areas, are weighed against the benefits of funds raised, of large turnouts of people, and of resulting participation of people who can contribute to the group over time. Obviously, the best recruitment method is one that costs little and yields many of the "right kind" of people, and the worst is one that is expensive and yields little. Inexpensive methods that yield few people do little damage, while costly methods that result in greater numbers of members have some rewards.

Personal recruiting, involving face-to-face and one-on-one encounters between the organizer and a potential recruit, is an expensive, time consuming method that generally results in many new members. The most common forms are door-to-door canvassing, community surveys, house meetings, and other formal or informal meetings in the community. This costly but high-yield method is supported by many organizers who feel the personal touch is vital to recruitment. The audience is "captive," and one can answer questions or objections people may raise. Personal recruiting often takes place during other activities, such as meetings or social events. Whatever the technique, the true purpose is to initiate a personal relationship that is difficult to reject.

Local organizers, are, by definition, more able to make personal contacts. They can canvass neighborhoods, make personal visits, hold house meetings, put tables up at a busy intersection or at a mall. National, regional, and statewide organizations are wise to look for opportunities when such contacts are possible. Some of these organizers follow up with people who write letters to the editor in newspapers or speak out at meetings. They then try to get these more vocal people to recruit their social network. Some organizers travel to local communities, identify local leaders, and train them to make personal contacts. While personal recruiting may be costly and expensive in staff time, if recruits then convince others in their networks to join the benefits are enhanced relative to the costs in time spent.

Formal group presentations are a less expensive approach to recruiting because the organizer can communicate with more people simultaneously. In group presentations an organizer retains the ability to answer questions and reassure prospective members, to tailor a message to a group's particular concerns, and to become known to them as a person with a reasonable and friendly style. Since a single presentation can address the questions or concerns shared by many people, they are less costly than individual discussions. Consequently, the member yield from this approach is likely to be relatively high, especially if the presentation is given or introduced by someone respected by the group. For example, in the parish ministry model, priests, rabbis, and ministers are encouraged to first discuss the organization from the pulpit. Subsequently, they introduce the organizer or member, who describes the organization and its work in greater detail (Boyte 1989, Joravsky 1990, Mondros and McGuffin 1992).

Another personal recruitment approach some social action organizations use is to proffer casework or group work services (e.g., advocacy counseling to women in the workplace who are coping with sexual harassment or discrimination, clinics for tenants who are facing eviction). Help is offered and clients are encouraged to join the group's organizing efforts. For example, an organization of the homeless uses its shelter and food as an inducement to homeless people to become involved in the activist opportunities (and obligations) it serves up along with the food:

> Food is a very powerful organizing weapon among homeless people. And good food—I don't mean that bullshit slop that they serve in most shelters and soup kitchens. It's a part of our philosophy, plus we use it to recruit. Like we will have fried chicken, potato salad, and greens; we'll have bacon and eggs for breakfast. We do that because we believe that's a part of dignity and, too, it's a tool for organizing.

Such services, however, can be very expensive to provide for a struggling social action organization. In some cases organizations purposefully sought funding for this work because they saw its potential for recruitment. In other cases the potential was realized after the funding and services began. In either case providing service is a method of getting funded to do the necessary organizational task of outreach.

Recruitment through written materials, (e.g., random direct mail solicitation, mailings and newsletters to members, and hand distribution of flyers), is a relatively inexpensive way to inform potential members about the organization—the issues or problems the group is addressing—or about a specific event or meeting. This type of recruitment, however, may not have the desired yield. "Cold" mailings to names on purchased lists are relatively common, and organizers talk of their group as having progressed to the point where they can finally afford to buy these lists. This somewhat indirect approach is dismissed by some organizers because it may only raise enough money to pay for the next mailing and doesn't really engage people. If funds are the only expected outcome, then a quick cost-benefit calculation in "dollars out" versus "dollars in" is possible. However, if less measurable products like commitment, ideas, and networks are desired, then the use of written materials is likely to have a lower yield.

Even in cases where flyers are distributed to reach particular populations, the yield in members may be low. One organizer tells of leafletting in unemployment offices for ten years. Seldom does this approach bring new recruits anymore—the approach is too old and there is no immediate issue to attract them.

There is some indication that recruiting by disseminating written materials is more effective with higher income groups. Most organizers use both personal contact and written materials, but the latter are used more often in organizations with middle-class constituencies. Personal contact and group presentations are more often used with lower-income groups. This organizer has experienced significant differences along these lines:

> We'd like to be involving more of the "powerless" people. We would like to be doing more work in the minority community, in the urban environments of the state. Resource-wise it's much more staff intensive to do that kind of organizing, and that's what you need to draw those kinds of people in. Now we have an agenda, we send out a newsletter, and if people want to fall into that, fine, we'll work with them. But it probably means we aren't going to reach the powerless folks. They have to do too much work to find us.

Perhaps the least costly method of recruitment is the use of the general media, including public service announcements, newspaper stories, and advertisements for events and meetings. There are no expenses involved when the organization receives television or newspaper coverage. Writing public service announcements and newspaper articles costs very little in staff time; advertisements will cost a little more. Organizations keep scrapbooks of newspaper clippings ("victory books"), which are then used in future recruitment to document activity and notoriety. The major advantage of using the media is that the message can reach large numbers of people, which is not possible when making personal contacts or disseminating written materials.

While costs are low, the resultant yield of new members through media exposure is questionable. Most organizers feel they have little access to or control over the mainstream media; indeed the media may not even report on an organization's activity, or may provide biased coverage. Public service announcements are often scheduled during odd hours and do not reach the right audience. Newspaper articles and ads might be on back pages. Further, since organizers seldom ask new recruits how they found out about the organization or what motivated them to join, the benefits of this approach lack strong documentation. Still, while using the media for recruitment probably cannot be measured, the "good coverage" that does exist may at least increase the receptivity of the general public, making it easier for the organizer and leaders to recruit individuals.

Because of the costs and benefits involved in each recruitment method, social action organizations typically combine them. The most common approaches are combinations of disseminating written materials and group presentations and disseminating written materials paralleled with personal contacts. While each method requires resources, multiple methods may serve to drive the message home to diverse prospective members, and have, consequently, higher yields. For example, getting a name, address, and phone number on a petition or survey allows a follow-up mailing or invitation to a group presentation. The organizer can personally contact those who have responded to a mailing or attended an organizational event. In every case the organizer's job is to communicate a message to prospective recruits and to build a bridge from their interest to the organization. One contact is not enough. The message must be repeated to the point where the individual is curious enough to attend a meeting or an event. It is, indeed, the initial access point.

This chapter has described the initial steps necessary to building the social action organization's membership base. While most organizers and leaders support the importance of recruitment, in practice they do not distinguish phases of a recruitment process as we have here, and they do not give special attention to each phase to ensure a constant flow of new members. Too many organizers envision "outreach" as a "soft" aspect of their work; they may worry about it but don't closely analyze or monitor it, and do not understand the inherent problems that must be remedied. Little active recruiting is actually done in many social action organizations; there is little analysis of who might join and why. There is little response to perceived discrepancies between actual and desired members. There is a tendency, instead, to routinize recruitment activities—constantly going back to the same "safe" constituency, reaching out with the same messages in the same ways. Intentionally or unconsciously, these organizers create either low access or ambiguous access organizations.

This is just the opposite of the purposeful individualized outreach we envision as most fruitful for social action organizations. Social action organizations can be strengthened when questions of access are considered at the earliest stages. This requires building bridges to people, reducing barriers to participation, and avoiding the use of gates too early. A few guidelines for increasing access are:

1. "Pools" of potential participants should be identified using principles of networks, representativeness, and special attributes.
2. A somewhat formalized way of assessing people's motivations to join should be established, and collected data should be used to craft recruitment messages that consider the member pool's interests and circumstances.
3. A range of recruitment methods should be used, paying attention to the costs and benefits, strengths and drawbacks of each.
4. Recruitment should be an ongoing part of the organization's work, and, as much as possible, joined with current issues and campaigns. In addition, the organizer and leaders must include the issues of newcomers on the organization's agenda if recruitment is to be effective.

These activities will be modulated by some pragmatic aspects of social action organizations themselves—size of staff, availability of members to become involved, geographic distance. We argue, however, that these should not be used as excuses to avoid the careful consideration of all the phases of participation and of the alternatives within each phase we have described in this chapter.

The attention organizers give to recruitment answers the question, Whose responsibility is engagement—the recruit's or the organization's? Although we view participation as a transactional relationship between the organization and the recruit, the relationship must be initiated, or at least responded to, by the organizer and leadership. That is the essence of the high access organization—it compels the organization to reach out and invite newcomers to enter.

The degree to which organizers and leaders accept responsibility for bringing in new people will influence how the first two phases of participation are pursued. Many of these themes become more pressing in the third and fourth phases, the initial engagement of recruits and the sustaining and deepening of their involvement.

CHAPTER FOUR

Maintaining and Deepening Member Participation

In the last chapter we discussed a number of issues affecting how social action organizations identify and recruit members. In this chapter we discuss similar issues affecting how these organizations initially involve members (phase III) and then foster their continued and intensified participation (phase IV). We further develop the theme of participation and discuss other issues that longer-term relationships occasion, most notably the development of leadership roles. This chapter, then, deals with organizers' most extensive interactive tasks as they work with individual members and groups of members, balance what may be conflicting agendas, and try to keep the organization prospering (Fisher 1984, Twelvetrees 1982).

Phase III: Initial Engagement

Tasks in the first phase of member involvement include identifying possible members and developing recruitment messages designed to reach them. Success in the recruitment phase produces people who show enough interest to join the organization. Their involvement at this stage may be quite minimal: they may have signed a membership form and sent a check, attended a meeting or demonstration, or agreed to write a postcard to a legislator. In contrast to the purpose of the recruitment phase the goal of the initial engagement phase is to capture the interest of new recruits so that they come to participate more regularly and intensively in the organization and its activities. The initial engagement phase is designed to form a bridge for the recruit from what is perhaps a transitory and passive interest in an issue to a sustained and active participation in the organization.

Much is at stake during this phase since initial interaction establishes the tone and expectations for the longer-term relationship between the new recruit and the organization (Henderson and Thomas 1980b). Recruits bring hopes for what they want to achieve by joining (e.g., they want a problem solved, they want to meet like-minded people), some degree of knowledge of the organization and its issues, and some ideas about the way they see themselves contributing to the group. Staff and current members may have their own vision of the individual's interests, tenure with the group, and the contributions they will be expected to make.

The burden for shaping a recruit's initial participation lies mostly with the organizer and current leaders. Their task is to capitalize on recruits' motives for joining by finding a way to marry those motives to opportunities within the organization. Barriers to participation can only be discovered and overcome through conscious efforts of the organizer and existing members. The bridges and gateways we mentioned in the previous chapter must be enhanced and opened. An emphasis on "high access," not only to the organization but to leadership positions within it, is reinforced during the early phase of member involvement.

As many organizers describe it, new recruits must be "plugged into" the fabric of the organization. This "plugging in," we argue, is a complex and delicate process that requires careful attention if the organization is to succeed in capturing the involvement of large numbers of new members.

Not all organizers give this stage such meticulous attention. In the flurry of activity and competing demands new member needs can easily be ignored. Organizers sometimes first identify the tasks that need to be accomplished and then look for people to do them. Often this results in selecting people known to and trusted by the organizer rather than the new recruits.

The problem with this approach is that it considers only the organization's needs and, at that, only the organization's *present* needs. While it may be an efficient way of completing immediate tasks and developing the skills of a few individuals, it does not attend to either the interests and needs of the new recruit or the organization's *future* needs for leadership. Instead, it conveys a message that members' interests are subservient to those of the organization. Symbolically, such an approach seems antithetical to the democratic ethos of social action organizing. Pragmatically, it can discourage member participation— just the opposite of what these member-based organizations supposedly intend.

Assessment in Initial Engagement

Essential to effective initial engagement is a careful assessment of both parties to the "plugging in" process: 1. assessing current and future organizational needs and matching new recruits to them and 2. creating and identifying organizational work out of the individual recruit's interests and concerns. The first helps ensure that organizational work is done and that new recruits commit and contribute to the organization's existing activity and goals. The second values new recruits by responding to their concerns and stakes, recognizing that the organization will be guided in its evolution by the interests and desires of its members. In this combined approach, for example, an organizer would question a new recruit about her or his skills. Discovering the recruit's talent in art, the organizer might involve the recruit in composing a flyer for an activity the group is planning. At the same time, however, the organizer would also suggest a new role in the organization—perhaps serving as cochair on a committee—while encouraging other more veteran members to endorse and support the recruit's activity in this new assignment.

The organizer's first step in such an assessment is to analyze several aspects of the recruit and of the organization in order to set up initial transactions between them. To be fully informed, the organizer needs to know several things about new recruits: their problems, concerns, desires, and needs, their interests in the organization, their skills and past experiences, their networks and connections to others, and their availability. This knowledge then is related to organizational factors: changing membership composition (attrition or turnover), staff and member dynamics, present and future roles to be filled, tasks needing immediate attention, and weaknesses in the current membership that could be strengthened by "new blood." These organizational and member characteristics are what organizers say they analyze when trying to engage members. Organizers typically include more than one of these factors in their analyses and emphasize different ones depending on what immediate pressures they face.

Organizers and leaders begin with little knowledge about recruits, particularly about how recruits will relate and work with existing members. Clearly, gaining this type of "feel" for a member will take more time, interaction, and information than is immediately possible. Yet quick assessments that harness a recruit's initial impulse to join are necessary for timely engagement. A fuller understanding of the recruit can develop only over time, which allows for adjustments in roles and task assignments for those members who continue to participate.

The majority of organizers appear not to use a formal approach for assessing new recruits. Their evaluation is largely intuitive, informal, and quick. It typically involves gathering only a small amount of data about the individual—just enough to make an assignment. For many organizers taking immediate advantage of people's interests and speedily plugging them into activities and structures is more important than a comprehensive assessment of their habits and needs.

Although speed is important in initial engagement, it does not necessarily preclude an assessment of the recruit. If recruits are put to work on tasks that make them uncomfortable (e.g., taking on a leadership role without preparation) or are assigned to committees in which they have no interest, the initial transaction is likely to fail. Instead, we encourage organizers to spend time getting to know new people. A modest effort will accomplish this goal. Much can be learned by having them fill out a questionnaire, by including them in a discussion of issues, by assigning a veteran member as a "buddy," or by simply talking with them privately to determine their talents, hopes, and interests. It is all too easy for organizers to forget how confused and isolating it can be for new people who are asked to "board" an already fast-moving organization. Initial interaction not only helps new people to feel more included and comfortable, but helps the organizer determine where in the organization the new person can get onboard most easily.

We suggest a few principles to guide initial engagement:

- the process should begin as quickly as possible with each new recruit, to take maximum advantage of the new member's motivation to join the organization;
- the process should be based in part on an assessment of the individual, so that the person's participation can be shaped by his or her own interests;
- the member's participation should be thoughtfully reviewed periodically, so that new or additional organizational opportunities can be offered.

Acting on Initial Engagement

If the first part of "plugging in" emphasizes assessment of recruits, the second part involves encouraging them to act and supporting them when they do.

Social action organizations vary widely on the activity they expect of new members. In fact, many social action organizations appear not to expect much from most newcomers. For example, social action groups frequently ask only that new recruits make financial contributions. Repeated appeals for more funds for a variety of campaigns or activities follow. Such solicitation requires little of new recruits. Further, they are not drawn into the work of the organization. In effect, the message is that the staff runs the organization and the members fund it. Such an approach does not enhance participation. Indeed, it is the finances, not the people, that are organized in such groups.

Other approaches to engaging new members require only passive participation. New recruits may be invited to attend organizational activities (e.g., fund-raisers, annual dinners, conventions, or mass actions). As these events may not directly relate to newcomers' initial interests, they are seldom experienced as "personal invitations." Newcomers are essentially asked to "show up," and are not introduced to the day-to-day work of the group and to its membership. Other organizers merely list existing committees available for recruits to join but fail to pave the way to active participation.

Some organizers support these passive approaches to engagement, arguing that they view members as more concerned with social issues than with participating in an organization working on issues, a distinction we do not accept. These organizers may, in fact, actually circumscribe potential participation. We believe that passive or tentative engagement approaches, where organizers have little or nothing for new members to do, is a serious barrier to continued member involvement. Such approaches give negative messages to new members concerning their value to the organization and often, we think, result in turning away all but a few "true believers."

We argue that social action organizations most effectively involve newcomers when they set expectations for active participation and then consistently reinforce them. Recruits can and should be expected to be active members rather than merely interested bystanders. Initial overtures that offer meaningful tasks and roles set the tone of the organization's hopes and expectations for new members. They reflect the organization's openness to new people with their own set of interests, ideas, and talents. And, most important, the more tasks and roles members assume, the more "hooks" there are to hold them to the organization and its work, reinforcing their commitment:

> People have to sign on to the concept that we have to build a group of people who are going to continue working on issues no matter what—that issues are never going to be gone and over. If we don't do that we aren't going to be strong, we're not going to be able to win any one issue. By coming out to meetings . . . by being willing to do fund raisers, by taking more of a role than just on their issue, by being willing to sit on a committee, by talking to other people about the organization and saying "Hey, you can get this done; if you've got neighbors together we can do it together." All this reinforces their commitment.

The most engaging initial activity is an immediate offer to carry out a specific task. Such an initial overture connotes respect for the skills new members bring and/or for their capacity to learn a new task quickly. It makes a clear statement that the newcomer is trusted enough to carry out a valid organizational task.

Recruits should not just "tag along" or be given meaningless or menial assignments. The initial overture should encourage the recruit to do real work with import for the organization: collect some needed information, discuss an issue with staff or other members, contribute to writing a letter or a brochure, be part of a delegation to meet with a governmental official or an opponent, canvass an area for issues and concerns. The message that the recruit is wanted and needed must be given, heard, and experienced. For example, newcomers to a tenants organization are paired with a veteran member to work as housing court monitors where they oversee and act as monitors in eviction hearings. This approach has the benefit of involving recruits in real work along with someone already committed to the organization.

An immediate offer to serve as a member of a committee or task force serves to tie the individual's concern for an issue to a subgroup working on that issue. The committee assignment attaches them to a structure and offers a participatory role in a context where they can interact with other members who have the same specific concerns. Even as new members they can influence the organization and its work. An opportunity to serve on a committee also affirms an expectation that the recruit will do something within the context and confines of a group. Thus, the message that the newcomer is expected to be accountable to a group is reinforced. Then too, as committee members new recruits directly interact with staff and veteran members. They get to know them, spend time with them, and learn about social action organizing from them. People become acquainted personally, enhancing in-group ties.

Common bonds are also enhanced when individuals share problems within a group so that these problems are experienced as "normal" rather than unique. People then understand their problems are systemic, that they are not to blame for the problem, and that only group action can resolve it. Leaders emphasize that talking about common problems openly is a way of helping people alleviate the guilt and shame associated with the problem. Here a leader of a disabled workers group talks about building camaraderie in this manner:

> Constantly at membership meetings, at board meetings, I'll ask, "What's the matter, what's the problem? Come on, let's talk, you have to say it to us, we need your thoughts to come out right now, because if we don't have them now you aren't going to call us or write us, so while we are here together let's talk about the problems: who hasn't got any food, who hasn't got any money, whose kid tried to kill himself, whose wife is divorcing him, what's going on out there?" If one person says a sentence, then another sentence comes from the other corner, and all of a sudden everyone will be talking. Cause everyone who goes to these meetings is injured, just got injured, or knows of someone who is injured.

Organizers have an important role in helping newcomers join a committee. They must spend time with newcomers beforehand, preparing them for participation by explaining the history of the committee and its issues, the current work of the group, its composition, roles of committee members, and any pertinent group dynamics. Such preparation helps new members move into the committee armed with information, and doesn't require the group to constantly reexplain and reexamine their efforts. The time spent with newcomers also allows the organizer to develop close and personal relationships with them, to provide support, encouragement, and inspiration.

Organizers must also recognize that when newcomers join an existing committee a great deal is asked of veteran participants. Established leaders must be willing to include new participants and give them time and attention until they acclimate. New participants invariably disrupt the norms and interactions of the group and may even threaten past work and relationships. The organizer must help veterans understand the importance of including newcomers, and help the established leadership reach out to recruits effectively. The tension between established leaders and newcomers is ineluctable in social action organizations, and we will say more later about how organizers can reduce the strain. The following practice illustration opens on the beginning of a meeting of a welfare rights group—where both the new recruit and the established leaders have been prepared—and shows how the organizer monitors and intervenes in the newcomer's entry.

ORGANIZER: Hi, Carmen. Glad you could get to the meeting. I think you'll find that other people are here who have the same problem you do.

CARMEN: Hi, Joan. I'm here but I'm afraid I'll have to leave early. I left the kids with my next-door neighbor.

ORGANIZER: Yeah, we all have that problem. We'll get out fast. Why don't you come and meet Louisa? Louisa lives in your area. Louisa, this is Carmen. She lives near you. This is her first meeting and she's coming because she has a problem getting a clothing allowance for her daughter.

LOUISA: Nice to meet you, Carmen. Where do you live? Oh, I know that area. Why don't you come sit next to me? I suppose Joan told you that we're working on the clothing allowance thing. You'll be very interested in this.

CARMEN: Well I think I'll just listen tonight.

ORGANIZER: Why don't you call the meeting to order, Maria?

MARIA: Okay, the meeting is called to order. You all have your agendas, right? Our first subject today is the clothing allowance. Mary, could you say what the response has been to our letter?

ORGANIZER: Maria, maybe you forgot Carmen, the new member in our group? Why don't we introduce ourselves to her? (Introductions are made around.) Maria, I told Carmen a little about this committee, but why don't you run it down for her again?

MARIA: Well, Carmen, I suppose you know we're a group of welfare mothers who try and work on things like "up the budget." We've worked on getting doctors to take medicaid and stores to take food stamps, and things like that. Now we're working on the clothing allowance, trying to get more money in it, and at least making sure that people get it for the right things. Know what I mean?

ORGANIZER: Carmen may not know what "up the budget" means.

MARIA: It means to increase the basic welfare grant.

ORGANIZER: All the women here have gripes about welfare. I know you had a problem too, Carmen. Want to tell the committee about the problem?

CARMEN: Well, my oldest daughter is going to college, and I need my allowance to get her things for school.

LOUISA: That's in the grant. You're supposed to get it. When I sent my son, I had a hard time getting it, but I finally did.

MARIA: Well, that's exactly our business for tonight. Now, Mary, could you tell us about the letter from the commissioner?

ORGANIZER: Mary, could you say first a little about why we wrote to him, and what we asked, and then tell about his reply? I have a copy of our letter, too, to pass around if anyone's forgotten what we asked about.

The final method organizers occasionally use to initially engage newcomers is to provide formal training. In the few cases we have encountered initial training is focused on specific tasks related to a group's current campaigns: training in house-to-house canvassing, in monitoring courts that deal with tenant-landlord cases, or in how to do a housing code violation survey. In some local parish ministry organizations, the organizer offers training to the members of churches or synagogues that have recently joined the organization. The sessions consist mostly of organizing training (e.g., the purpose of organizing, how to recruit, how to select issues, how to do action research, how to plan strategy, how to negotiate with targets).

While training initially offers newcomers the opportunity to participate in an activity and get to know others, it does define new people as trainees—as needing information before they can contribute. There is less consideration of what initially brought people to the group and less utilization of new members' own unique talents, skills, and interests. We support early training, but only alongside other task or committee opportunities that capitalize on recruits' skills and experience. In fact, organizing training may be of greater value later, as newcomers themselves experience their need to know more.

Supports for Action

Once expectations are established the next task for organizers and veteran members is to create and maintain supports for new people to take on active roles and work. While organizers love to recruit veteran activists with honed skills, and are prepared to use them with little hesitation, most know that these people are rarities. Most new recruits need support and encouragement when taking on new tasks and working with new people.

Organizers who assume that newcomers can do their assignments without assistance may create another barrier to member participation. They assume, unrealistically, that if newcomers are invited to meetings, sent information, or given a task to do they might make their own way into the organization.

Organizers who assume people can do the work asked of them might think their "hands off" approach promotes a sense of independence and projects a feeling of trust. This argument, we feel, merely rationalizes the organizer's inattention or possibly disinterest in truly engaging new members. While these organizers don't exclude anyone from joining, they don't encourage people to actively participate. Much more needs to be done to help people make the transition from member to activist.

Briefing before new recruits take on a task, and debriefing after these tasks are the most common supports organizers offer to encourage participation. It is also not uncommon for an organizer to perform a task along with the newcomer. Organizers who use initial training to involve newcomers argue that by offering skill training they help people feel more competent to perform a task, and peer support becomes part of the initiation process. The practice illustration below shows an organizer helping a new member to take on a task before and after she has made a report at a meeting.

ORGANIZER: Debbie, Sam and Emma asked me to ask you if you would make the report about the housing survey at the next Housing Committee meeting Monday night? They feel that you did the lion's share of the work and are the best person to do it.

DEBBIE: Oh, you know me, Roger, I don't mind doing the work but I don't like to speak in front of groups. I get too nervous.

ORGANIZER: I know you do, Debbie, but you do know the details better than anyone else.

DEBBIE: Can't Sam do it? He's been around longer and he's a good speaker.

ORGANIZER: Well, Sam is going to have a lot to do that night, he's chairing the meeting. And people have heard Sam. They want to know other people are doing the work. But it's a good idea to do the report with someone else. Didn't you work with Fred?

DEBBIE: Yeah, Fred is good. Anybody but me.

ORGANIZER: Maybe you and Fred could do it together? Why don't we see if there are things that would make you feel more comfortable? How about if Fred, you, and I meet and we talk about what you want to say in the report? Then you could write it down, and if you get too nervous, just read your part.

DEBBIE: Okay, if I have to.

ORGANIZER: Listen, Debbie, I know this is hard. But you know this stuff better than anybody. And it's just our little group. Fred and I will help you. It's always hard the first time, but let's see how it goes.

DEBBIE: Okay. I'll try.

(After the meeting)

ORGANIZER: Well, how do you think it went, Deb?

DEBBIE: It went good I think. We got a lot done.

ORGANIZER: Your part went real well. People were really interested in the results of the study. They couldn't believe the number of vacant properties and the amount of back taxes owed.

DEBBIE: Yeah, it's pretty serious.

ORGANIZER: How did you feel about speaking? Were you as scared as you thought you'd be.

DEBBIE: Well, it wasn't as bad as I thought once I got into it. Except when I lost my place. I was sure glad Fred was there to help me.

ORGANIZER: I don't think anybody noticed that slip. It's good to have a buddy, though. I thought you did real good for your first time. People felt like you knew what you were talking about. And it does get easier, I promise.

DEBBIE: Well, I guess so. Anyway, at the next meeting we should be able to report the license and inspections stuff. We're moving on.

In sum, the degree to which a group can effectively bring in new people depends on staff and leaders' willingness to share rights and powers and ability to consciously create opportunities and supports that encourage participation. Often organizers and leaders ask how many new people have *joined* the organization and are satisfied with numbers. The real question is "How many new people have been *working* with us lately?" If, over time, the numbers are small, an evaluation of how the organization handles initial engagement is in order.

Phase IV: Sustaining and Deepening Member Involvement

Once newcomers are participating, an organizer's concern shifts to sustaining and deepening their involvement. This shift occasions several critical questions:

1. Is sustained involvement of members necessary?
2. Why does member attrition occur?
3. How can member attrition be countered?
4. Why do some people remain involved, and how can their involvement be enhanced?
5. How is leadership defined and developed in social action organizations, and who are the people who take on leadership roles?
6. How is group identity and cohesion strengthened?

The Necessity of Sustained Involvement

It has been estimated that less than 2 percent of a potential constituency will ever be engaged in a social action organization, and that large numbers of people will drop out after their initial interest fades or their problems are settled (Delgado 1986, Von Hoffman 1966). Yet people—the essential resource for power—create the capacity for ongoing action, for the growth and power of the organization, enabling the organization to influence targets and issues over time. It is understandable, then, that there is widespread concern over the maintenance of continued member activity. Burghardt (1984) describes an organizer's nightmare: "An organizer offers a familiar complaint: one million people show up in New York in June 1984 for an antinuclear rally. It is the largest march in U.S. history, writes the activist; but three months later organizing activity is at a snail's pace" (31).

We are convinced that there is a difference between sustaining and deepening involvement. For us *sustained involvement* refers only to an individual's continuing participation. We define sustained members as those who, perhaps for years, renew their memberships and attend meetings, actions, and events. They need not be involved in decisions, but are valued because of their reliability, attendance, and availability within the parameters of what they and the organization deem appropriate. In contrast, members whose involvement has deepened take on a greater number of tasks, and accept roles that are more demanding (e.g., spokesperson, chairperson). More requests are made of them to be active, and they increasingly assume roles that bring both the obligation and opportunity to make decisions that direct the organization.

Consequently, they receive a greater investment of staff's time directed at enhancing their leadership skills. While sustained members may be the heart of a social action organization, these "deepened" leaders are its mind and soul.

Differential participation by members of social action organizations appears to be a fact of life. Organizers use various terms to describe member tiers. Most common is the distinction between a "core" of leaders and a "periphery" of members. The distinction derives from the time and energy an individual invests in the group, and the consequently different levels of recognition they receive from staff and peers. The core group commits their time, talent, and energy to the organization; they are involved in discussions and decisions. "Periphery" members may be members of several organizations, attend periodically, and are generally involved only in the activities that interest them. The presence of the core group is constant; they step forward to express their thinking and to work on solving current problems. Members on the periphery make few contributions because they are seen only periodically, and seem to choose when and how they will be involved.

Some groups distinguish between nonsalaried participants ("constituents") and "contributing members," who give money, and active members. Some organizers differentiate between "volunteers," who generally perform office tasks, and "members," who are issue activists. Finally, some organizers describe members in terms of their place in the organization's structure. There are board members, advisory group members, committee chairs, members of committees or task forces, and general members. Each respective category suggests a decreasing level of activism.

Organizers naturally work more closely with members who are active. They talk glowingly of the personal relationships that develop with "core" members with whom they spend the most time. Consequently, active members are ingrained in communications loops; they more frequently hear about events and opportunities and are more often involved in making decisions. Conversely, those on the periphery receive less communication, may not learn of opportunities to participate, and are excluded from decision making.

It is very common for the organizer to rely on and use experienced and dependable leadership totally and almost automatically. These veteran leaders are politically sophisticated, and consequently able to relate to the organizer's concerns and analyses. Members on the periphery may have potential, but need more support to be effective, and thus may become too burdensome for the organizer. Organizers may, consciously or unconsciously, develop a pattern of excluding new members from much of the group's work. Left unattended and ignored, these new members may not only never mature into activists but become disgruntled with the organization.

Where organizers take major responsibility for promoting participation they consciously structure organizational levels that require progressively greater participation and responsibility. It then becomes the organizer's job to encourage and "groom" members to make the transition from one level of participation to a more active level. These organizers view all members as potentially top leaders, and actively draw people in from the periphery, moving them toward the "core" of the organization by assuming deepened leadership roles:

> I get scared making a distinction between membership and leadership. I think if we do that then we don't challenge that person to be a leader, we let them be those people over there who don't have a say in the inner circle. . . . I think part of my role is to try to look at who those people are and involve them. Try to catch myself when I'm always going to the same people; and then also encouraging the people who are more active to have that same role of involving others. Some people are just going to be sort of followers, but there is a lot of potential for some of the people to move to leadership or take on bigger responsibilities.

Because social action organizations rely so heavily on members to accomplish tasks and goals, member attrition means more work for the organizer. If large numbers of members are continually lost, the organizer must recruit new members for every new issue. Clearly, a good percentage of people must stay involved. Given the importance of retention, it behooves us to examine why some people end their involvement and why others maintain it.

Member Attrition and Longevity

Organizers do not keep records on member attrition, so the average tenure of members is unknown (Wilson and Mondros 1985). Nevertheless, organizers are rarely happy with the continuity of their membership. They frequently talk about the problems created when members drop out. Particularly problematic are people who join a group out of self-interest and leave after their individual problems are solved, and people who cycle in and out of the organization, getting active then "burning out." Both groups leave a "hole" in the organization.

Organizers from local and grassroots groups complain that people often join out of self-interest and then leave after their problem is solved. These organizers argue that the ability of their groups to deal with public issues hinges on a significant portion of members moving past their individual needs to embrace more collective interests. Organizers and leaders can make conscious efforts, to be discussed later, that will ensure this happens. Yet, organizations composed of members where there is a "natural" termination to involvement (when students graduate or when unemployed workers find a job, for example), often must accommodate such attrition. While the attrition is likely to continue, these organizations can at least plan their recruitment efforts with this trend in mind. Student groups can recruit freshman and unemployed workers groups can solicit union members who are interested in the problem.

Episodic involvement of members is more likely in lobbying and mobilizing groups. Organizers describe people "burning out" after a period of activism, either because they are frustrated with their ability to solve issues or because other life events take precedence. People may get involved only in specific activities or around specific issues or get totally immersed for a period of time, only to drop out for a long hiatus. Organizers complain of the resulting difficulties in building an ongoing campaign with people who are often "missing in action."

Organizers appear, reluctantly, to accept such episodic involvement, but wish for a solution to this problem. Again, while some people may come and go, there are methods organizers can use to protect leaders from burning out. One way is to ensure that no leader is overburdened with work, that work is shared among many. Other clues to how to keep people active may be found by examining what organizers call the "diehards," those who continue their involvement over time.

We have discussed that people join voluntary associations for a variety of reasons, and most often for several reasons. We also find that people stay involved in organizations for different reasons than those that initially prompted them to join.

There are five primary reasons why people stay involved. The most commonly expressed of these is an increasing belief in the importance of the work of the organization. This reason comes closest to Gerlach and Hine's assertion that the degree to which an ideology is mutually held among members and the intensity of that belief ensures the continued involvement of people (Gerlach and Hine 1970). Sidel and Sidel (1976) stress this point for small organizations, where sustaining members and group survival are virtually synonymous: "The pattern of rise and fall of small (social action) groups is evidence that without some common purpose to keep them going, the group cannot be sustained by isolated special interests and special purposes" (Sidel and Sidel 1976:69).

A second major reason that many people maintain their connection to a group is the organization's effectiveness, i.e., the organization's victories. Having a track record and the ability to solve problems on an ongoing basis can be a potent drawing card for members.

The sense of community or peer group that evolves out of these relationships is often cited as another reason for continued involvement. Some organizers consciously form personal relationships with members so that, minimally, members will feel obligated to the organizer to continue working. Organizers encourage new recruits to work with current members so that relationships can form. Gerlach and Hine (1970) write that people engage in and deepen their commitment to an organization because of the interpersonal ties that develop among members. Such a rationale is particularly relevant in social action organizations, which commonly deviate from prevailing thought and norms. It is difficult for most people to take an opposing stance. They are afraid of being seen as "radical" or "aggressive." They worry about being outsiders or different. Part of developing the peer group is to offer a new reference group with new norms and views to replace old relationships. The organization becomes a new reference group, where their new convictions are both valued and validated.

Organizers also sometimes report that people stay involved because they feel that they are doing interesting tasks, making a contribution, or are made to feel important as a result of their work in the group. This supports O'Brien's (1975) argument that organizations must offer members individual benefits beyond the general benefits that accrue to a wider public. He allows that these rewards may be expressive benefits. For example, appearing on television or being quoted in the press or being on a first-name basis with the mayor are often cited as individual benefits related to status.

Knoke and Wood (1981) suggest that participation itself is a major reward and reason for people's continuing involvement in social action organizations—people who are involved in making organizational decisions commit to that organization.

No one motive is operant for every member; all probably apply to some degree. This housing organizer captures the myriad reasons members continue to participate:

I think they stay involved because of the relationships that they've formed. I think they stay involved because they have fun. They stay involved certainly because they see the organization accomplish things and they see the organization doing things that they never thought could be done. I think they stay involved, again, because the organization is bigger than them and bigger than anything they—or even members of their ethnic group as a group—could accomplish; and that it aspires to values that they feel are important, like justice and love and dignity of people. . . . I think they stay involved because they learn things personally, they develop skills and they feel that they are growing as people in the organization. Habit . . . ritual, in a sense. And a shared kind of history.

The reasons people stay involved in a social action organization may differ markedly from the reasons they initially became involved. As people work within an organization, their motives may be confirmed, changed, or replaced. We believe that people often join social action organizations with a vague sense that they can get help with a problem or like something about the organization. They stay involved because they become invested in the issues and purposes of the group, they see the organization can succeed, and they reap some benefit from contributing to those successes. Also, with increased experience of the organization, members find additional reasons to stay (e.g., friendships, feelings of personal worth and competency, commitment to a group purpose and effort). Their sense of what's at stake and what can be gained is extended.

Enhancing Member Retention

As organizers recognize the factors that lead to member retention, they can consciously work to strengthen their investment. We now examine organizers' methods to counter attrition and retain members: the use of member entitlements and roles and reward systems.

Member Entitlements and Roles As we have argued all along, members cannot be retained in an organization if they don't participate actively. Participation gives members a personal stake in the organization and offers status and recognition to individual members. By participating along with like-minded others, the notion of an organizational reference group is reinforced. The question is not who participates (that is a "right" of joining), but who participates in what, and how division of labor between members, leaders, and staff is determined.

Member rights to assume responsible positions and decisional control within the organization can be codified formally in by-laws or constitutions. Such documents offer members the opportunity to become involved and acknowledge their rights to hold organizational roles. The documents reinforce the understanding that members are competent to perform important organizational duties. Many organizers have a deep appreciation for what members can do in a social action organization.

Typically, however, rights to real control, i.e., to participate in key organizational decisions, become available to members only as their involvement increases, as they "prove" themselves as bona fide organizational leaders, trusted enough to make crucial determinations. If organizers and current leaders feel this way, however, it becomes incumbent on them to help newer members take on decision-making roles, because these new people will not do so otherwise. The constant need to include new people in decisions, to give them the kind of information and support they need to join the inner sanctum of decision makers, is explained by this organizer:

> I think you've got to be able to challenge leaders to be able to do everything. But you've also got to challenge yourself to include them. It's easier for an organizer to work with a trusted group. But if you're truly going to develop leaders you need to spend time with newcomers, tell them what you're working on, talk with them about the different options, and what's at stake in each one. You have to elicit their ideas and have them discuss it with others. Then they too are prepared to join the discussion.

While organizers must monitor and thoughtfully distribute the roles of members and leaders, they also must perform a careful balancing act between their own role and that of leadership. Organizers carefully safeguard their own involvement in key decisions, for they understandably have a stake in protecting the organization and its work. To avoid mistakes that might jeopardize the organization, they must exert influence over important decisions, a task more easily accomplished with established leaders than with lesser known members. Yet exclusion and manipulation will turn away newly active members and, we might add, veterans with strong opinions. Consequently, organizers must strike a balance between having influence and fostering participation. A rule of thumb for many organizers is to let members have their way when their ideas will do no or minimal harm and to try to influence members when important decisions are at stake. If the organizing is going to continue for a long period, however, organizers will often allow members to make major errors and point them out in debriefing. In that way they hope members will learn from experience.

The practice illustration below shows an organizer working with a group of students, one of whom has written a letter to a university official. The organizer feels the letter is too long and too strident for a first request, but must convince the group of this. At the same time the organizer must spare the letter writer's feelings and encourage his continuing participation.

> ORGANIZER: Well, we have David's letter to look at, and maybe we ought to do it together. Let's read it and see what we think. (They all read the letter silently.)
>
> JERRY: It's a great letter, David. Very well written.
>
> SUSAN: I think so too. Very strong, David.
>
> ORGANIZER: I think it's a good start, too. We can see you put a lot of work in, David. And you write very well. I have a question, though. Do we really want to be so strong right now?
>
> DAVID: I think we do. We have a right to make our problems known. We pay a lot of money for our education, and he should know, in no uncertain terms, how we feel.
>
> ORGANIZER: What do some of you others think?
>
> ANN: I guess the question is how do we think he'll react to this letter?
>
> ORGANIZER: Good question, Ann. How might he react? After all, he doesn't even know we exist. And he doesn't know what our problems are.
>
> DAVID: I can't believe he doesn't know. I'm sure the provost told him. And anyway, he'll never do anything if he doesn't see how determined we are.
>
> ORGANIZER: The problem is if we are nasty first, he can refuse to deal with us on the grounds that we are nasty. If we ask politely, he can't refuse, at least on those grounds.
>
> SUSAN: Well, could we be both strong and polite at the same time?
>
> ORGANIZER: Let's see if we can. Where do you think your letter is the strongest, David? Let's see if we can change a few words here and there to make it softer.

DAVID: Well, I guess the two middle paragraphs could be softened.

ANN: I was thinking maybe the letter was a little too long.

DAVID: I don't think so. It takes time to explain all this.

ORGANIZER: Why do you think the letter is too long, Ann?

ANN: I think he might not read such a long letter.

ORGANIZER: What do the rest of you think?

JERRY: I think we need to keep it short but hit all our points.

DAVID: I'd say that's impossible.

ORGANIZER: You're right, David. It's going to be hard. David, why don't you take us through it line by line, and let's see if we can make suggestions for both brevity and softening the tone. Is that okay, David? You did a great job for us. All we need to do is a little editing.

Too often, the thoughtful intervention of the organizer above does not occur. Organizers, wanting respect for their knowledge, skills and commitment, tend to assert their prerogatives in making decisions. As Delgado (1986) found in interviewing staff and members of ACORN, when the tendency to claim democratic control of the organization is probed, staff, in fact, make most decisions, at least on strategy. This leads us to explore the appropriate role divisions between staff and leadership.

Certain tasks are almost always done by organizers, no matter the size of the organization: general office management, financial management (financial accounting, grant writing), personnel management (personnel decisions, staff performance evaluation, job descriptions and contracts, and assigning work to individual staff members), and issue research. All but the last are administrative tasks. Staff clearly carry major responsibility for organizational maintenance, and this is probably inevitable in social action organizations.

Members generally have responsibility for governance. They draft the constitution and bylaws of the organization and fill the elected offices. In addition, they most often carry the visible roles (e.g., chairpersons, spokespersons), with staff acting in an advisory capacity. This arrangement reinforces the sense that social action organizations are owned and operated by the people.

Members are also the sole or primary generators of issues in most social action organizations. It is commonly conceded that it is more difficult for an organization to proceed on any issue that has not been raised or, at least minimally, considered and approved by members.

Public actions and pressure activities are almost always carried out by members. The most common approach is for leaders and members to play active roles, with staff acting "behind the scenes."

Staff share work with members in a number of areas: determining organizational directions and objectives, creating operating policies, generating and assigning work to members, selecting issues, targets, strategies, and tactics, recruiting and educating participants about issues, working with the media, providing services and information to constituents, and fund-raising (except grant writing).

Principles exist to guide the allocation of task responsibilities among staff and the membership. Staff accountability, for instance, is raised by some organizers as the basis for division of labor. Some organizers assume that because they are paid, they must perform certain tasks. They don't expect the same time commitments from volunteers, and therefore are less likely to ask them to assume responsibility.

Other organizers use member control as a guiding principle. In this model organizers act as "coaches," giving logistical and strategic advice to members and providing continuity within the group—activities that support members' more visible roles. These organizers refuse to do tasks members can do, and try to help members do the tasks they are unequipped to perform.

Other organizers acknowledge the trial and error of creating a balance between their own work and their members. They manage a blend by encouraging people in their projects but filling in the gaps when volunteers are absent. Still, the delicacy of this balance is clear, and fine-tuning is often needed.

The principle of members' visibility may be severely tested when leaders are not available for tasks that require immediate action. Some organizers would not assume roles rightfully accorded to members, but many would be visible themselves rather than forego an opportunity to act. This organizer takes the second choice in this dilemma:

> You should have membership speaking on the issues. Staff should cut them, and so forth. Like I said, that's what should be, but not necessarily what is. Unemployed people should speak on the issues themselves. We do that, but when we don't have it we continue anyhow. Staff will take that role, and we'll move the issue anyhow. Sometimes it's more important to move the issue than this developing of somebody; that's important, but not more important than the overall issue.

We believe that this organizer's choice has serious implications. As organizers perform tasks rightfully belonging to members, they unconsciously give the message that members are not competent to perform them, that the organization can function without their participation, and that they don't have to work to achieve desired ends. Instead, we suggest several other methods of handling the need for immediate action.

Organizers should educate leadership and membership about their responsibilities and obligations. Orientation and training sessions for new members on this difficult area of staff-member relations can educate newcomers. In briefing and debriefing with veterans the organizer can call attention to and reinforce their responsibilities. One organization has even developed formal job descriptions, not only for staff but also for volunteer board members, to help clarify their respective roles. Finally, if members seem to have become too dependent on staff, refusing to carry their responsibility, the organizer can simply refuse to take on the assignment. It is fair play for an organizer to say, "This is not my neighborhood, this is not my group. It is yours. And you have to work for it. I won't do it alone."

In sum, members of a social action organization should have both the right and the obligation to participate in meaningful and visible ways. The true role of staff is to help members competently assume those roles. Organizers can and should have influence on decisions, but be constantly wary of dominating the group. The more the organizer does, the less the members do, and the less reason they have to remain active and involved.

Rewards Rewards to members for increasing their involvement can also help sustain participation. For the most part organizers are comfortable with the idea of rewards, although some organizers feel strongly that the opportunity to work on important issues should be reward enough.

Ironically, organizers admit that often the only "reward" for a leader's accomplishments is an increase in organizational responsibility. They acknowledge, however, that not everyone recognizes more work as positive recognition.

While leaders may be aware of the irony of being given more work in compensation for past efforts, the burden may be mixed with a sense of pride at being entrusted with important roles and tasks, and the associated status in the eyes of staff, their peers, and others in the community.

A major problem in these organizations is the fact that some re-wards given in other organizations—money, trips, posh conferences, etc.—are not available. Still, there are other possible rewards: expres-sive rewards to individuals, expressive rewards to the collective, in-strumental rewards to individuals, and instrumental rewards to the collective (Mondros and Wilson 1986).

Individual expressive rewards are fairly widespread in social action organizations. These include giving plaques, testimonials, exposure in the media, and the conferring of formal titles. Few people join social action organizations looking for such rewards, but the recognition im-plicit in these rewards can be among the most important and cherished events in people's lives. Of course, there is a danger of recognizing one individual over others. Jealousy can become a problem, and the organizer must be careful not to undercut the ethos of the group by giving rewards to some and not others, unless there is common agreement about the recipient.

Praising, recognizing, and complimenting members are other indi-vidual expressive rewards that can be given freely without fear of con-flicts. They are daily reminders of one's value to the group, which may have much greater meaning to people than the occasional testimonial. Public expression of thanks and complimenting people privately and in group settings are small but meaningful.

Parties and celebrations are collective expressive rewards that allow people who have worked together on a task to acknowledge and enjoy their efforts. This could include bringing in food and wine to celebrate what has been accomplished, going out to eat with people who have been active in a project, and, of course, holding the yearly holiday party. These collective, positive expressions increase cohesion and em-phasize the enjoyment people get out of working together. The organi-zation is not only powerful and successful. It is also fun.

Few social action organizations appear to use instrumental rewards for individuals. Resource limitations of these organizations, and the real potential for divisiveness between recipients and nonrecipients limit their use. Some individual instrumental rewards are less problem-atic, however. The groups that use a "casework" approach may be said to be providing individual instrumental benefits. And some individual benefits can be used to reinforce group membership: one citywide ten-ants' rights organization had the innovative idea of offering a "benefit package" of discount services from local locksmiths, home repairers, lawyers, and others to their members. A few organizations hire members for salaried positions and reimburse members engaged in campaign or office work for lunch or carfare.

Instrumental rewards that accrue to the collective membership are present in all groups: these are the victories the organization achieves. New members especially need victories to reinforce their belief in the value of membership. However, leaders also accrue prestige as they grow to be seen as "winners" in addition to "fighters."

Rewards are, in general, underutilized by organizers as a means for sustaining member participation and supporting leaders' deepened participation. The likely reason for this is that organizers themselves rarely look for rewards outside the satisfaction derived from the work itself and therefore tend to forget that others are not necessarily so motivated. Veteran leaders can contribute to this perception if they take on the style of the organizer and themselves eschew the need for rewards. Staff and leaders can easily come to associate the need for rewards with weak member motivation. Most of the rewards we have seen are both inexpensive in terms of resources and time expended yet very meaningful to recipients. They merit more attention from and use by organizers.

As members continue to participate in the organization, organizers begin to concern themselves with deepening their involvement, i.e., developing them into leaders. We now explore the subject of leadership: what it is, who becomes leaders, and how the organizer attempts to help people make the transition from member to leader.

Leadership in Social Action Organizations

"Leaders" can be defined as those in positions of authority, e.g., executive board members, committee chairs, formal representatives to other groups (French and Raven 1960, Wrong 1980). Leaders can also be defined by the quantity and quality of their roles and tasks, i.e., they have decision-making power within the group, actively accept responsibility and visible roles, and serve as role models for other members (Heifetz and Sinder 1988). We define leaders as nonsalaried members who have not only sustained their participation in a social action organization but have deepened it as well, actively shaping the organization and its endeavors and exuding a sense of organizational "ownership."

For Alinsky the term "leader" applied to all members other than paid staff and is used to connote the sense that all participants make valuable contributions, have equal access to leadership roles, and that members have the major stake and responsibility in social action organizations (Alinsky 1971). Piven and Cloward's (1977) analysis of leadership and membership dynamics in the welfare rights movement offers a view of a leadership driven by pragmatic operational concerns, including having only a few members available to assume leader roles. We believe both principle and reality should impact on how social action organizations define their leadership.

Problems with leadership are common in social action organizations. The democratic belief in having many leaders may run counter to concerns for efficient decision making. Multiple leaders can be a recipe for conflict and delay. The merits of developing leaders, to some analysts and organizers, must be weighed against needs for quick action or expertise that do not allow for leadership development. This debate goes to the heart of the organizer's gatekeeping function: does the organizer restrict or promote member access to leadership roles?

Few members enter an organization with fully developed leadership skills. Those who do may not best represent the views and needs of the members or constituents. Indeed, it may be dangerous to initially entrust newcomers, no matter how skilled they appear to be, with great organizational power. Leaders may also use their power in ways that limit others' participation (Mosca 1939), and become a "power elite" running the group largely in its own image (Michels 1966). While the existence of this "elite" experienced group may be helpful to the organizer, reliance on them may become an obstacle in recruiting "new blood" with fresh ideas, talents, and networks.

Consequently, most potential leaders will begin as members and must evolve into leaders. The task of the organizer is to recruit and groom members for leadership roles, monitoring that the dedication and productivity of the few does not become an obstacle to the participation of others. At the same time developing new leaders cannot block needed action.

While organizers believe that all members can potentially become leaders, they have definite ideas about the qualities and talents most useful in leaders. These qualities often become the "calling card" of a new member, signaling to the organizer whether she or he is worth developing.

Leaders, like organizers, are viewed ideally as multidimensional actors who bring many skills and attributes to the group. The best leaders are politically astute, reliable, energetic, dogged, articulate, and loyal to the organization. These "movers and shakers" infuse energy into the organization, and articulate its causes effectively. Organizers see leaders as rare people with special qualities who model for others desired democratic attitudes and behaviors.

Organizers especially value leaders' ability to relate to, motivate, and inspire others. They know that leaders are the most effective recruiters, engaging their peers and holding them accountable in ways the organizer cannot. The existence of such a cadre of leaders consequently removes some of the burden for membership maintenance from staff. While the skills of the organizer frequently set them apart, the skills and commitments of leaders are inspirational to newcomers. Leaders act as role models for new recruits; as they watch the sophisticated actions of their peers, they begin to believe that they, too, can and must perform similar roles.

For organizers, leaders' technical proficiency is less important because the organizer offers the needed in-house expertise. Leaders confirm the need for the organizer's expertise, and view loyalty, dedication, and the ability to recruit members as leadership's most important contributions.

Organizers and leaders, therefore, do "quick assessments" of members, sizing up who may have the native qualities that would make them likely candidates for leadership. An organizer describes her group:

> I don't look to have all the qualities and talents in one person, but it's great if they're all there in the group. When I meet people I try to figure out their strengths and deficits, and use what's strong. Then I use the others in their weak points.
>
> Lynn is brave and strong. She's great with targets, but the others think she's a little abrasive. Jan is the peace maker—everybody loves her. Susan is the motivator—she can get people to do things and cuts through the crap fast. Martin is the intellect—he can write, he can think, he can speak, but he isn't patient with the others. Jenny has time, but she gets scared.
>
> So I try to get Lynn and Martin up there with targets. I try to involve Jan and Susan when people are feeling tired or scared.
>
> And I steer Jenny to work that doesn't need guts. One by one they all have strengths and weaknesses. Together, they're unbelievable.

The organizer will spend a great deal of time with a member in the process of developing him or her into a leader. In private conversations the organizer will draw out the member's interests and questions and explain detailed information.

Organizers also eschew professional distance from their leaders.

They develop intimate relationships with them, know their families and tribulations. They take the time to listen to members, ask questions of them, get to know about their families and lives. As one organizer says, "I take the time to do that; to be there for them. And if I'm there for them, they'll be there for the organization."

The organizer will offer roles as chairperson or spokesperson, and if the member is insecure or uncomfortable, carefully review with them what the role entails. After the member has performed the task the organizer provides praise and feedback, reinforcing the importance of the activity and making suggestions for improvement. An organizer talks of her work with a new member:

> We agreed she was going to testify in city council hearings, but she was very nervous. So we sat down together and wrote her testimony. We talked about what should be said, then she wrote it in her own words, then we edited it and added ideas, then she gave the speech to me, and then to the committee. Afterwards, we went out for coffee, and I got her to talk about how good it felt, how she had overcome her dread, and how successful she had been. She was so pleased with herself. I also suggested she might want to go see Harris again, taking some others with her. I wanted her to continue working, build on that good feeling.

While the relationship between leaders and organizers is very important, the organizing process also entails strengthening relationships among leaders. Leaders are supported and validated by their peers. The group serves both to legitimate their leadership (i.e., giving them people to lead) and prop them up so they are not acting alone. Both external and internal interactions with peers reinforce the leadership role. Whether the leader is negotiating with opponents and speaking to the media or chairing a committee meeting and holding committee members accountable for tasks, they lead in the context and at the behest of the group. Part of the task of the organizer, then, is to foster group identity and strengthen group cohesion. In the practice illustrations in this chapter one notices that even while the organizer is focused on one member, all members of the group are encouraged to participate in discussions and decisions. In this way each individual is tied to the others in the group.

Enhancing Group Identity and Cohesion

Common bonds among members build solidarity and a sense of empowerment among the "victims" of a situation and encourage people to lead. Panzetta describes common bonds in communities in terms we accept for social action organizations:

> [They] are characterized by an implicit bond which relates person to person. Like the extended family such a community is held together by common values, affection, mutual dependence, respect, and a sense of status hierarchy. There are no formal rules of relationship and the roles of the members of the community are set by traditions and cultural expectations of the group. (Panzetta 1975:38)

Panzetta warns that such bonds may be an anachronism. Social action organizations might be formed at least as "islands of closeness," an idea that Bellah et al. (1985) seem to support from their analysis of Americans and public agendas. And the organizational style that most organizers subscribe to does reflect the qualities Panzetta describes. Yet such a sense of community or "shared fate" does not occur naturally. The organizer and leaders must create it.

Ethnic and class antipathy are deeply instilled in people. Diverse constituencies often feel themselves to be very different, and tend not to appreciate similarities they have with others. For example, it may be difficult to get white, middle-class gay men to see commonalities with lesbians who are not as privileged or with people of color. Neighborhood organizers often struggle with racial and age differences and tensions between homeowners and renters.

There are several techniques for overcoming these differences. While formal business meetings reinforce different levels of skills and knowledge, informal socializing that occurs around meetings and at special events minimizes such variations and breaks down stereotypes people may hold of one another. These social periods encourage friendship and camaraderie among people who generally see themselves as dissimilar.

Organizers can also use organizational history as a means for building collegiality. The special history and significance of the group is retold, and—by implication—the importance of the future, and members' special obligation to serve, are fueled. For example, an organization in a multiracial community had fought an arduous battle with the city around vacant homes and tax delinquent properties. At the group's annual convention a few leaders and an organizer devised a skit. In it a leader, dressed as the movie character Rocky, entered to the movie's theme song, punched down vacant buildings made of cardboard, and finally knocked down the city's housing commissioner. The skit was a big hit; it reaffirmed the group's collective history and sense of future purpose. It continues to be remembered fondly in the community even ten years later.

Involvement in making decisions also builds a sense of ownership in the organization. Yet the sense of group purpose and cohesion can quickly erode when a group gets bogged down in details or can't come to a decision. In this case organizers need to help leaders ensure that members have had time to become familiar with what's involved and all have had their say. Watching people's body language will help the organizer determine whether people are becoming bored and disillusioned. When that happens it is time for the organizer to suggest coming to a conclusion by focusing on the group's common goal.

Perhaps the most difficult task of an organizer is to orchestrate relationships among leaders and members when there is internal conflict. No matter how positive and intimate the relationships, how strong the common ties, how effective the rewards, how well crafted the participation, at some point problems, disagreements, and tensions will arise. Conflicts can range from those that are merely a healthy by-product of full member participation to those that threaten the very existence of the organization. Still, any conflict, if left unattended, jeopardizes the common ground developed in the organization. Whatever the source of the friction, it is the organizer's job to attempt to resolve it.

Groups with interracial, multiethnic, and interfaith memberships may find that prejudice is sometimes a tense undercurrent in their organizations. When it occurs working together, reaching for common issues, and socializing together often reduce antipathy.

There can be power struggles among participants and staff that involve who controls which decisions, who must take responsibility for what, and who can hold whom accountable. Board-staff conflicts are common, and usually arise around how much the board is involved in setting policy versus doing fund-raising and program work.

Veteran leaders are probably more apt to struggle for control with staff over new directions. Newer recruits with less history and investment will more likely withdraw from the organization at the first blush of such conflict. All disagreements with staff, however difficult they may be, should be viewed as positive because they reflect the investment people have come to have in the organization. Staff-leadership friction may suggest, however, that the leaders are uncomfortable with their limited roles and questioning staff dominance over decisions. In these cases it is incumbent upon the organizer to reevaluate the division of labor between staff and leaders.

Veteran leaders can also come into conflict with new members around leadership succession issues (Burghardt 1982b). People who have led the organization may view new people as threats to their prerogatives. Organizers need to help established leaders understand why new people must be brought into leadership positions, and help them to accept their role in bringing new people along. When necessary organizers must also create additional "emeritus" roles for veterans so they are not merely moving out of a role but into another equally prestigious one.

Conflicts also can arise among different units of an organization or, very commonly, among coalition partners or between the national office and local affiliates. The autonomy of each group is often at stake. Guidelines that lay out areas of autonomy and interdependence and what is expected of each unit can eliminate some of this type of strain.

Personality conflicts are most often petty differences, not the type of conflict that endangers a group, but they may cause individuals to leave the organization. Since organizers have great influence on strategy decisions, conflicts around strategies or tactics are rare. When they do occur, conflicts over strategy appear to reflect basically different approaches to applying pressure. Some members want to be more aggressive and confrontational, while others support a polite, collaborative approach. Full and ongoing discussions of the various strategic options should help air these differences and allow people to at least go along with a consensus view.

The most common friction among leaders is generally around workload (typically who is not doing enough, who is dominating the group, and who is doing things independently), what the priority issues should be, and how organizational resources should be allocated. Such conflict is normative and probably inevitable. Yet, when left unfettered, such conflicts can seriously undermine the good feelings and work of the organization.

Organizers have developed a large number of ways to address, deflect, or ignore this last type of friction. Skilled organizers help leaders concentrate on heading off disagreements before they become openly conflictual and on working toward compromise when conflicts do flare up. Group discussion and communication should be used to avoid misunderstandings in the first place. One organizer says, "The greatest skill is avoiding: talk, look for compromise, try to smooth over conflicts to keep people working together."

If open discussions are not working, organizers may try individual private discussions, getting people to come in and talk over their positions. The organizer then can serve as a broker by interpreting one member's opinions to others with competing views, looking for compromise while avoiding face-to-face confrontations. Sometimes such conflicts can be referred to leaders who are respected by the competing factions. Officers or board members can negotiate the differences.

Most organizers can recount times when the conflict threatened to overwhelm the organization, and little could be done to stop it. Sometimes a large group of leaders leave the organization, and the organizer must recruit new members to replace them. In other cases the conflict destroys all sense of common ground. In these instances it is probably most effective to build an entirely new organization.

In sum, friction and contention spring necessarily and unavoidably from participation. Yet, such conflict must be monitored and controlled so that members' fighting spirit continues to be directed outward at targets and opponents and not inward at peers and staff.

This chapter and the previous one have examined what we envision as a four-stage process for involving people in social action organizations. We have described how pools of possible participants are identified, how recruitment messages are crafted and disseminated, how newcomers are "plugged into" the organization through activities, committees, tasks, and how members are sustained and developed into leaders.

There is a good deal of evidence to support the existence of such a process in social action organizations, and we argue that the more fully each phase is consciously developed and implemented the more likely the organization will succeed in attracting and retaining members.

While organizers and leaders support the importance of these phases, in practice they do not give special attention to each phase. Instead, work with membership is viewed as a less important aspect of their work. They may worry about it but not closely analyze or monitor it, and they tend not to understand the inherent problems in each phase. Many organizers do very little in these phases. Rather than recruit new members, they are like wallflowers at a dance, waiting to be chosen. Recruits come almost by happenstance. Other groups are conscious about early phases, aggressively recruiting new members yet doing little to involve them. They tend to view joining as an end, rather than as the beginning of deepened investment. Grassroots organizers and those who support countervailing institutions' beliefs manifest the strongest member outreach, leader development, and retention strategies. Their orientation demands active member participation—this is the sine qua non of their organizing. These organizers succeed in developing relationships with and among leaders, members, and new recruits. Obviously, this is easier to do in local settings, which allow for proximity. However, the creative and resourceful statewide or national organizer who refuses to use distance as an excuse can find ways of enhancing participation. Regular conference calls and the use of computer "mailboxes," having organizers and leaders travel around to keep communication going, newsletters that report on local activities and acknowledge individual leaders, and regularly scheduled conferences that bring people together are all ways of keeping distant members and leaders in regular contact.

CHAPTER FIVE

Issues

The changes social action organizations seek are not solely the abstract ones of empowering people, developing leadership, and educating the public. In addition, social action organizations work toward changes on selected issues.

Social action organizations work on public issues, not private troubles. According to C. Wright Mills, "Troubles occur within the character of the individual and within the range of his immediate relations with others" (Mills 1959:8). Public issues "have to do with matters that transcend these local environments of the individual and the range of his inner life" (ibid.). For example, the individual who has a mental disability has a private trouble, but the inability of the welfare and mental health system to provide housing and services in the community is a public issue.

Social action organizers also accept that defining public issues is not solely a scientific process, but that issues can also be defined subjectively by those who are experiencing them (Biklen 1983). Evictions by unscrupulous landlords may constitute an issue to the neighborhood and the people left homeless, but may not be defined as a problem by the landlords. Put simply, social action organizers help people define and take on those conditions which make it difficult for them to live decent, productive lives (Center for Community Organizing 1989).

Thus, the process of defining and agreeing on organizational issues becomes the content of the organization's work and the substance of its efforts to pursue social change.

The process of defining and agreeing on organizational issues can be described in four stages:

Phase I: Generating and Identifying Issues In the first phase a variety of possible problems for work are identified. The major goal of this phase is to discover problems and people interested in them. Discovering problems may be done in many different ways and the sources may vary, but essentially the organizer, as representative of the organization, must listen for problems requiring change.

Phase II: Selecting Among Issues and Developing a Working Agreement for Organizational Priorities From the many problems identified an issue or a set of issues are selected as "issues for work." * The major goals of this phase are to determine which problems will be taken on, based on some criteria, and to form a working agreement among participants around the selected issues.

Phase III: Collecting Information and Deepening and Extending Commitment During this phase the major goal is to become more informed about the issue, its causes, and implications. At the same time people's interest in the issue is deepened, and others are persuaded of its importance.

Phase IV: Monitoring Organizational Issues During this phase the major goal is to evaluate how effective the organization's "package" of issues is; whether many issues can be handled simultaneously, whether a new issue is warranted, and whether and, if so, how issues can be linked together in order to keep people motivated.

Each phase in the process of developing issues has goals related to the issue (an instrumental end) and goals related to people (an expres-

---

*Social workers employ a similar process in working with individual clients, families, or groups. People come with a whole host of problems, and the worker and client must select a "problem for work." Shulman (1991) describes this as "the common ground or overlap between the services and help offered by the agency through the worker and the felt needs of the client" (46). Shulman goes on to say that "clients often start with 'near problems' or safe issues to test the worker. Once the worker has demonstrated the capacity to help, once trust and a sound working relationship exist, the client may expand the working contract and begin to take help in more difficult areas" (48). We postulate that issue identification in social action organizations is a similar process.

sive end). Brager and Specht (1973) suggest that organizers are required to handle two tasks simultaneously: technical tasks (selecting feasible organizational issues) and expressive tasks (recruiting and developing a constituency to support them). This formulation assumes a need for a constituency to advocate for an issue. The existence of an organizational issue gives the organization purpose and takes those involved beyond the realm of a social club or reference group. Conversely, an organization with an issue but no loyal following has little chance of realizing a desired change (Grosser and Mondros 1985).

This process and role for the organizer are, however, only general guidelines. Indeed, there are many variations. First, because organizers guide it, the process is grounded in what they value, think, and do.* Second, the process is affected by the organization's environment, by the geographic domain of the organizing, and by unpredictable social, economic, and political events. Consequently, not every phase of issue development entails both expressive and technical tasks to the same degree for every organizer.

What follows is a description of how social action organizers and leaders in their organizations can envision the process of issue development, and operationalize expressive and technical tasks in the process. While we have organized this chapter according to this process, we will also pay attention to nuances and differences that suggest other ways of working.

Phase I: Raising and Identifying Problems

Almost any public issue offers opportunities for social action organizing. Neighborhood groups work on such issues as getting banks to reinvest money for low-income housing, pressuring for job opportunities, enforcement of fair housing codes and inspections, obtaining foot patrol in high-crime areas, and ridding the community of drugs. There are metropolitan groups that work on rent stabilization and better police treatment of minorities. State and national organizations fight for laws protecting reproductive rights, and fair and equal treatment of women, gays, and the disabled. National groups work for disarma-

---

*The influence of orientation on defining problems has been noted in other types of practice. Germain and Gitterman (1980) write of the influence of the clinician's orientation on problem definitions. If clinicians locate problems within the person, then clients' problems are defined as pathological, and psychotherapeutic interventions are used; if workers locate the problem within the environment, then clients' problems are defined in social-institutional terms, and a social action model is used. Because of this influence, problem definition is seen as a critical feature of practice.

ment or to stop nuclear dumping. The marketplace of issues that can comprise an organization's change agenda is almost limitless and often changes over time.

For an organizer the first phase of issue development is to discover problems on which to work. This initial phase entails searching out the universe of possible problems that could potentially translate into organizational issues and become the substance for pursuing social change. Tasks include determining how problems can be identified and finding reliable sources to suggest them.

Commonly, there are three ways organizers discover issues. Many organizers generate issues directly from people, believing issues that are deeply and widely felt to have the greatest ability to motivate people and create the most loyalty to the issues and to the organization. In this traditional approach organizers knock on doors, make telephone calls, and visit community members in an effort to elicit complaints. The organization's issues emerge from these grievances. In this model the technical task of finding an issue and the expressive task of interesting people in them are merged.

An unyielding emphasis on generating issues from people has however, certain disadvantages that a second model attempts to correct. People may experience and complain about the high cost of health care but are not likely to attribute the problem to federal regulations and budget cuts. The organizer who rigidly adheres to issues that people experience and express may not attempt to analyze the causes that are also valid issues for organizing. Consequently, organizers can begin with issues people generate and then look to convince people of the importance of related issues. For example, an organizer may have found that people with whom she is working are concerned about vacant buildings. Forcing the city to use its authority to take over and rehabilitate the buildings becomes the work of the organization. As that is being accomplished the organizer begins to think about the need to improve the community's housing stock by obtaining reinvestment money and trying to negotiate with area lenders to provide low-rate home improvement loans. The people, however, have not expressed this concern; indeed, the lending process may be outside of the experience of most residents of the neighborhood. Yet the organizer sees it as a natural extension of the work the organization has been doing. In this model the organizer then seeks to explain the connections between banking policy and neighborhood deterioration and to persuade the people that this issue does indeed directly impact on the quality of life in the neighborhood. The organizer first performs expressive tasks, followed by the instrumental task of further issue definition, and once again returns to the expressive task of educating people.

In a third model organizations are either established to work on certain predetermined issues or born out of the need to work on an issue because some economic, political, or social event has demanded a response. Organizations that advocate for the homeless are examples of the former, while organizations that developed in reaction to the Vietnam War exemplify the latter. In this model the organizer's task is to persuade people that these issues deserve their allegiance—to find people who are interested in the issue, to deepen their interest, and to engage people who have not thought about the issue before and convince them that the issue personally impacts on them. The instrumental task of issue identification precedes the expressive task of persuading people of the issue's importance.

Though it is sometimes valid to have a predetermined issue, it is dangerous for organizers to rely too heavily on their own judgment about what issues are important or to have too much control over the selection of issues. Sometimes organizing staff have formal influence by holding seats or voting rights on the governing bodies that identify issues, or they have small committees, which they use as sounding boards for their ideas. Organizers offer many reasons for this influence: they are the ones with daily operational responsibilities and expertise, members are open to influence, the issues are easy to discern anyway, the organization's mandate is already clear, the organization covers too great a geographic area to involve members effectively, when staff decides issues the organization can act quickly and nonbureaucratically. In our opinion these are not good reasons to refrain from generating ideas directly from the people with whom they are concerned or at least exploring ideas with members. Too often organizers will see situations through their own personal lenses, and these are often young, white, middle-class male ones. They will notice situations that offend them, but not necessarily the ones that offend the people who live with the problems. In extreme cases organizers may find themselves organizing in opposition to what most of the community wants. An organizer who worked with Hispanic parents explains how she caught herself making this mistake,

> I had determined that we should pressure the school board for a bilingual kindergarten. After all, how could these kids be expected to learn when everything was in English and their first language was Spanish? It seemed so obvious to me. So I talked to a couple of the

mothers, and they were very sweet, and nodded their heads, and said sure, they'd come to a meeting. The first meeting only Rosa showed up. So I thought, OK, I picked a bad time, the publicity was bad. So I called another meeting, and no one came. I was fed up and thought these people just don't want to do anything. I was complaining to Rosa, and quietly she said, "Some of the parents *want* their children to learn English. They get the Spanish at home." And I suddenly realized that the bilingual English class was my agenda. I never asked what they wanted.

Several rationales support the viewpoint that the "best issues" are those generated by the people with whom organizers work or issues that people routinely experience as burdensome. First and foremost is the belief that the organization should reflect the needs and interests of its constituencies; that people are best able to define the salient issues that affect their lives. Often these are not the issues that the organizer deems most important. Protesting for the installation of a stop sign or the removal of no parking signs may hardly seem significant in the face of overwhelming social problems. Nonetheless, these issues are most painful to the people with whom they work. Many organizers struggle to reconcile their own perception of what's important and what they consider the relatively low aspirations of their members. Sometimes they find themselves advocating for an issue that their members are less concerned about or accommodating themselves to working on issues they consider less meaningful. An organizer working with the homeless explains this struggle and why he finally accommodated to the desires of his members.

We were organizing to sue the city, and we were saying we need affordable low-income housing, we need jobs. We had meetings and rallies, and homeless people were saying, "Right on, right on, but let us tell you about these God-damned shelters." We'd go to another city and talk about housing and jobs, and people would say, "Right on, right on, but what about these fucking shelters?" What people were saying is that yes, we need housing and we need jobs, but right now staying in a God-damned shelter is killing us. We need to deal with that now. To be relevant to them, we had to go with their most pressing issue first.

There are other reasons for stressing that people should generate their own issues. Self-expressed issues are thought to intensify the sense of urgency to act, increase the credibility and legitimacy for the organizing, immediately empower people by offering them an active role in issue selection, and give focus and meaning to people's participation. Organizers feel that when issues come directly from people there is less need to "sell" the organization, its issues, or the need for participation. As an organizer says,

> People are so rarely asked in our society what they think about anything. Most of what we do is as spectator rather than participant. When we organize around something that comes from the community it immediately opens the level of participation in a way that people unfortunately just don't experience in our culture. I think the fact that we try to take the time to find out how people feel and draw the issues from the community makes a big difference in how strong and powerful the organization can be.

People's grievances, however, do not usually simply "bubble up" into an organized protest. To the contrary, people are reticent to express problems, particularly to a stranger. People often accommodate to oppressive conditions, may not give them much due or even notice them. For example, a polluting factory that emits a foul stench may go virtually unnoticed by long-time residents. People also often experience public issues as private troubles and feel ashamed at their inability to cope with them. The worker laid off from a plant closing may experience it as a reflection on his competency as a breadwinner rather than an organizing issue. Finally, people may even recognize an issue but believe few others suffer from it or feel nothing can be done about it or leave it to others to work on. All these factors inhibit people from expressing their complaints.

Consequently, organizers have to be active in discovering and eliciting problems. They act as receptacles for the collection of common problems. They make contacts with people and ask them to identify issues or test out issues, which people then judge for their relevancy. These contacts allow them to really hear what people are concerned about. They also have to have contacts with many people to avoid the trap of hearing only idiosyncratic concerns or, worse, only those people who agree with their perspective about significant issues. The practice illustration below shows an organizer meeting for the first time with a neighborhood resident to whom he had been referred by the parish priest. The resident is reluctant to express his grievances, and the illustration shows how the organizer carefully elicits his concerns and frames them as neighborhood issues.

Father Joe had suggested that I visit with Bill. Bill was an active church member who served as the leader of the church's boy scout troop. He had lived in the neighborhood all his life. My hunch was that he had never seen himself as a community leader. I thought he might care about the neighborhood kids, and might be interested in things like recreation. Despite Father Joe's introduction, he might feel hesitant about getting involved in anything beyond scouting. I would have to reach for his concerns and interests. I introduced myself to Bill, and explained that I was the organizer for M.A.P., and a little about what M.A.P. did. I said M.A.P. tried to work on problems in the community. I used my calling card and said that Father Joe had particularly wanted me to meet with him to learn more about the community. I mentioned that I knew he had lived here for many years, and was active in the church and boy scouting. I asked him how he found living here. He answered very noncommittally, saying "Well, it's been home all my life." I asked him to tell me a little about what the neighborhood had been like in his youth, hoping that by making comparisons between then and now, he might raise some problems. He reminisced with feeling about the neighborhood of his youth. After letting him go on for awhile, I asked him what he thought had changed for kids today. That question was like opening the floodgates. He told me about the drug dens in the area, the fact that parents didn't care what kids did anymore, that there was no discipline in the schools, that everything in the community was being vandalized. I picked up on his last concern and asked him what he thought kids did for recreation now; after all the recreation center had very limited hours since the city's budget cuts had gone into effect. He said that, except for scouting, there was very little for kids to do in the neighborhood; that's why they were always getting into trouble. I said a lot of people in the neighborhood seemed to think the same thing. I asked if he thought that was something worth working on—getting the recreation department to keep the center open longer, especially during the summer. He seemed noncommittal again, and I sensed his hesitancy. I said I believed that it was important to work together on problems and to propose solutions. Still hesitant, Bill said he didn't see what we could do, if the city didn't have the money. I said I knew that some recreation centers in the city were open longer hours. They apparently either had clout or had made a case for it with the city. Rather sarcastically, he said they probably had clout. I said I thought we might be able to have clout, too, if we had a lot of people working together and could make a good case. He seemed a little more optimistic. I asked him if he knew other people who might care about this, and he listed a few people at the church who worked with kids. I asked if it was worth at least trying to get them together to discuss this, and he said he thought we could do at least that much. I could sense that he wasn't sold yet, but he did agree to call five people and see if we could get together next week. I suggested we ask Father Joe to sit in on the meeting. He thought that was a great idea, and volunteered to call him. I left thinking that I had made a good start with Bill.

As the illustration above shows, the task of eliciting grievances is not usually a systematic need assessment. While surveys and studies may help in fund-raising and establishing an organization's legitimacy, they aren't required to really hear people's grievances. Instead, the organizer has informal conversations with as many individuals and groups of people as possible. Traditionally, organizers have done door knocking, although this approach is less effective in areas where gaining entry may be difficult. Organizers hold open meetings or meetings of churches, senior clubs, or dorms, encourage phone calls to the organization requesting help, and set up "gripe tables." Some organizers have tried more rigorous ways of discovering issues by conducting formal interviews or surveys. An organization of working women conducted simple interviews in places where women office workers were likely to travel—on subways, in the city's business district, and in the cafeterias that secretaries frequent. A welfare rights organizer reviewed case applications for SSI benefits to discern common welfare issues among her constituency. These more formal assessment methods may be needed to reach a population that is not geographically fixed.

The way the organization is structured can also help in issue identification. A fairly popular approach is for the social action organization to solicit institutions such as churches, senior clubs, or campus chapters to join the organization and send representatives who serve on governing bodies. They then establish action or issue committees where interested individuals or members of the institutions can serve. Many people are connected to the organization, and there are a number of places where issues can be raised. An organizer from a senior citizen group describes how issue identification can work in such a federated structure:

> We have member groups, issue committees, and a steering committee. Sometimes the issue committees identify an issue, sometimes the member groups, sometimes the steering committee. Issues come up a variety of ways, and people with different connections to the orga-

nization all have a say. Later we funnel the issues back through the multilevel structure so that people in the member groups can still work on something identified at other levels.

Even though the ideal is to generate issues from people, it is not always practical to do so. Physical proximity to one's constituency allows an organizer to hear problems directly from people. When the access to one's constituency is limited, as it is in statewide and national organizations, techniques must be developed to overcome the obstacle of geographic distance. These organizers can rely on local organizers to offer ideas about issues or travel to local groups to "keep their finger on the pulse." They can mail questionnaires and conduct telephone interviews, which, while costly, have the added advantage of allowing for individual contact and give-and-take discussion. They can create local or statewide chapters from which issues can emerge. Finally, they can hold national conventions, which has the benefit of both allowing problems to percolate up and persuading people in the grass roots of the importance of a national issue.

Often, national and statewide organizers use other avenues to supplement hearing concerns directly. They analyze economic and social data to determine what might concern their members or watch for political events that affect their constituents. Once the issues are identified, people can be attracted to them. Recognizing that data collection can not substitute for issues that are generated or affirmed by people, these organizers must find other ways to hear people's complaints. They may make visits to local chapters or visit places where people experiencing the problems are likely to congregate. In that way they learn what the local manifestations of the problems are and can call on those people when they are working on national issues.

It is also not always possible to wait until someone raises the problem. Some issues, such as prisoners rights, are not likely to be raised spontaneously. Moral issues do not always directly impact on the majority of people, and many issues involve prejudices that obviate against them being expressed. The people who experience these problems may be afraid that raising them will subject them to retaliation. The principles of equity and social justice that undergird the issue are more important than how it gets raised or who raises it.

It is also sometimes necessary to raise an impending issue before the effects of it have been felt. A proposed legislative bill that will limit welfare entitlements, plans to build a highway through a neighborhood, a case of police brutality, should not necessarily be held until "someone brings it up." The organizer will have to identify the issue.

In these cases organizers will have already identified the issue, and their task is not to generate other ideas but to attract adherents to the current problem. In such circumstances the traditional methods of door knocking, open meetings, and individual contacts may be quite frustrating. Organizations that send staff to knock on doors merely to solicit funds are neither generating issues from people nor urging them to get involved in some substantive way. They may have an issue, but will not have attracted people to work on it.

Obviously, organizers need to be aware of moral and emerging issues, and most hold potential for organizing. However, attempting to persuade people to predetermined issues poses certain obstacles. Despite the predetermined nature of the issue, the organizer can still find people who are likely to care about it, can determine its attraction for people, explore it with them in more depth, and engage their interest. Those who work on the problem professionally, advocates for the population, and members of progressive churches are likely to be interested in the issues for moral or professional reasons. Contacts with them can be made through professional associations and churches and these institutions can be a starting place to explore how the issue is perceived and to attract interested people. The most obvious population to reach will be those who are at risk of experiencing the problem directly, even though they may be reticent to talk. The organizer's task is to find those people—to engage them in a discussion of their problems, explore the ways in which the issue affects their life, show that the problem goes beyond their individual situation, and educate them about their right to their concerns. In some cases a self-help group comprised of people who suffer with the problem may already exist. An organizer who works with parents of children who are developmentally delayed explains his approach,

> When you're organizing this population you will find a million professional advocates and politicians. You could spend all your time organizing them. And they're nice people, they care, but they pull in and out, depending on grants and vacations and other priorities. The parents don't pull out because they live with this problem everyday. But no one talks to the parents, no one ever asks what they think about the service system, the schools, the plans made by the experts. I try to say to them this is not a problem you should be ashamed about, you have a right to be concerned, and who knows better than you what the problems are with the system, and what

your kid needs. I work with the professionals, sure, I go to their meetings, and they come to ours, but my real base is the parents.

Phase II: Selecting Among Issues and Developing a Working Agreement

Commonly, in the first phase of issue development a variety of problems have been raised and people have many opinions about what caused them and what should be done. The second stage of issue development entails selecting an issue or a set of issues from the many problems identified and developing a level of agreement among people that allows work on the issue to continue. These decisions are based on some set of criteria that governs which issues are most effectively pursued by the organization.

During this phase the organizer must decide who must agree and how much consensus is necessary for work to continue. As people participate in selecting the organization's issues and come to agreement about causes and solutions, the sanction for the organization to pursue its work is widened and deepened.

When people select an organizational issue, agree on the causes of and solutions for the problem, and decide to work on it together, their individual investment is affirmed by peer support. The process of selecting issues emphasizes their roles as participants and organizational decision makers rather than spectators. Having made the decision to pursue an issue, they are more likely to want to work on it and are more committed to sharing the work that will have to be done. Finally, as they air differences they come to understand that compromise is possible, that their individual interests and opinions may be blended or traded with others or even changed. They value the reality of compromise among peers rather than demand total unanimity. This negotiated settlement is what we call a "working agreement."

To reach a working agreement the organizer helps people see their problems as organizational issues rather than individual concerns. To do this, people must come together to discuss the issue. If distance prevents this, multiple structures can be used so that issues can be sanctioned by many people at the local levels of the organization. In these discussions, organizers encourage people to decide *among* issues, to identify common grievances, to determine priorities, and to assess the organizational feasibility of an identified issue, choosing those that are best suited to the organization. The organizer poses the questions that encourage agreement: Which issues are most important to people and why? What are the root causes of the problem? and most important, What would solve the problem and what would be the consequences of such a solution? By eliciting different ideas, offering information, focusing on a common issue rather than differences, the organizer actively helps people move toward a working agreement. As a thorough, public, and open decision-making process takes place, a working agreement emerges and becomes a commitment for all (Mondros and Berman-Rossi 1991).

Yet, it is often difficult and time-consuming to achieve such a working agreement. Some argue that staff members are better informed on issues, know best what the organization can handle at any given point in time, and may have a national perspective that supersedes local sentiments. Middle-class people may particularly emphasize the necessity of expertise. Perhaps they don't feel the need to participate in issue selection because their rights are confirmed in so many other areas of their life.

It is certainly true that circuitous discussion that leads nowhere is demoralizing to most people, especially to those who doubt that anything can be done about the problem anyway. And it is equally true that as more people are involved in the selection of issues, the risk of endless discussion is increased. Yet, as organizers choose the organization's issues or limit the number of people involved, the process of gaining sanction and investment is abridged.

Consequently, organizers have to attend to both participation and efficiency at this phase. Total consensus is probably an unreachable ideal, but there needs to be enough agreement among participants for the organization to act and retain the support of its members. At the same time the decision-making process must be time limited and structured. It is the organizer's job to insure a "working agreement" that allows action.*

Even with the organizer's encouragement, however, people may not come to agreement. People often bring interests and needs that are not easily put aside. All the organizer's efforts to persuade people of the importance of a selected issue may fall on deaf ears. In cases where

---

*The idea of reaching initial "working agreements" or contracts is used by other practitioners, particularly clinical social workers. Much of the literature argues for the client and worker to develop a "contract" that specifies mutual goals and roles. In a way similar to the working agreement suggested here, a contract seems to enhance a client's continuing involvement and ensures that worker and client are working toward the same ends. Contracts, as working agreements, evolve and are elaborated over time (Maluccio and Marlow 1984, Seabury 1976).

people have different priorities about which issue is most important, two or more "issue committees" can be established that allow people to pursue the activities they feel most committed to. The organizer can encourage people to barter their interests and provide support for each other by suggesting that people agree to work on one issue with the promise that another issue will be taken up next. Where conflict around status exists, leadership roles can be shared or rotated, or people can be offered different roles with equal status and visibility.

The most challenging situations are those where there seems to be vast disagreement about which issues are important, who is at fault, and what should be done about them. Increasingly, organizers face the problem of trying to bring together people who should have the same interests, but are extremely hostile to one another. Often, the conflict is racial, but such antagonism exists between other groups, such as working women and homemakers or the working poor and those who receive government benefits. Organizers are understandably disheartened by such antagonism and discouraged by people's inability to see beyond their own needs. One dangerous response is for organizers to work only with people who are already of like mind. In this approach unanimity is relatively easily achieved, but it is obviously a case of "preaching to the converted." The process of building a working agreement, eliciting differences, and coming to compromise are simply avoided.

Organizers need neither avoid these conflicts, nor work only with those who already agree. Instead, an organizer can look for an issue, *any* issue, around which there is agreement, and begin bypassing some of the differences. In these situations organizers can also appeal to the "common good" to convince people that an issue is worth their effort, despite their differences. An experienced organizer who began working in Yonkers, New York, during a time of extreme racial strife used both strategies. Initially, he avoided the issue of public housing, which was the area of greatest conflict, and instead worked with people on a co-op conversion law, rehabilitation of parks, and a public information system for the city. Working through area churches and synagogues, he established "Nights of Harmony" where ethnic music and food were shared. After six months, he appealed to members' religious values and helped people to work on a comprehensive housing plan for the city that focused not only on public housing but also on multiunit dwellings, low-interest loans for homeowners, and luxury development.

Criteria for Selecting Issues

All social action organizations have some criteria that govern the decision about which issues to undertake. These criteria, based on the particular values, needs, interests, and resources of the organization, become the standards against which each issue is measured. Issues are examined in relation to these criteria during the process of building the working agreement. The job of the organizer, then, is to work with people to select not just an issue, but the best issue among the ones expressed, for that will be the focus of organizational work.

Organizers measure the viability of issues according to five criteria: 1. the relevancy of the issue for the organization's membership or constituency, 2. the ability to successfully pursue an issue, 3. the feasibility of the issue, given the organization's resources, 4. the importance of the issue in the environmental context and the likelihood of some public receptivity, and 5. the ability of the issue to further social change goals. These criteria are not mutually exclusive. As we have suggested earlier, developing leadership (a constituent-oriented criterion) is often viewed as a way of building power and therefore related to social change. Similarly, assessing the social and political climate's receptivity (an environmental factor) may also be a way of analyzing the prospects for success.

The most important factor in issue selection is the needs and interests of the organization's constituents. "Good" issues are those which are broadly and deeply experienced by members or constituents, hold the promise of valued benefits, and have a great deal of support. This criterion is particularly important when working with low-income or working-class people who do not have the luxury of spending time on abstract or secondary concerns (Brager 1963, Brager and Specht 1969, Haggstrom 1969). Moreover, organizers assess issues according to people's willingness to work on them, on their ability to involve new people, and the potential for developing and educating leaders around them. These are litmus tests that go beyond mere interest in an issue. They are questions that examine how deeply people feel the need for action is, how many other people can potentially become part of the effort, and whether the issue spurs people into taking on leadership roles. It is also necessary that the issue be important to all quarters of the community, especially if the community is fraught with ethnic or racial tension.

In organizations where issues are selected by staff or a small board, it is very important to assess whether people are interested enough to actively work toward change. Without their willingness to become engaged, the organization will remain a paper tiger. An environmental organization, for example, chose to work for enactment of a bill that allowed refunds on glass bottles, not because this was its most important environmental issue, but because it was popular, would build membership, and allowed coalitions with other groups.

A second important factor in issue selection is the prospects for pursuing an issue with some degree of success. Here organizers are assessing whether something specific can resolve the issue, whether someone can be held responsible for the problem, whether it logically suggests a goal or an action, and whether it can potentially be "won" in a foreseeable time span. These are practical considerations that assess an issue's "do-ability"—that it can be resolved in some way. Here organizers are not only concerned that people are interested in the issue, but that they can experience some success by acting on it. As issues are resolved, members learn they can competently solve their own problems.

There have been many criticisms about the "quick fix" approach to community organizing (Eaton and Scharff 1979). Critics have charged that organizers who focus on easy victories avoid the basic social injustices that are by definition much harder to remedy. For the most part organizers have come to agree with this view and moved away from the classic Alinsky (1972) dictum that issues must be winnable. Yet, to involve people initially in a long and difficult struggle has the potential of undermining their self-confidence and faith in the ability of the organization. The answer to the problem lies in a more developmental approach. To build confidence in people, begin with issues that are easy to resolve and later tackle more demanding issues that require more faith and endurance. In this developmental approach people are continually educated so that their self-confidence does not ride on constant victory, and they recognize the efficacy of taking on more complex issues. In the illustration below an organizer describes such a developmental approach.

The first thing I wanted to do in Homesburg was to get people involved in something they cared about. I didn't care what it was. I wanted to show them they could work together on something they cared about and win. So the two first things we did was get the city to remove the no parking signs across from the park so that people could park there, and we got the dogcatcher to patrol the neighborhood once a week to capture stray dogs. At that point we had a committee of about twelve people, but they felt good about their successes. I thought we could go on to something a little bigger, but it still had to be directly tied to their interests. They brought up the issue of the vacant lots, and we got the city to clean and seal them. We involved the people who had vacant lots on their block in that. That took maybe three months, and near the end of it I started talking with them about who owned these lots, and it would be interesting to find out whether they had back taxes on them, and how vacant lots and properties affected land values. So I got several people interested in that and we surveyed all the vacant properties in the neighborhood, who owed back taxes, and we had a major campaign with the city to collect the taxes. That campaign took almost a year and by now the group was almost two hundred active folks. We held a community convention, and almost seven hundred people attended. The people presented various resolutions on things like education, housing, and safety. We worked on those things—foot patrol in the neighborhood, a new building for the alternative school, special sanitation efforts. After about two years of pretty regular organizing and a slew of successes, we agreed to work on arson in the neighborhood. We were going to have to take on the fire company and insurance companies in the nation to do it, and it was sure to be a long fight. But by then over one thousand people were involved and we had leaders who had been around three years. We were ready to do something bigger.

Another important factor in determining issues is organizational resources. Does the issue fit within the organization's mandate or take it too far afield? Will the issue require spending scarce organizational resources? Is the issue "worth it," given the limits of time and money? Does the organization have the expertise needed to pursue the issue? Does the issue duplicate the efforts of other organizations or allow the organization to work in coalition with others? Does it enhance the organization's visibility? These criteria are ways of assessing the costs and benefits of an issue.

Organizational concerns are generally given more weight by organizers than members because it is mostly their labor that will be spent. Organizational concerns are also often seriously considered by middle-class leaders, some of whom may manage other organizations. While these are indeed important considerations in issue selection, they should be balanced with the relevance of the issue for the members and constituents. An organizer who is overly attentive to resources and not to people's desires may soon find herself with a bureaucracy devoid of members.

Another factor considered in selecting issues is the larger political and social environment. Issues that present an imminent danger as a result of a social or political event, such as the nomination of a supreme court judge opposed to abortion, cannot be evaded. Too, an analysis of the sociopolitical climate may suggest that the "time is ripe" to pursue a certain change. For instance, the passage of federal legislation that offers states matching funds for establishing comprehensive service programs for families "at risk" opens up opportunities for many organizations already active in the child welfare arena.

The degree to which the environment is considered when selecting issues says a great deal about the way organizers and leaders perceive the relationship between the environment and the organization's work. Some organizers believe that an organization is more aggressive if it controls its own agenda rather than marching to the tune of outside forces. They seem to agree with Sam Rayburn that "any jackass can kick down a barn door. But it takes a carpenter to build one" (O'Neill 1987:4). For these organizers the larger environment is an unimportant criterion for selecting issues. Their notion is that whatever people care about is important, and the organization will force the environment to take notice. Other organizers monitor social and political forces and select issues reactively to what's going on around them. They resign themselves to contending with the reality of an ever-changing environment at the same time they try to raise their own concerns.

Finally, there are organizers and leaders who monitor environmental events and actors to discern issues, usually those they consider "most dangerous" to their constituency. These organizers describe themselves as being "caught up in the riptide of events" with "very little time to sit around and figure out what to do next." For these organizers and leaders the environment really defines the organization's work.

Organizers who neglect social, economic, and political events may be doing a disservice to their organizations. It is essential for the organizer to know and warn people about events and trends that will affect them. Some events cannot be ignored, so potentially threatening are they to the concerned constituency and members. Equally as often, however, a piece of legislation or financial news can offer opportunities for organizing or complement an existing issue.

However, social, political, and economic events cannot be the sole determinant of what issues an organization will undertake. Organizers who only choose issues by reacting to the environment will miss important opportunities to place issues on the public agenda that have not yet been recognized. For example, organizing around AIDS was begun long before the public, government, or the media took notice. Indeed, it has been argued that the organizing forced them to take notice (Padgug and Oppenheimer 1992, Shilts 1987).

The final factor used by organizers to assess the viability of an issue is its relationship to their vision of large-scale social change. This factor is, however, dependent upon how the organizer believes social change occurs. Organizers who believe that the development of leaders and a strong countervailing organization is the way social change occurs will emphasize the prospects of the issue to extend the organization's membership and build the organization's power. Organizers who believe that social change occurs incrementally by slowly changing public opinion will stress the ability of an issue to sensitize and educate the public to the point where lawmakers must respond. Organizers who believe that social change can occur only during auspicious moments stress the ability of the issue to increase the number and quality of activists they have on hand so that the organization is more ready to move when the political, social, and economic environment suggests. In all cases the ability of the issue to further social change goals is associated with other specific factors that in some way advance the organization and its cause.

As organizers and leaders examine possible issues and select some for work, all these criteria are weighed. Constituent interest is important because people must be able to "buy into" the issues either before the selection or after. The prospects for success on an issue and the organizational resources are also assessed. Social, political, and economic events are monitored to suggest both danger and opportunity. Finally, the ability of the issue to further social change is assessed.

Phase III: Collecting Information and Deepening and Extending Commitment

In the third phase of issue development the organizer's instrumental task is to research the issue so it is understood more deeply and comprehensively. At the same time the organizer's expressive task is to help people who have been involved to gain a better understanding of the issue and its consequences so they can deepen their commitment to the issue and act knowledgeably. New supporters must also be recruited.

Researching Issues

Once problems are identified and an organizational issue selected, "issue research" begins (Biklen 1983, Collette 1984, Douglas 1984, Kahn 1992, Trapp 1979). Five factors are considered when performing issue research: the place of information in organizing, who collects information, the types of information collected, how information is collected, and, finally, the audiences who consume it.

The Place of Information in Organizing Organizers place different emphasis on the collection of information. Some see the gathering and disseminating of information as the primary work of the organization. These organizers produce substantial policy reports and white papers that are widely disseminated. At the other end of the spectrum are organizers who put little emphasis on issue research. They feel that an angry crowd that visibly and loudly proclaims its sentiments is far more effective than data. For others information is an essential prelude to action, but not an end in itself. As one organizer says,

> Doing research doesn't mean you're going to be effective. If I do research and nobody knows it or buys into it, then all I've got is knowledge. If I do research and I can effectively convince the legislature that my research is correct, important, and helpful, then I have a chance to sell what I want to do. If the press picks up the research and recommendations, then it becomes legitimate and people talk about it. Then I've got at least a small chance of getting my recommendations through.

Along with many others who write on organizing, we see issue research as a major weapon in the arsenal of a social action organization. When organizations do solid fact gathering and use that information well, it strengthens the organization's ability to negotiate and weakens the opposition's (Trapp 1979). People who meet with a government official or corporate executive without good information will be easily outmaneuvered.

On the other hand, research cannot supersede action. With rare exception, facts by themselves hold little hope of galvanizing support or convincing the opposition. It is necessary to have enough information so that people can act in an informed way, but an organizer need not collect every last shred of information before moving into action. Organizers can use the following four questions to guide them about how much information needs to be collected around any issue:

1. How much information is sufficient for people to feel comfortable discussing the issue and taking a position on it?
2. How much information is sufficient for a good, though not foolproof, case to be argued against an opponent?
3. How much information is sufficient to counteract arguments or claims made by others such as the press or opponents?
4. How can this piece of information help move the organization into action or aid in what's already been done?

Who Collects Information Issue research is not usually the favorite task of most organizers or leaders because it is difficult work. Frequently the information an organization wants is not made readily available, and it may even be concealed. It may therefore require ingenuity to find sources and doggedness to track down concealed data. Data collection can require long hours of going through complicated materials such as legal briefs or city budgets. It can be tedious, for example, as when organizations find they need to go through title searches or tax records. In some cases research institutes can provide material, and the organization need not "reinvent the wheel." Yet, in many cases, the information is not readily available, and someone in the organization must collect it.

In the majority of cases it is the organizer who collects the data. Organizers have the sanction to do research as part of their jobs, may have more knowledge about where the data can be obtained, and may be better able to comprehend complicated material. Yet, there are rationales for the organizer to involve and help members collect the information. By collecting information themselves people again participate in the organizing effort rather than watch it as spectators. They go through the process of discovering the information for themselves, digesting the complexity of facts and relationships, and perhaps even recognizing how much others wanted the information to be concealed. For example, one organization used members to perform a housing survey where every lot on every block in the neighborhood was checked for occupancy and being up-to-code. The members then went to city hall, and learned to look through deeds and tax records to ascertain the absentee landlords and tax delinquent properties. In the subsequent negotiations with city officials, members understood the neighborhood housing situation intimately and could answer sophisticated questions. They were also pleased with their new skills and new knowledge. In the example of a women's organization working on sexual harassment, information was not readily available. Members designed a survey and administered it in places where women congregated (e.g., supermarkets, lunch cafeterias frequented by secretaries). The committee spent many hours analyzing the results. Again, their report was delivered with authority and competence, and they felt themselves to be and were treated as experts on the issue.

Because of limited time and expertise it is not always possible to engage members in collecting information. In cases where it is not possible, organizers can do some of the groundwork by collecting data and engaging members in the analysis phase.

Types of Information Organizers generally try to collect three types of information: research on the issue, on the target, and on political factors.

It is important to collect as much information as possible about the issue itself. Here organizers research such areas as the numbers of people affected by the problem, the relevant demographic information, the history of the situation, the laws that govern the problem, the public's perception of the problem, what solutions exist, and how effective and cost efficient existing and alternative programs have been. Commonly, problems exist because some group has a vested interest in maintaining the status quo. For example, many large industries such as insurance companies and banks depend upon a cheap supply of female labor, and will fight against efforts for pay equity. Good questions to answer are "Who profits from this problem?" "How much money is made from this problem?" and "How much does this problem cost us as taxpayers?"

Another important part of issue research is to discover who should be the organization's "target," i.e., who is responsible or can be held accountable for the problem, and who has the power to resolve the issue. It may seem easy to determine who this is, but most large bureaucracies will try to obscure who makes the real decisions. Many people carry important titles with no decision-making responsibility. Public relations types with no real authority will be used to deal with social action groups. In government bureaucracies one branch may blame the problem on another. Discovering the decision maker may, in fact, take some digging. It is sometimes possible to also discover "secondary targets," people who are not directly responsible for the problem but can be influential with the primary target (Brager and Holloway 1978). For example, when the union found itself ineffective in its attempt to negotiate a contract with J. P. Stevens, members went to the boards of other prominent institutions on which the J. P.

Stevens chairperson served, and asked them to remove him. Feeling the heat, these board members put pressure on him to begin negotiations.

In addition, it is also often helpful to know a lot more about the target. Where their vulnerabilities lie (e.g., if they haven't paid taxes) and who they associate with (e.g., what clubs they belong to, what boards they serve on, whose campaign they contributed to) can often be helpful information in negotiations. For example, a group had been told by the parks commissioner that their park could not be renovated because there were no funds in the budget. The organization discovered that forty city employees, including the parks commissioner, were living rent free in luxurious homes located on park ground and gave the story to the newspapers. The commissioner quickly capitulated to the organization's demands.

In many cases the issue of the social action organization will involve the enactment of laws or the resources of government. Here, politicians and legislators are the key actors to influence, and information should be collected about them. It is important to know who the key public officials are, their political proclivities, and which ideas might find greatest receptivity. The timing of legislative calendars, other pending legislation, budget surpluses and deficits, and potentials for trade-offs and compromises within the legislative system will also be important data.

How Information Is Collected Most issue research is not scholarly or objective. Such rigorous methodology would supersede action. Further, issue research is done to make a point, to provide data to support a group's position. Therefore, data must be drawn from a variety of sources and in a variety of ways, depending on the issue. Sometimes information is readily available and all one needs to do is ask. It can be as simple as reading *Who's Who in America* or going through the *Wall Street Journal* archives. It may require requesting reports through the Freedom of Information Act. Legislative issues require checking voting records and campaign contributors. More complicated issues may require legal research, data collection and analysis of demographics, or reading the corporate reports of major companies and reviewing reports filed with the Securities and Exchange Commission. In some cases the research may not be available and the organization may want to carry out its own simple survey. A women's organization designed a survey about salaries, job descriptions, petty office tasks, and sexual harassment, and interviewed women on street corners to produce a report that gave them the necessary data. Some organizers have employed focus groups to collect data on public sentiments. Because the method of the research is dependent upon the organization's issues, issue research is most akin to investigative research, where the detective goes from one clue to another.

Who Consumes Information Information is collected with three audiences in mind. First, and foremost, information is directed at the organizations' own membership. As people understand the problem they can use the research to formulate solutions to their problem and to suggest what they might do to pressure targets to comply. Again, having the information makes them actors rather than spectators. An organizer says, "People tend to see problems as 'Either we can do this or that.' Then we do research and all of sudden it's 'Well we can do this, this, this, or this. What do we think will work best?' "

The second audience for the information is the organization's opponents. The information is used to counter their claims and positions and force negotiation. Organizer Shel Trapp writes about this purpose.

> In a meeting with a bank the residents were told, "We can't make loans in your area because it is a high-risk area and we have to protect our depositors' money." Research done by the organization had revealed that the bank had lost 30 million dollars last year on land tract development loans in another state. Confronted with this, the bank's position was weakened, if not totally destroyed. Today the institution is making loans in the community. (Trapp 1979:5)

The third audience for information is the general public, and the goal here is to influence public opinion. This is, of course, most easily accomplished through positive reports in the media. Developing good relationships with reporters, "feeding" them facts and public interest stories, and keeping them interested in the group's activities and issues not only gets the word out but also builds sympathy for the organization and its issues.

Paradoxically, organizers often give more attention to providing information to their opponents than they do to communicating with their own members. Staff may knowledgeably debate with a legislator, but people who are not informed may well believe what their public official has said. Far too often members are given scanty information before meeting their opponents and members of the press. They can easily appear foolish, and will be angry with the organizer for putting them in such a vulnerable position. It is important that the information collected by the organization be given to and consumed by all three audiences.

Deepening and Extending Commitment to the Issue

While the technical task of an organizer is to research the issue, the expressive task is one of deepening and extending people's commitment. During this stage the organizer's job is not only to increase people's commitment to the issue but also their investment in working collectively toward a solution with others within the context of the social action organization. Commitment to the issue deepens and extends to peers and to the organization itself.

Disseminating the collected information is a useful way of furthering all these investments. It can inform and increase members' allegiance to the issue. The knowledge and expertise "banked" in the organization can increase the group's legitimacy in the eyes of members. Further, people generally have a great capacity to learn—whatever their background—and are eager to do so when there is an opportunity. Acquiring information can make members feel like a specially expert group, giving them a status they are seldom afforded. It can also convince previously unaffiliated people that the issue is worthy of support. Information can also be shared in many ways: in face-to-face discussions where the information is discussed and analyzed, through written communications such as fact sheets or newsletters, or through reports in the media. The purpose of the data suggests how it is best shared. If, for instance, the intent of the information is to convince unaffiliated people that the issue is worthy of support, a more public venue like the media is used. On the other hand, if the information is designed to motivate members, personal methods of sharing are more effective.

Data are shared so that people can understand the issue better, deepen their concern for the issue, and begin to map strategy for solving it. This process of understanding and using the information begins early, when members are involved in collecting the information. When this is not possible, the information collected by the organizer can be discussed with individuals and with groups of participants in meetings. The information can have a dramatic effect on the way the issue is viewed and the opportunities people see for solving it. As people come together to discuss, analyze, and debate the information, they reinforce their reasons for being together within the organization. One technique, when time or expertise is limited, is for the organizer to go over the research in detail with a small group of people, and then have them present it to a larger committee. Members grasp the information better as they report it to others.

However, as more people become involved, it is probably not possible to hold individual discussions with everyone or have everyone attend meetings. A particular problem arises when many new people who were not involved in the planning attend a meeting with a target. Having no background, they may feel that the organization's spokespersons are being unnecessarily rude. One way of remedying the situation is to design a simple "fact sheet" listing the organization's complaints, including important information, and reviewing the organization's progress. Fact sheets have the advantage of updating the newcomers about the information quickly, without delaying the work of those who are already informed.

Social action organizations often publish other types of written materials to keep members informed. Newsletters and special reports about a particular issue are regularly mailed to all members. The preparation of such material is less time consuming than conducting individual discussions and meetings, and probably allows an organization to reach a larger audience, including those who are only tangentially involved. These written materials, however, don't allow for the intense discussion and understanding that the more personal approaches of sharing information do. They are best used to supplement discussion and to reach those who cannot participate.

Geographic distance is obviously an impediment to sharing information personally. A local group can easily hold discussions about research, as they are by definition more accessible to their constituents. A national organization, with a far-flung constituency and a centralized staff, is naturally more dependent on written communication. Yet national organizations need not give up totally on the more personal approaches. We have mentioned the importance of multiple-level organizational structures as a way of identifying and sanctioning organizational issues. These structures can also be used to deepen commitment on issues. Even though issues may be decided and researched centrally, they can be communicated to the "grass roots" through chapters, affiliates, or primary networks. One organizer employed by a statewide chapter of a national organization describes this process.

Our issues are mostly selected at our national conference. We have, however, a state council, which meets every six weeks, comprised of state chapter presidents and some additional people. At those meetings we review where we are on legislation and other issues and brainstorm about strategy options. Then we share those ideas with the local chapters. I travel to different chapters, and if a campaign for school-based clinics in Cambridge has gone really well, I share that with Springfield so that they can replicate it. The ideas for the pay equity campaign and the equal representation campaign were developed at the state level, and then we developed organizing kits that were shared with local chapters and at the national conference.

While there are many ways to inform an interested constituency and deepen their understanding and commitment to an issue, a major problem for organizers is how to extend the information to and attract the interest of those who have no affiliation with the organization. That is, how do organizers influence the way the general public views their issues? Obviously, public venues such as television, radio talk shows, and the print media must be used. Although most organizers "play to the media," they don't put much stock in influencing public opinion through it. In general, social action organizations have little access to the media and even less control over what will be said or written. Instead, they are forced to rely on more informal "hit or miss" public education such as leafletting, using tables to disseminate litera-ture, or holding speakers series. Demonstrations that are visible to those who pass by may get the word out to the public, but they can be equally offputting and disruptive to the very people whom the organi-zation would like to attract.

Clearly, the most effective way of educating the public is through the mainstream media, and yet this is not easily accomplished. Orga-nizers need to develop relationships with media people so that the facts of an issue get receptive treatment in the press. One leader on the Lower East Side of New York talked about how she developed such a relationship with a *New York Times* reporter:

> Every time we had something going on, I'd invite him to sit down with us. And I always made sure we had two things: good facts and good food. We'd sit in my kitchen, and we'd have fact sheets, so his job was easier and he didn't have to take many notes. If it was win-ter, I had a hot toddy for him; if it was summer, it was a mint julep. I always looked for his byline, so I could tell him what a nice job he did reporting on such and such. I'd ask about his family and how things were going at work. We told him other stories unrelated to our organization which would make for "good print." We made him feel that every time he came down, he was getting something for himself. After awhile, he'd call us and say, "Are you doing anything I can write about?" I think he was really missing my mint juleps.

During the third stage of issue development it is crucial that the organization deepen the commitment of members about the issue and extend that commitment to others. This is especially true if the issue has not been generated directly from constituents and members. Organizers often find, much to their dismay, that people are easily swayed by an opponent at a meeting or, worse, that open disagreements among the members ensue. Others wonder why so few letters are sent to legislators about a pending bill or a march is not well attended or few people come to a meeting after a demonstration. Often, if organizers are honest with themselves, they may realize that they did little to communicate information and deepen commitment at this important stage.

Phase IV: Monitoring Organizational Issues

The last phase of issue development consists of monitoring organizational issues. We refer here to the assessment an organizer makes of the organization's "package of issues"—how many the organization should be working on, whether new ones should be added, how issues link to each other, and how these issues connect to the issues of other organizations and to larger change goals. During this phase the technical task of the organizer is to ask "How are we doing?" by evaluating what else needs to be undertaken. The expressive task is to keep people motivated around the organization and its issues.

While we include this as the final stage of issue development, such an assessment is an ongoing process. Many organizers begin organizing with the idea of having multiple issues, adding new issues, and drawing connections among issues, and only timing is assessed. This intention is based on values about the purpose of organizing and beliefs about what is most effective. Alinsky, for example, writes that organizational vitality relies on a broad and integrated agenda to which new issues are constantly added (Alinsky 1974). For many organizers, however, decisions about the number of issues, new issues, and linkage among issues is a more pragmatic concern, based on an assessment of what the organization "needs" at any point in time. These organizers reflect back on an organization's process or assess its current state to determine *whether* to do something new, to add on, to make a linkage.

Multiple and New Issues

Political analysts and media have made much of the existence of single-issue interest groups, but not many organizers support single-issue organizing. The majority believe multiple issues are necessary. Some organizations take up many different issues related to the needs and interests of their constituencies. For instance, neighborhood groups work on housing, crime, and drugs, since these issues are raised by their members. Many other organizations have a single focus, such as homelessness or reproductive rights. Even in these organizations, however, the single focus is a way to categorize and capture a number of smaller related issues. For example, organizations representing the developmentally disabled work on federal disability policy, which includes health insurance, mainstreaming in the schools, guardianship, SSI benefits, vocational rehab, and ombudsmen programs.

There are many advantages to working on multiple issues. Through working on many issues people learn they can understand and act on many things that affect them. When people take on a single issue, they tend to see it as merely solving a problem. When they take on a number of issues they are more likely to understand that they are, in fact, involved in making social change. As one organizer says, "I think people learn more about what institutions are making decisions in their community and how their lives are controlled when they see it time and time again in a variety of different situations."

There are also many practical reasons why organizations need to take up many issues. In many cases the constituency they work with (e.g., seniors, parents of disabled) simply have many issues that need attention. One issue may naturally lead to another, as in the case of groups that work on code violations and become involved in fighting for low-interest loans and grants for homeowners. In order to attract funding organizations may also have to work in a new area. Often some social or political event will either demand work on an issue or create new opportunities. For example, a recent New York state law mandating that hospitals identify and serve the health needs of the surrounding communities offers an opportunity for neighborhood groups to make health care a concern.

Working on several issues also helps an organization attract a larger base of support. Different issues attract different people, and by working on many issues the organization can bring together a diverse group of people with similar but not identical concerns. A new issue is also a way of attracting new supporters. Organizers also use diverse issues to avoid boredom or demoralization. Some organizers support the notion of multiple issues because it is "simply too risky to put all your eggs in one basket." Delays and setbacks on one issue can demoralize members, impede other work, and tarnish the image of the entire organization. Other issues where there is more success act as motivation to maintain activity.

Despite the advantages, working on many issues poses potential organizational problems. Fears of being overwhelmed and rendered ineffective, lack of focus, diluting central concerns, and spending scarce resources are worries of many organizers. Frequently, organizers worry that organizational resources will be "spread too thin." Although organizers must be aware of these dangers, these concerns should not be seen as insurmountable. Focus can be achieved as people are helped to set priorities among issues important to them. One organizer describes the process of priority setting this way,

> I think about how to work on many issues like using the burners on a stove. I work with members to decide which issues are most important to us, and those issues are on the front two burners. Say we're actively working on gay bashing and freeing up funding for AIDS research, and they're bubbling away. We also choose two other issues to put on the back burners—say an antidiscrimination law and gay adoption. We can't work on them right now, but we've got them simmering. When we finish working on the first two issues, we move the others up, and put two more on the back burners. I think about two bubbling and two simmering all the time. That way our energy is focused, but we won't lose people who want to work on something else.

Another method organizers can use to work on multiple issues without diluting all their resources is to link issues. For example, an organizer working on peace and disarmament talked in what now seems to be a visionary way about how his organization focused on what American intervention in Central American might mean for subsequent foreign policy decisions around the globe.

Finally, coalitions can be developed. Coalitions allow an organization to pay attention to other issues without diluting efforts on its primary issue.

Sometimes an organization must stay with an issue for a long period of time, either because people want to continue to work on it or progress hasn't been made. In these cases keeping people motivated and reducing boredom can be accomplished by changing something other than the issue itself. As one organizer for a peace group that organized around the war in Vietnam says,

> We worked on the Vietnam War for a decade, and it would have gotten tired if we kept doing the same thing. But we were always trying new approaches, new organizing attacks, new methods of opposition. There were demonstrations and marches and draft card burnings and sit-ins and symbolic bombings of ITT in 1972. Different tactics, different targets, and organizing against it in different ways helped spur people on to continue to do things and to do them more creatively. That sort of variety is essential.

It is likely that social action organizations will always take on new issues and work on several simultaneously. The practical needs of organizations to keep members involved, to recruit new people, and to respond to new events and opportunities makes single-issue organizing a luxury most organizations cannot afford.

Connections Among Issues

It is helpful to think about linking issues in three ways: 1. connections can be made among all the issues that the organization is working on, 2. connections can be made among organizations working on similar issues, and 3. connections can be made so that a local organization works on the national implications of its issues or, conversely, a national organization works on the local implications of its issues.

Almost all organizers try to identify and help people understand the connections among the issues the organization has undertaken. In many cases there is a natural connection between the issues. For example, parents of developmentally delayed children are naturally concerned about issues that will arise later in the child's life. These connections then help the organizer to unify a diverse constituency. In some cases placing a particularly controversial issue among other more palatable issues helps develop a more positive frame of reference for members and the general public. For example, abortion rights may be placed in the context of the need for child care and family leave, creating a package of rights for families and children.

Perhaps most important, connecting issues helps educate people about their power and rights across many areas, and teaches social responsibility. It allows people to feel they are working on systemic change rather than individual problems. While multiple and new issues are valued for their pragmatic returns to the organization, linking issues expresses the central social change mission. As one organizer says,

> I think that when people understand the connections among issues it gives them a sense of their power. By making those connections people become conscious of the organization and the purpose of its work, not just the issue. If you are just looking at an issue, you come to a meeting and then you go. People need to understand that what they're doing is building a group of people working together to change their neighborhood, over and above any single issue. In every committee you've got to help people understand that we are working on this issue but we're also developing our power. It may be important to work on one issue at this time or do fundraising, but everything that we do is to strengthen the ability of the organization to improve our lives here.

It is generally much harder to work with other groups around a common issue. While there are some positive experiences of pro-choice and peace groups working together, neighborhood groups all focusing on housing seldom report working with other neighborhood groups or statewide tenant groups or organizations working with the homeless. Most national groups report working only with their own affiliates. Certainly groups reap benefits by joining coalitions. They allow organizations to share resources. To the extent that they bring together more people or different groups of people, coalitions make the organizing effort that much stronger, and perhaps broaden the support of each group involved. Yet, organizers also find that when they work with others their issues can get lost and different organizational philosophies and approaches must be negotiated. A group's views are more likely to be subject to compromise, and the process of reaching agreement is often protracted (Carden 1989, Kaplan 1986, Weisner 1983). Finally, there is the issue of who does all the work and who gets credit for the victory, because the organization's resources and image are at stake.

Most organizers feel it's especially important to relate the everyday individual issues people experience to larger social issues. Local issues have national ramifications, and policy made on the federal level has a direct effect on the lives of people living in neighborhoods. When organizers draw connections among local and national concerns it is often the most direct expression of their social change goals. If there is any chance of "building a movement," people will need to understand the relationships between issues.

Yet helping people to see these connections is not easy. It is often difficult to get people to enlarge their perspective beyond the neighborhood, and equally difficult to get someone with a national perspective to care about a local concern. Organizers find, much as Bellah et al. (1985), that Americans have lost the sense of "collective good." Tenant organizers wonder how you legitimately raise issues of foreign policy with low-income tenants who are having problems getting heat. And peace and disarmament organizers are seldom interested in vacant lots and foot patrol.

There are not many ideas about *how* to connect larger social issues with local concerns. Organizers themselves should certainly be conscious of the connections between local and national issues, have information about the connections on hand, and try to discuss it with people when they can. Some work here can be done as organizers talk with leaders and members about the "bigger picture," helping them to understand "who the decision makers are, the basis on which they make their decisions, and how to have influence on them." Some organizers have tried to develop campaigns that symbolically discuss local issues in the context of national policy. One organizer describes a campaign where an effort was made to tie the issue of hunger to military spending and the tax system. Another helped people design a "neighborhood defense budget," which compared the cost of maintaining the housing stock in his Bronx neighborhood to the cost of building weapon systems. A few national organizations reach out to local groups, offering research and organizing staff when a local issue is raised.

Perhaps the most innovative approach was developed by a voter registration organizer. His voting rights organization solicited the participation or accepted the invitations of local community grassroots groups and sent an organizer to work intensively with the members of those groups to design, plan, and execute a registration campaign around a local issue. After the local activity had been accomplished, the organizer maintained ties with the staff and leadership of these local organizations, later encouraging them to register voters during national elections. The organizer saw this model as a way to gain local sanction for national issues, fulfill his own organization's objective of registering new voters, and develop the leadership competency of the grassroots organization. This informal structural relationship, in which each organization has its own interests served, seems to us a very inventive idea, and one worthy of replication. Still, there aren't many ways of creating the public dialogue that Bellah and his colleagues (1985) urge. It is a problem that continues to frustrate most organizers.

As we have described it the process of developing issues is both technical and expressive. It requires both good research skills and the ability to make people care about the issue and want to do something about it. The information and interested people accrued during this process strengthen the organization and make success more likely.

We conclude this section by noting two especially problematic areas that need greater attention by organizers and writers on the subject. First, organizers don't have many ideas about how to reach wider audiences and unaffiliated people with their message. Mass media is often not accessible, and outreach is described as "catch as catch can." We don't seem to have good methods of reaching beyond a rather small core of "believers."

The other area that we feel needs attention is how organizers can attempt to connect local issues to national agendas and vice versa. This gap is particularly important because the divisions seem to be based on class. Local organizers work mostly with low-income and blue-collar communities on "bread and butter" issues, while state and national organizations tend to work with middle and professional classes on issues of national or international import. While it is clear that there are connections among the national issues of peace, environment, and feminism and the local issues of housing, unemployment, and crime, organizers don't know how to make those connections understandable to their members. Innovations in this area will be essential if a broader social change agenda has a chance of realization.

CHAPTER SIX

Strategy Development

Once an issue or a set of issues is chosen the ability of a social action organization to realize its goals for change depends on the development and implementation of effective strategies. Inducing the types of changes desired by social action organizations is a daunting and arduous task. Since strategy is fundamental to an organization's ability to bring about change, and therefore requires extensive review, we devote chapters 6 and 7 to its discussion. In this chapter we focus on strategy development. We first define strategy and tactics. We then examine the four considerations essential to the development of effective strategy and tactics: the influence of organizers' change orientations, the establishment of goals, the selection of target systems, and the identification of resources. Finally, we discuss the process social action organizations use to select strategy and tactics. The next chapter describes the execution and evaluation of strategy.

Defining Strategy and Tactics

The literature includes many different definitions of strategy and tactics, ranging from rational cause-effect ones (Biklen 1983, Cox, Erlich, Rothman, and Tropman 1970) to those which are more dynamic. A linear view of strategy stresses the development of strategy apart from contextual factors such as the actions of targets, public sentiment, and social and political events. Cox et al. offer a definition that is more complex. They write,

The word "strategy is derived from game theory, which distinguishes games of individual skill, games of chance and games of strategy—the last being those in which the most effective course of action for each player depends upon the actions of other players and the players' anticipation and assessment of those moves. As such, the term emphasizes the interdependence of allies and adversaries' decisions and their various expectations about each others' behavior. (Tropman and Erlich 1974:161)

This view portrays the actions and reactions of multiple players and multiple strategic decisions. Implicit, too, is the idea that subgoals, related to a larger desired end, may be fashioned during the strategic process.

Typically, tactics are defined as specific and short-term events or behaviors that are used within a strategy. Alinsky (1971) defines tactics as "consciously deliberate acts." Cox et al. (Cox, Erlich, Tropman, and Teresa 1984) write that tactics are "specific interventive devices or means that contribute to the operationalization of a strategy" (preface).

For us, strategy is a plan for action that links problems and solutions and depends on an ongoing assessment of the actions and sentiments of other actors, including one's own constituency, the target system, and the general public. To borrow a sports analogy, strategy is a "game plan." It is offensive in its attempt to achieve a goal and defensive in that it is influenced by the perceptions of allies and adversaries. Strategy development responds to two important questions: What are the organization's goals? Who are the organization's targets?

If strategy is the "game plan," then tactics are the actions or events that execute the plan. The choice of tactics is governed by considerations about the resources of the organization and the perception of the target's resources. Organizations escalate the contentiousness of tactics as they face resistance. Both strategy and tactics, therefore, are preplanned but constantly and consciously modified in reaction to shifts in an environmental context.

We find that organizers frequently confuse the terms strategy and tactics, and decisions often involve the merger of both. Criteria used to select them are remarkably similar. Strategy development does not seem to follow the more dynamic model suggested by many authors. Many organizers repeatedly employ the same strategies and tactics. Despite opposition, there may be no effort to "up the ante."

As the literature suggests, most organizers consider goals, target systems, and resources in their development of strategies and tactics.

However, the divergence between the literature and practice appears to be explained by the fact that organizers' "action plans" are critically influenced by the organizer's values. Therefore, the development of strategies and tactics is influenced by four major considerations. First, strategy development is fundamentally influenced by the organizer's change orientation, which influences what the organizer views as the most effective means to change. Second, strategy development includes the establishment of outcome and process goals. Third, strategy development entails the selection of a target system. Finally, tactic selection includes an identification and assessment of the resources a social action organization can call on throughout the strategy. These four considerations describe how organizers plan strategy and tactics. We now turn to each of these areas.

Change Orientations and Strategy Development

There has been much discussion in the literature on social action organizing about the influence of organizers' values on what and how they choose to organize (Biklen 1983, Lindeman 1921, Pray 1948, Ross 1967). On the one hand, Alinsky's (1971) chapter "Of Means and Ends" defines the goal of social change as superordinate, and assumes these goals will be hotly contested by an intransigent opposition. In his fifth rule he describes his view of resources, when he writes "that concern with ethics increases with the number of means available and vice versa" (Alinsky 1971:32). Clearly, Alinsky was describing his orientation toward change: an intransigent opposition, a need for conflict, and evaluating resources according to what's available to use against the opponent. There is no doubt that these views about change generated the "Alinsky model"; selecting individual targets, confronting them directly, and moving to achieve an organizational victory.

On the other hand, writers such as Murray Ross (1967) and Kenneth Pray (1948) insist that the democratic process of organizing is primary. They stress the therapeutic value of bringing together different interest groups, encouraging a group to self-determine their goals, and the process of reaching consensus. Clearly, Ross argues for a collaborative process—a community therapy of sorts—which is reflected in the local development model he proposes.

Organizers, we find, are uncomfortable discussing their values about change in such abstract terms. Instead, they are more likely to point to specific actions they consider totally unacceptable. Sometimes these activities have to do with ideological principles; they wouldn't use racism as motivation for a campaign, for instance. Sometimes they refer to actions they are unwilling to take such as bribing public officials or stealing information. They may judge the morality of an action based on how they and their members subjectively view it; the assumption is that people won't be comfortable with morally reprehensible actions. In other cases the litmus test is whether an action will enhance or harm an organization's credibility. Since such practices as tapping phones or bribing officials are beyond their resources, they argue that the means that would truly challenge their values aren't accessible to them and consequently they are seldom faced with significant moral dilemmas.

Values are clearly a part of every strategy decision. Beliefs about how amenable a target will be to influence, and the role of conflict and confrontation in the pursuit of change influence strategy development. In chapter 2 we referred to these beliefs as the organizer's change orientation.

Change orientation, although often implicit and unarticulated, is particularly influential in decisions about strategies and tactics. Change orientation may set the basic parameters for action, so that for some organizers many of the decisions about strategy and tactics are, in a sense, pro forma. The organizer's change orientation may restrict strategic alternatives, promoting one option over all others despite contextual evidence that would suggest other views. Because change orientation is ideological, it seldom changes, and consequently has influence in the organization over time.

For example, in chapter 2 we defined the countervailing institution change orientation as one that suggests that people with power make decisions that affect the lives of people. Power holders are individuals who are the accepted targets of change efforts, and it is understood that they will resist efforts to modify power arrangements. Numbers of people directly confronting them is the only way to wrest power from them. The more organizers embrace such a view, the more their strategies will consist of personalizing a target, creating so much trouble for the target that an organizational victory is achieved. The organizer who holds such views is less likely to consider collaborative or persuasive approaches, even when the possibility exists to develop influential allies.

On the other hand, a pluralist pressure change orientation suggests that the major arena for change is government, and therefore the obvious change targets are the institutions of government and individual legislative, executive, and judicial actors. These governmental targets are viewed as "powers to be persuaded," rather than enemies to be confronted. Consequently, the organizer who embraces pluralist pressure views will tend to select governmental targets, monitoring the legislative, executive, and judicial processes for any opportunity to persuade and negotiate with these actors. The organizer will tend to form a cadre of experts who can use their knowledge to convince governmental officials of the efficacy of the organization's goal. And they are less likely to consider other targets or to use confrontation, even when there seem to be few other alternatives to effect change.

The mass education change orientation, like pluralist pressure, accepts government as the appropriate change target. However, power holders in this view are seen as highly resistant to change. Change can only occur at opportune moments. This orientation suggests that an organizer essentially carries two orientations: one allows for maintenance during conservative periods and the other allows for disruption during more conducive times. Organizers who embrace this view will tend to work with this dual perspective in mind. During maintenance times they will try to persuade potential supporters while confronting power holders when the climate allows. By waiting for the "window of opportunity" to open, they may overlook opportunities to provoke change.

Consequently, as organizers develop strategy out of their unique set of assumptions and beliefs, the influence of change orientation may explain why strategy and tactics seem so merged in practice and why so many organizers seem to employ the same strategies over and over. It may also explain why, despite resistance, there seem to be few attempts to escalate tactics.

Because change orientation may play such an important role in the determination of strategy, it is incumbent upon organizers to examine the beliefs they bring to their strategy work. Organizers need to know what they believe, and to be able to articulate their opinions. Beliefs and values, after all, are not easily put aside in professional endeavors. They provide us with some direction for analysis and action so that we need not reinvent the wheel with every new situation. As organizers clarify and understand their beliefs about change, they are more able to communicate with members why they believe a certain strategy is more efficacious, and in doing so, they hold their beliefs up for discussion and debate.

It is equally important, however, for organizers to constantly scrutinize their biases. Rothman (1969) has noted that there are inherent risks in each of his three models of community organization. Rothman's work suggests that rigid adherence to a particular practice model and, in our view, to a change orientation, can place considerable constraints on the assessment of strategic options.

The task of making social change requires contextual analysis. Organizers will face situations that demand a deviation from their own biases. No one can afford to have only a single play in their "playbook." There can be various target systems, not all of whom will always be amenable or resistant to change. The pluralist pressure organizer will sometimes discover targets so resistant to change that at least the threat of confrontation will be necessary. Such was the case when Planned Parenthood, the National Abortion Rights Action League, and the National Organization for Women threatened a potato boycott because of the proposed restrictive abortion legislation enacted by the state legislature in Idaho. (The governor quickly vetoed the bill.) Organizers who support countervailing institution views should not be surprised to find corporate allies. Goal perceptions may shift, and all potential resources must be considered. When organizers are more flexible in their beliefs, they are more able to escalate or deescalate the contentiousness of their tactics when necessary. The more organizers remain fixed in their attitudes about what is assessed and what can be done, the less creativity and inventiveness they bring to their members and organizations.

While organizers probably cannot put aside their values, they can limit their impact on strategy assessment so that all possible strategic options are evaluated. To fully assess strategic options we suggest the three remaining questions to be answered: 1. What are the organizer's and organization's goals in this effort? 2. Who are the targets of this effort? 3. What resources can the organization bring to bear in this effort? We turn our attention to each of these questions now.

Goals in Strategy Development

The literature on organizing is preoccupied with the subject of goal setting. Rothman (1969), Ross (1967), Brager and Specht (1973), and Warren (1977) have all dealt with the subject of establishing goals. Strategy development, in particular, raises considerations of goals, most important, the organization's perception of the goal and how the organizer believes the target perceives the goal. Here the question is, "How can we make change, given the way we and our target system see this particular goal?" Goals are referenced to the organizing strategy, and benchmarks and outcomes are established for each step of the process.

In developing strategy organizers consider four types of goals: long-term or ultimate outcome goals and short-term or partialized outcome goals and long and short-term process goals.

Outcome goals refer to the desired solution to the problem the organization has identified earlier. In the literature these goals are called task goals, environmental change goals, instrumental goals, or content goals. These long-term goals include both the organization's priorities, and the desired results. A welfare rights organizer offers an example.

> Each year we have a general membership meeting, where people talk about what will be the goals for the coming year. Will we continue to work on increasing the welfare grant, will the focus be the bill or the budget? We want to focus on the budget this year, as opposed to the bill, because that's where we get the money, but always keeping in mind that what we are ultimately looking for is guaranteed minimum standards for welfare benefits.

To some degree establishing and evaluating long-term outcome goals accepts the standard rational planning model as a way to measure accomplishment. However, unlike most profit and nonprofit organizations that set goals for products and programs, the achievement of outcome goals of social action organizations is fundamentally influenced by the larger sociopolitical environment. Social action organizations seldom have complete control over goal achievement. This is particularly true for lobbying organizations that are dependent on legislative calendars.

How the target perceives the organization's outcome goal is also a very important consideration. Questions here include What is the target's opinion on this subject? How strongly are these views held? Is there room for compromise? Are there other ways of influencing the target to behave differently? Sometimes the answers to these questions can be uncovered through research. For example, a review of the voting record of a politician or the decisions made by a judge or the charitable contributions of a corporate leader may yield much about their beliefs and investments on a variety of issues. In other cases the target's views are uncovered during the organizing process, as leaders meet face-to-face with targets. Consequently, strategy must be reconsidered.

The target's view of the goal may, in fact, cause the organization to reformulate its goal. When a target is totally opposed to a goal, and no amount of pressure will change the opposition, the organization may have to settle for a compromise and declare it a success. For example, an organization that failed to win a campaign to retain transportation fares at current levels, but succeeded in gaining more corporate taxes for transportation, declared its campaign a victory.

Despite the dependency on targets with power, the organization can control activities that may promote a desired change. These activities are based on short-term outcome goals, sometimes called *objectives*, that partialize the long-term outcome goals. Getting three hundred people to a neighborhood meeting about the park, encouraging four thousand people to write their congressperson, or holding a dramatic demonstration that increases the visibility of the organization are intermediate outcome objectives. These efforts pave the way to the ultimate desired change. Shorter-term outcome goals that offer more certainty for success are particularly important when working with low-income members. Often they are less able to sustain interest and energy if benefits can be achieved only in the distant future (Brager 1963, Brager and Specht 1969, Haggstrom 1969). While short-term outcome goals are certainly more under the control of the organizer and members, it is probably equally hard to measure the organization's effectiveness in reaching them. As one organizer says,

> It's very hard to evaluate goals. What makes a strategy a success? If our ultimate goal was to stop one hundred million dollars' aid to the Contras, who says what one particular strategy worked? Did this demonstration push people a little way? Was it the letter writing campaign? Was it the exposé NBC did on it? It is very hard to determine.

Organizers also establish process goals, referred to as "sociotherapeutic" (Ross 1963) or "institutional goals" (Brager and Specht 1973) in the literature. Process goals are desired ends that focus on the process by which the organization becomes more and more able to effect its outcome goals. Long-term process goals go to strengthening the organization, educating leaders so they are more competent advocates, increasing the membership of the organization, and building public awareness. An organizer identifies long-term process goals, evaluating how a strategy will affect the strength of his organization:

> It may be quicker to make some progress on a goal with one or two people who are always the spokespeople and always the leaders. That doesn't build an organization, that doesn't build new leadership, and that doesn't broaden the organization. There are some folks who would impress the targets, but we may not use them be-

cause there are other people who have to grow. We have to pay attention to the process because we are developing and building an organization and building people's capabilities.

Long-term process goals are particularly important to organizers who are working on large and highly complex changes where the outcome goals are not easily nor quickly achieved. Here it is particularly dangerous for members to focus on only instrumental ends. An equal emphasis on process goals helps members understand that although the road to change will be long and hard, there will still be benchmarks along the way.

It is also helpful to partialize process goals, to set benchmarks for the organization and for members in each activity. Short-term process goals include objectives for involving more people at every meeting and for gaining more media attention. Identifying and training new leaders, helping members to interact, insuring that members learn something, gain confidence, and are a part of something that excites and motivates them are also short-term process goals. An organizer focusing on these says: "We want to involve a lot of people and train a smaller group in everything we do. We ask: how many people do we want to come to this meeting? How many 'first timers' do we want? These questions are very important. They teach people to think critically about the organization's development, and give people a sense of accomplishment."

Strategy development, then, considers long- and short-term outcome goals, and long- and short-term process goals. Outcome goals set long- and short-term objectives for goal achievement, while process goals set long- and short-term objectives for strengthening the organization. In the illustration below a neighborhood organizer describes a two-year campaign to save a movie theater, the Midway, in the neighborhood. His discussion includes short- and long-term goals for process and outcome, and has much to say about targets and tactics as well. Certainly the illustration manifests that strategy is dynamic and evolving.

Our organization had been around about three years before we tackled the issue of the movie theater. We had been through a lot of successful smaller neighborhood fights around vacant lots and houses, police protection, schools, and sanitation. We claimed to represent about twenty-three neighborhood churches, block clubs, and senior groups (about 40,000 people), but I would say we had a cadre of about 150 competent leaders. We were at a level, organizationally, where we could take on a larger- and longer-term issue without our folks becoming demoralized, and I believed our leaders would benefit from the stretch. Before they built movie complexes in the suburbs the neighborhood had ten movie houses. The only one left was a huge art deco structure on the corner of the neighborhood's major intersection. Even though it had gotten pretty seedy, folks were pretty sentimental about the theater—it really was the "last picture show." One day the theater just shut down. There was a rumor around the neighborhood that it had been sold, and plans were to turn it into a rock concert hall. I talked with some people, and no one thought we needed a rock concert hall. People thought rock concerts would bring drugs, traffic, and garbage. People cared about it, so it seemed like a good issue.

At the time the city's mayor was trying to get the city charter changed so he could run for a third term of office. In order to solidify a constituency for his campaign, he was making promises to predominately white neighborhoods that "no neighborhood had to take what it didn't want." Of course, he applied this principle to things like welfare offices, but I figured we could use it too. And, of course, the converse of the mayor's principle is that neighborhoods could have what they want. I figured that a strategy for the theater could use both principles. I knew that if we took on this fight it was going to be a struggle, and people would have to realize that this was going to be a long campaign.

An article appeared in the local paper saying that there would be shops at the site. The first thing I did was find out who had bought the property, how much it had cost, who financed the mortgage on it, what title companies and attorneys had been used. I discovered that the new owner was Paul Breezy. So we got a committee together, discussed the sale and my research, and decided to invite Breezy to a meeting to ask him what his intentions were for the site. Leaders and I did a lot of recruiting, and we had about 150 come to the meeting with Breezy. When he said he was planning to make the site into a rock concert hall, the people were furious. After the meeting, the committee decided to do a simple survey to find out what neighborhood people thought the site should be used for. The survey was given out through churches and block clubs, and we probably reached 1,000 people. The survey also gave our leaders an opportunity to talk with others about the theater so that interest in the issue was building. The survey results showed that people wanted to keep their movie theater.

We started doing more research. First, we discovered that Breezy was an associate of the mayor, and had given ten thousand dollars to the mayor's campaign. We also looked into this particular theater, and discovered it had been designed by a famous architect and was the last example in the city of art deco theater architecture. Further, we looked into building codes, necessary building permits, and zoning laws which might affect the theater.

Remodeling work on the theater had begun. The committee, which was now about 75 people, met to discuss the research and the survey results, and especially to decide what should be done. In order to save the theater, our ultimate goal, we had to stop the remodeling work. The committee decided to invite the commissioner of licenses and inspections to meet with the group. At the meeting, which about 125 folks attended, we demanded that work on the theater stop because of permit violations. We had good press coverage at the meeting. The commissioner agreed to tour the site the following morning, and several leaders said they would accompany him. The tour, too, was covered by the media, and he agreed to pull the permits on the remodeling. Right after work stopped, two kids entered the building through an open back door. Breezy pressed charges, and both kids committed suicide, apparently in reaction to the charges. That sure fueled the emotions of our members.

The committee was now meeting weekly. People went to the fire department and asked for a "pre-arson" inspection because of their fear that the building would catch fire. We went to the American Institute of Architects and asked them to investigate the historical significance of the building. They said it could be considered a landmark, so we went to the Historical Commission to ask they designate landmark status to the building. We went to the bank that held Breezy's mortgage and asked them to foreclose on the property. Basically, we were targeting everybody we could think of. At this point, about eight months after we began, we were in the press almost every day; the organization and the issue were recognized throughout the city. Breezy finally gave up and sold the property. Burger King became the new owners.

I thought now that we could at least claim we had stopped rock concerts in the neighborhood. But there was the potential of a fight to have the building used for what neighborhood people wanted, rather than just another fast food joint. The committee met to decide what we wanted to do about the property now. People remained firm that the building should be a theater, but thought there might be other uses as well, e.g., shops, offices, space for senior citizens and kids. This decision set off more research. We researched who owned Burger King, where their investments were, who was on their board of directors, their corporate structures, etc. At the same time, we looked into the possibility of the neighborhood developing the property, i.e., what municipal funding sources were available. We discovered that the Industrial Development Corporation (I.D.C.) had financed movie theaters in other neighborhoods. The committee then arranged a meeting with the city's managing director to discuss the use of these funds. At first he said the I.D.C. funds could not be used that way, and he refused to meet again. The mayor was in the neighborhood for a rally, and our leaders tried to tell the mayor, using his principles, what we wanted in the neighborhood. Our leaders weren't allowed to speak, and his goons broke our sound system. We met the managing director's aides and got nowhere, so we again invited the managing director to a meeting in the community. He agreed to come, but canceled a few hours before. We arranged buses for about 200 people to take us to city hall, and when he refused to meet, we went to his house. People passed out flyers to his neighbors describing our plight. Once again, we had great press coverage.

While this was going on, we also went after Burger King. We wanted them to save the structure of the building, and to have the structure include space used for other purposes, along with the restaurant. Burger King, a Florida corporation, was then owned by Pillsbury Corporation, a Minnesota corporation. We invited the corporate heads in Florida to a meeting, and they refused. Then we had our members send postcards to the corporate headquarters at Pillsbury, demanding a meeting. I think about four thousand cards were sent, but they still refused. We asked the city zoning board to withhold the zoning permits from Burger King, and they refused. We found out which Burger King was the busiest one in the city, and on a busy Friday lunch hour, we took 500 people to it and people paid for their lunch with pennies. We tied up the restaurant for about three hours. The press that day was terrific. The headline in the newspaper was "Community Group Has It Their Way," which was Burger King's ad campaign at the time. We then asked another community group in Minnesota to ask for a meeting with the corporate heads of Pillsbury. They sent letters and tried to meet with corporate officials.

A few days later, United Way, which was one of our funding sources, called to say they could no longer fund us. The managing director said that the city would no longer take up a collection unless they cut our funds. We demanded a fair hearing, and organized that. A few months later, the United Way found in our favor, and stood up to the city.

This whole campaign had lasted almost two years. It was clear that Burger King was probably going to have it their way. We were involved in a lot of other issues by then, and we had done a lot of fundraising. Ten new groups joined the organization, we had brought in at least

500 new members, and our core of competent leaders had doubled. The organization had increased visibility and name recognition. City officials reluctantly had to respect our tenacity and power. The city charter was not changed and the mayor was defeated. So the committee decided to end the fight. We agreed that although we hadn't saved the movie theater, we had stopped rock concerts, and we claimed that as a victory. We may have lost on our ultimate goal, but we won an intermediate goal, and the organization benefited in many, many other ways.

Targets of Change

We define *target* broadly: as the person or people the organization must influence in order to make change. This definition is widely accepted (Brager and Specht 1973, Sieder 1956, Warren 1977). There are several ideas about who can comprise a target system. As organizers define the target system they say something about their change orientation, particularly about who they see as amenable to change. When change orientation is rigidly followed, however, their views also unnecessarily restrict who should appropriately be influenced. As organizers assume who the target *should* be, they often overlook who the target *could* be.

Some organizers see targets as the organization's supporters and other potential activists who support the organization's cause with their time and energy. This definition merges the target and action systems, i.e., those who will make the change are themselves the focus of change. For these organizers other activists are the people most highly amenable to change.

It is a quixotic notion to say that changed people change the world. If the definition of a target is those who can make a desired change, one's members cannot be considered targets. It is certainly part of an organizer's work to alter how people perceive their own power. We have defined this work, alternately called conscientization, education, and leadership development, as attention to empowerment goals, maintaining the distinction between those who desire change and those who can actually make it happen. Other organizers define the general public as the target. These organizers understand that change occurs by influencing public opinion, and their focus is on changing the American perception of a problem. As one lobbying organizer says clearly, "Part of what we believe to be the case is that public attitudes influence the way legislation gets shaped." In this view, neutral or apathetic people may be convinced otherwise. They are approachable with the right message.

On many major issues, however, the primary power holders continue to make decisions that go against the views of the public. For example, numerous surveys have been taken about the general public's support for abortion, and yet many legislatures continue to pass restrictive legislation. We, therefore, consider the public a secondary target, i.e., one capable of influencing the primary target system, perhaps, but not in a position to make the ultimate decision about a change.

Two other definitions speak most directly to the target's ability to make change. Some organizers define government as the appropriate target. These organizers are likely to try to persuade powerful legislative, executive, or judicial actors to act in manner supportive of the organization's cause. In this view, government is the logical protector of rights and entitlements, and, as representatives of the people, government officials can be persuaded to do the organization's bidding.

Logically, government has the ultimate power to set policy and enact protective regulations, and there are numerous examples of persuading government officials to support a cause. Yet to only focus on government may mean overlooking other potential targets. Further, legislators are frequently not persuaded by arguments alone. In the case of a restrictive Idaho abortion law, it was the threat of a potato boycott that identified farmers not legislators as targets, which ultimately moved the governor to veto the bill.

The broadest way to define a target system is to look for power holders, i.e., anyone with authority to make decisions. In this definition the target is likely to change as different issues arise. The target could at one time be the commissioner of a government agency, at another a private landlord, and at still another time the president of a corporation. The issue determines the target. This definition encompasses elected representatives and government bodies when appropriate, but does not insist that they are the only possible targets.

Many who hold this view see their targets as very resistant to change, calling them "enemies," and believe that targets will only make change if they are forced to do so. The danger of this belief is that these organizers may move too quickly into an adversarial stance, before assessing the target's willingness to negotiate. Even during a campaign someone who was an opponent can become a very useful ally. Changes during the power struggle can suggest opportunities for alliances that were once not available. Organizers and leaders must also watch for those possibilities. In the illustration below an organizer explains a strategy in which just such a shift from target to ally occurred.

Our national staff and leaders decided to target Aetna Insurance Company for our reinvestment campaign. Aetna is the second largest insurance company in the world and has a great deal of interest in keeping their policyholders happy. They want to be known as a civic-minded company, and they especially do not want to be federally regulated. Our strategy was to have a big national kick-off to the campaign, and follow it up locally in six neighborhoods in four cities. So we started out aggressively, with lots of press. Our national organization held a big confrontational meeting with their president with about 600 community people attending. We followed up locally by inviting their representatives to tour six different neighborhoods in Chicago, New York, Cleveland, Philadelphia, and Baltimore. Our local tour ended with a meeting with about 150 people, and although we were polite, our leaders were tough on them. We demanded that they invest five million dollars in the neighborhood. We had a lot of press coverage on that too. A similar action was taken in the five other cities. Along with the media attention there was always the implicit threat that our national organization would lobby for regulation and since we had just won some federal banking regulations, the threat was a real one. Finally, they agreed to commit two and half million dollars of reinvestment money in each of the six neighborhoods. We agreed to help them publicize these "civic efforts." As the projects succeeded, they became good allies. They had an investment in our neighborhoods and they didn't want to see the money go down the tubes. They went with us to banks to negotiate the financing and to foundations for operating funds. Those people are my good friends today, and they've reinvested in almost seventy-five other neighborhoods since then.

There are also differences of opinion about whether targets should be individuals or institutions. Alinsky (1971) makes a strong argument for individual targets when he writes, "The other important point in the choosing of a target is that it must be a personification. . . . It is not possible to develop the necessary hostility against, say, City Hall, which after all is a concrete, physical, inanimate structure . . . which has no soul or identity" (133). Others suggest that a target can be "a group, organization, community or society toward which an innovation is directed" (Rothman, Erlich, and Teresa 1977:158).

Organizers who believe that individuals should be targeted offer many rationales for their view. They argue that an individual target helps to structure decision making by identifying who must be influenced, who must be held accountable, and who the organization is "up against." It is often easier to apply direct pressure to an individual than an institution. For instance, many organizers have successfully embarrassed the president of a corporation by petitioning neighbors or fellow church members. An individual target also offers someone members can confront directly. Personalization helps to develop members' anger and contradicts the belief that problems are caused by abstract systems rather than individuals.

Other organizers focus on institutions, offering rationales that directly counter the rationales given for selecting individual targets. These organizers believe that institutional targets are more visible and acceptable to members. They say people have a harder time developing an understanding of systemic problems if individual targets are used. An organizer argues, "If you get people focused in on an individual person, then all their anger and what they want to do is directed at that person as opposed to directed at the source of the problem, which is a policy." These organizers may also see focusing on individuals as more dangerous, risking the loss of allies and causing the target to harbor revenge.

To some extent every social action organization must target individuals. A congressional vote is always the sum of individual decisions and lobbyists must persuade individual legislators to vote on their behalf. Universities don't made decisions; the board of trustees does. The chief executive officers make most decisions for corporations; only the most major decisions go to the board or shareholders. Consequently, it is individuals who must be persuaded and influenced.

To us, the debate about whether to target an individual or an institution is to some extent a debate about the role of conflict. An individual target implies direct confrontation, while an institutional target implies greater distance and reserve. Organizers, we think, understand the need to influence individuals. It is the implied conflict and the attendant consequences from which many shy away. We will return to these views when we discuss the evaluation of resources and tactic selection.

Identifying Targets

Selecting targets is, on one level, a relatively simple process. In most cases the process of collecting data about the issue will suggest who has the authority to make desired changes on issues. The institution, and a particular person within it with the authority in a given area, is the most obvious target. An organizer says, "When I'm working with our members I always try to get them to go through the thought process of who makes the final decision, where does the buck stop. That's the ideal target."

In many cases, however, there are a variety of possible targets. Usually, city, state, and federal actors all have roles. Or, in the case of the reinvestment campaign illustration described earlier, there were many possible banks and insurance companies who could have been targeted for action, though Aetna's concern with their corporate image made them a particularly attractive target. According to Alinsky (1971), the target initially selected seldom matters. He writes,

> Any target can always say, "Why do you center on me when there are others to blame as well?" When you "freeze the target," you disregard these arguments, and for the moment, all the others to blame. Then, as you zero in and freeze your target and carry out your attack, all of the "others" come out of the woodwork very soon. (133)

However, the selection of a target is seldom so casual. If there are many possible targets, each will have attributes that render them more or less vulnerable. Organizers therefore look closely at other aspects of targets: e.g., their voting record, visibility, background, and the experience others have had with them. They may also look for others who have influence on the primary target (i.e., secondary targets). They will try to discover connections among their targets, as was the case when the organizers of the boycott against manufacturer J. P. Stevens attacked major charitable and cultural organizations who had Stevens executives on their boards. A feminist organizer reports the process of target selection for the Equal Rights Amendment campaign:

> With ERA, the ultimate power is with elected representatives. We realized that to influence legislators, we needed to influence people who persuade legislators. So we looked at economic interests who opposed us and influenced legislators, to see what we could do to diminish the opposition of those interests. One of the big opponents of the ERA was the insurance lobby. They are the largest lobby in most state legislatures—one of the largest employers of women— and they profit from discriminatory benefits and payments. They were actively trying to defeat the Equal Rights Amendment by giving

money to legislators. So we decided in Massachusetts and in other places to go for unisex insurance legislation, figuring that if we won that, or at least gave them trouble on another front, we would diffuse the activity of the insurance industry on ERA.

It is also important to assess how members of one's own constituency will react to a target. Members may be sentimentally attached to or in awe of a target and unwilling to ask anything of them. Who would agree to target Santa Claus or Mother Teresa? On the other hand, members may already be angry with a possible target and want a chance for revenge. Such was the case when a national organization for the homeless targeted the Veterans Administration. The organizer knew that many people have negative feelings about the military and that fair treatment of those who give service for their country is widely supported. They began a campaign to stop the Veterans Administration from evicting veterans who could not make their mortgage payments. The campaign garnered a great deal of support and met with much success.

In many cases the target may be quite formidable and beyond an organization's initial capacity to influence. In these cases the organizer will often choose to begin with a less formidable opponent, someone lower down in the hierarchy, and later, as the campaign builds strength and greater support, target the key decision maker. For example, on issues such as health, transportation, or environment, it is wise to meet first with local and regional officials. If there is no resolution locally, members can then attempt to meet with the state commissioner. If still no agreement is reached, the group can go on to the state board, or, failing there, to the political officials who appoint or confirm board members. For each meeting organizers and leaders can involve more people, so that the group is large, strong, and representative by the time meetings with the state officials are held. Meetings with local officials may also disclose information and arguments that will be helpful with the more powerful decision makers.

Our description thus far supports the idea that in the game plan of the organizer's strategy, it is important to initially identify at least one or two potential targets. Experienced organizers, however, are also watchful for opportunities when targets present themselves. A "window of opportunity" may open when a particular person seems suddenly accessible. There is a chance at least to influence public attitudes if not necessarily achieve the desired goal. An organizer for a national women's political organization says,

Sometimes you have to seize an opportunity that presents itself. We will sometimes support a candidate who we know perfectly well is going to lose. First, she may be a candidate we can work with in the future, so we're investing in a career, not just an election. Second, we realize that her race may raise issues which will be beneficial to our overall goal. Third, we realize we might change some public opinion with her. Gerri Ferraro running for vice president in 1980 is the best example. We knew that her race would be enormously beneficial in terms of what we do. We hoped that she'd win, we did everything we could to help her win, but the investment in her career was well worth our time.

In sum, selecting a target entails both a research process and some additional analysis. Change orientations that prescribe who the target should be and how resistant they are will unnecessarily curtail the kind of comprehensive and thoughtful analysis necessary. A careful review of who can make the desired change, who is most vulnerable to pressure, and who is the most formidable should yield a beginning sense of the appropriate target. It is also important to look for secondary targets who can influence the primary one, scout for serendipitous opportunities to press a target for change, and, at times, select a target who may be advantageous to the organization in the long run.

Resources in Tactic Selection

Once the organizer and members have ascertained the goal of the strategy and the targets who need to be influenced, the next question is, "What tactic will be effective to influence this target to make the change we want?" Tactics are largely determined by the resources at the organization's disposal and the resources the target system is perceived as having. That is, to choose among tactical alternatives the organizer considers what resources the organization can bring to bear that might offset the resources of the target. The resources of both the target and the organization can change during any strategy. A breaking news story, an election, an "inside tip" may alter resources significantly. The selection of tactics, therefore, implies constantly looking for both offensive and defensive opportunities.

Brager and Specht (1973) note that the choice of tactics depends on three related factors: 1. the goal as it is perceived by the organization and the target, 2. the perceived resources of the organization and the target, and 3. the relationship between the organization and the target. They describe three types of tactics: collaboration, persuasion, and

contest. Collaborative tactics include problem solving, education, joint
action, and mild persuasion. Campaign tactics include political ma-
neuvering, bargaining, negotiation, and mild coercion. Tactics that violate social and legal norms are understood as contest tactics. Tactics
can be escalated as resistance is met.

Too often, however, organizers do not employ a variety of tactics,
nor do they escalate activities in the face of resistance. Further, organizers do not seem to have the sense that their tactics reflect different
degrees of contentiousness. Organizers and members describe both letters to public officials and confrontational negotiations as "mild persuasion." A march and a press release are called public education. Few
organizers believe they support tactics that "violate social norms," despite the frequent mention of civil disobedience, pickets, and demonstrations. Organizers often claim their tactics are not contentious, and
seconds later tell stories of direct confrontation. For example, one organizer described her organization as employing the more mild tactic
of persuasion, but followed with this story of direct confrontation:

> Last year we delivered a casket to the governor representing the in-
> creasing infant mortality rate and its relationship to low welfare
> grants. We had some political theater around the statehouse at
> Thanksgiving time—"the tale of two tables"—where there was a
> Thanksgiving day table for those who are making it in Massachu-
> setts and a table for those who aren't making it. Then we delivered
> an empty cornucopia to the governor. We also did a Labor Day
> picket at the Department of Public Welfare, with again the demand
> being that DPW request of the governor that welfare grants be
> brought up to poverty level.

Initially, this organizer appears misguided, describing strategies as
persuasive and executing ones that are clearly confrontational. Indeed,
as Brager and Specht (1973) suggest, this organizer may be simply
atheoretical. The authors' notion that insurrection or contest depends
on the social climate may be operant here. Those tactics, once highly
controversial, have been used frequently in the last twenty-five years,
and may now be viewed normatively, given the more violent protest
the country has witnessed. We think, however, that this confusion is
attributable to the biases in the organizer's change orientation. As we
have seen, many organizers view their targets as amenable to influence,
and do not envision confrontation as the appropriate means for making change. The biases brought by their change orientation account
for the repeated use of persuasive and educational tactics, despite the

opposition's refusal to change. These organizers would prefer to use collaboration and persuasion, but the intransigence of their targets and the power of the "system" to deflect, co-opt, and otherwise avoid change sometimes make it necessary to "up the ante." While organizers may use tactics that deviate from their norms, they frame them in terms acceptable to their change orientations.

A full and open assessment of resources requires the organizer to recognize that there are many ways to pressure for change, all of which can be used based on the target's behavior. Sometimes conflict and confrontation is necessary to obtain the goal of the strategy. In most cases the assets of the target system (i.e., wealth, legal authority, access to the media, political connections) are far greater than the assets of a social action organization. Powerful and wealthy targets can use these assets to co-opt members of social action groups. City officials can offer particularly outspoken members lucrative city jobs or appoint them to prestigious "advisory" commissions. When other methods fail, targets often have ways of harassing members. It is not unusual for the home of a leader of a group pressing for changes in housing legislation, for example, to be visited by a tax collector or a housing inspector or have his or her car ticketed on a regular basis. It is incumbent upon the organizer to remain open about all the possible resources that can be employed in response. A social action organization has innumerable resources that can be used to good effect. These must be considered in any evaluation of possible tactics. We describe five of the most important assets and considerations here: 1. the availability of members to carry out the tactic, 2. the timing and sequence of a tactic, 3. the dramatic effect of a tactic, 4. the existence of a favorable social or political environment, and 5. the organization's staffing and budgetary resources.

People as a Resource The major resource an organization has in its attempt to pressure for change is probably numbers. Numbers of people signify to the opposition that the organization is strong and has a great deal of support for its position. A demand for change can easily be denied if it is made by only a few people. When the demand comes from large numbers it is harder to ignore. This is especially true for politicians who must continue to garner support to get elected. One of the first assessments any target will make is about the number of people supportive of the organization and its demand for change. And frequently the opposition's initial attack will be an effort to question or downplay the organization's support. A student recalls such an incident:

> We sent a little delegation in to ask the dean for a change in course scheduling. The first thing he asked was who do we represent, were we a part of the Student Union, did we legitimately represent the student body? This theme kept coming up over and over. He said we were only six students, he knew of many other students who felt differently, and implied he had a stack of letters from them. He said he couldn't concede to a change requested by six students—we had to show him that this was really a problem. We were very demoralized until we realized that this was a ploy to get out of making the change. The next time we'll have numbers when we meet with him.

In general, the more people a tactic involves, the more effective it will be. Devising tactics that can include a large number of people and attract new ones is a critical part of tactic selection. However, as we have seen, people don't always feel ready to carry out a tactic, particularly if it involves conflict and confrontation. Interestingly, middle-class people tend to be more wary of confrontation than lower-income and working-class people. As a general rule of thumb, people must feel comfortable with a tactic in order to execute it; it is a classic Alinsky (1971) dictum to "never go outside the experience of your people" (127). In order to assess a tactic's potential organizers need to examine key factors: Will the tactic involve and attract a large number of people? Are people willing to carry out the tactic? Is it something that people can feel comfortable doing? A good example of this principle is made from the campaign we described earlier to save the Midway theater. During the campaign, city officials refused to either stop the sale of the building or take ownership of it so that it could be turned into a community center. The organizer suggested to leaders that since their own government refused to help them, maybe they should request help from the Soviet consulate. He argued that the action would be dramatic, humorous, and certain to attract press attention. But the suggested tactic was offensive to the community leaders, who considered themselves true American patriots, and it was quickly defeated. Had the organizer insisted on employing the tactic, it is almost certain he would have visited the Soviets alone. Indeed, the organizer might have been in far greater trouble with his leaders if he had not been working successfully with them for ten years.

While it is generally true that people must be comfortable with a tactic to execute it, organizers should not underestimate what people are willing to do. Leaders are often more willing to try new tactics than their organizers anticipate. Who would have predicted that in 1963 a community of African-Americans in Montgomery, Alabama, would agree to boycott the public transportation system?

Frequently, people can be encouraged and supported to take a courageous action. Through discussion of tactical options, particularly if more collaborative and persuasive efforts have failed, people can themselves decide to try something new. For example, students had been protesting for almost six months when it came time for graduation. Leaders of the protest were very concerned. They felt that tactics could be effective at graduation given its large audience, public setting, and presence of the university officials who were their targets. But the students were obdurate in not wanting to ruin the event for relatives and other graduates and, out of respect, had decided to do nothing. The organizer convinced them to at least survey the student body to determine whether the majority of students were willing to employ a dramatic tactic at graduation. The results were overwhelmingly positive, although students wanted the tactic to be respectful and not conflictual. They came up with the idea of wearing black buttons, a quiet symbol of their protest. Almost every student wore one, the audience and the targets got the message, and the students felt they had behaved with strength and decorum.

Having particular groups of people involved in the tactic can also be a major resource for the organization. Professionals and experts in the issue area can be effective in arguing an organization's issue. For example, the disarmament movement was given a boost when Physicians for Social Responsibility organized. Celebrities, too, can stimulate interest in an organization's cause, as when Elizabeth Taylor became active in fund-raising for people with AIDS. Finally, the involvement of clergy, who have a special spiritual authority, can be helpful in promoting a group's issue. A citywide housing group, for example, organized a delegation of the city's most prominent priests, ministers, and rabbis for a prayer vigil for the homeless outside the governor's mansion on Thanksgiving. While these "special groups" can all be used to good effect, they seldom, in our view, supplant the need for large numbers.

Timing and Sequence as a Resource The timing of a tactic and the sequencing of tactics are other important resources for bringing about change. Certainly, legislative and electoral calendars create important opportunities for organizational activities. The daily and yearly schedules of constituents are another important consideration. For example, it is difficult to carry out any tactic over the Christmas holidays or at the end of the summer. Exam schedules need to be kept in mind when organizing students. Workers will find it difficult to attend a daytime event, but it is hard to get senior citizens out in the evenings. Finally, there are religious considerations. Religious Jews and Seventh Day Adventists cannot attend Saturday functions, and many Catholics and Christians are not available on Sundays and on certain feast days. An organizer working in a multiethnic neighborhood found himself planning events on Saturday nights!

Organizers can also think about sequencing tactics so that they have greater effect. Generally, tactics are escalated; more confrontational tactics are employed as a target resists. Innocuous activities such as small meetings or letter writing campaigns can be used initially, and rallies, public hearings, or boycotts used when resistance is met. Escalation of tactics has several benefits. First, early tactics are "polite" and nonmenacing, making it difficult for the target to gain sympathy or discredit the group as "glassy-eyed radicals." When the more aggressive tactics are used, they are more likely to be viewed by the public as justified, given the target's resistance. Second, the target's intransigence can be used to build support for the organizing, allowing new people to join along the way. Finally, escalating tactics give members a sense of moving toward a goal. As one organizer says, "No one wants to write a letter after they've been through a major demonstration."

Finally, it is sometimes effective to use several tactics at once, involving different targets and using different methods of approach. Such a technique makes the organization less predictable and appear ubiquitous, giving the organization the aura of power. In the Midway theater case several tactics directed at different targets were used simultaneously. The organization was demonstrating against the city's managing director, attempting to negotiate with the Historical Preservation Society, and attempting to influence corporate officials at Burger King. City officials could not go through the day without some contact with the organization's leadership. When members of a community group in Minnesota visited Senator Pillsbury, the arms of the organization must have seemed long indeed.

Drama as a Resource Another useful resource is a tactic that is eye-catching or dramatic. Symbolically, the drama brings attention to the organization, helps members understand the issues more clearly, and portrays the target in a poor light. Creative, interesting events or ways of portraying a problem or demand are another way of making the target uncomfortable. Targets, particularly when they are people in public office, learn how to react to demonstrations, and can be caught off guard by something unexpected.

Drama is also exciting, interesting, and humorous for the people who participate in the activity. People will be more likely to continue to work in organizations if they are having fun, as well as doing important work. For example, a citywide organization was working on getting banks to make mortgages and home improvement loans in working class and poor neighborhoods. They planned a meeting with the president of a large bank that had a particularly bad record for lending. Members brought along a giant "report card on lending activity" and as the president denied their requests, they wrote in failing grades. Such a dramatic tactic is fun for the people who participate, enhances the assertive tone of the meeting, and plays well in the press.

It is important, however, to consider how people will react to these symbols. Some symbols will appeal to people and the media, catching their imagination and sense of humor. The use of the report card on lending activity and paying for lunch at Burger King with pennies are examples of effective drama. Some symbols are counterproductive. They repel people rather than engage them. The hangers and pictures of dead fetuses used by different sides in the abortion debate are examples of drama that are probably counterproductive.

Environmental Resources There are occasions when the social, economic, or political environment shows greater receptivity toward an organization's goal. Indeed, Piven and Cloward (1977) may be correct that the achievement of social change has more to do with environment than an organization's efforts. In such a climate the organization's message is likely to find a receptive public audience, and news coverage is apt to be more positive. But even in less receptive times events occur, or some information is released, that can be exploited by the organization for its own benefit. For example, the New York City Chamber of Commerce released a study of businesses deciding to leave New York, citing two of the major reasons as the lack of affordable housing for employees and the increasing number of homeless persons threatening clients and workers. The report was used by many New York City advocacy groups for the homeless to demand that the city increase its low-income housing stock.

Occasionally, such news is especially fortuitous. A neighborhood organizer tells of one such story,

> We wanted to do something about the park in the neighborhood, but we were having a hell of a time getting anybody to listen. At the time the city budget was in trouble, cops and teachers were being furloughed, and it was hard to build up sympathy to renovate our swimming pool. Then an investigative reporter did a story on all these officials living rent free in these luxurious old city-owned homes in the park. They didn't even pay for fuel, and this was during the oil crisis. All of sudden, our campaign took off. After all, if the city could spend that money, they could certainly repair our pool. By tying the two things together, the city was embarrassed into making the repairs.

Though it is often luck that brings such evidence to light, organizers obviously need to be alert to such potential news. As one says, "I skim six newspapers a day and every magazine I can get my hands on. Anything that's out there, I want to know about it."

The Organization's Resources Finally, the organization's resources, particularly its budget and staff, also need to be considered when selecting tactics. Here organizers examine whether a tactic is feasible given organizational resources and time schedules. Some tactics clearly are more time-consuming and costly than others. A demonstration or meeting takes weeks of preparation time, time spent making arrangements, recruiting people and working with them, and ensuring publicity. Much of the work will ineluctably fall to staff. The already overburdened organizer will simply not be able to attend to all the details. On the other hand, organizers and leaders must continue to promote activities; they are essential to furthering the organization's instrumental goals, recruiting newcomers, and developing leaders. A careful balance must be struck. As one organizer says, "Tactics must take you to the limits of your abilities, but not push you over the precipice, where you end up doing something detrimental to the organization."

The Process of Selecting Strategy and Tactics

Thus far, we have described the questions and considerations that guide organizers in making strategy and tactic decisions. What remains is to describe how organizers work with leaders and members to reach mutually agreed upon decisions about strategy.

There are diverse ways of reaching strategy decisions. Organizers whose work is designed to influence government suggest that targets and strategies are self-evident. Decisions emerge from an understanding of an issue and the analysis of the governmental body involved in the issue. In some organizations organizers make decisions about strategies and tactics. Their right to make decisions in this area is based on their greater expertise and the need for expediency. In other organizations strategy and tactics are selected mutually by the organization's staff and board. Arrangements range from highly formalized processes that involve reports and voting to informal "checking out ideas with a few key people."

In our view strategy and tactic decisions should never be determined by the organizer unilaterally or decided by a small, select group of individuals. Strategy and tactic development, like issue development, should be determined by the staff, leaders, and members conjointly. There are many rationales for such thorough discussions. First, while instrumental goals are the substance of strategy discussions, expressive goals are realized as members engage in discussions about strategic options. Strategy discussions are yet another opportunity to engage, empower, and educate members. By mutually establishing what can be expected out of a meeting, how they should respond to each alternative, and marking progress, members, both individually and collectively, come to "own" the decisions, and increasingly invest in the organization. In this way, people learn how to plan strategy and gain both a sense of control and accomplishment.

Organizers working with low-income people and minorities more often describe involving members in selecting targets, strategies, and tactics than do organizers working with middle-class or professional constituencies. Perhaps what is suggested here is that organizers who work with lower-income groups see education of their members as a priority, and therefore engage them more in discussions and decisions about strategy. Organizers working with middle-class and professional people may assume their members are educated and need only to be motivated to act. We think organizers need to be careful about assuming that members are educated about strategy development. Even if members are astute, their knowledge can only enrich the discussion, and their motivation can be enhanced through such debates.

A second reason for involving members and leaders in strategy decisions is that, as we have seen, organizers often design strategies according to their own biases. Full and open discussion with leaders and members mitigates organizers' proclivities to limit their analysis by bringing other ideas into play. For example, an organizer may overenthusiastically envision a march with massive numbers of people participating. Through group discussion, however, it is ascertained that a lobbying strategy might be more effective. The organizer's biases are put aside, and members may be spared the demoralizing effect of a time-consuming and ineffective tactic.

Third, through discussion of tactical options, members have an opportunity to discuss their fears and reservations about a particular activity. This is especially important when the tactic is confrontational and implies some risk taking, such as a sit-in or a visit to a city official. In strategy discussions it is especially important for the organizer to be honest with leaders and members. They need to know the risks inherent in any strategy, the potential benefits, and most important, that no strategy or tactic ensures victory. In such a frank discussion the organizer makes clear that the strategy is not a primrose path. When promises are made or risks are realized that have not been discussed beforehand, members can feel angry, frustrated, and demoralized, and less willing to take subsequent action.

In these discussions the organizer helps people assess their realistic chances for success, offering options that may increase their chances or at least stretch their thinking. The organizer can introduce new ideas to members—ideas that they may not have considered, or even those that may be initially distasteful to them. By voicing their worries about the possible risk and potential benefit of any tactic beforehand, members have an opportunity to explore and possibly accept more confrontational tactics. On the other hand, the organizer is quickly dissuaded from planning tactics that people are unwilling to execute. An organizer stressing this point says,

> I think the organizer really has to play an agitator role and lay out for people: we ain't going to get where we want to unless we try this. You also have to be real honest. The worst thing that you can do is sell people on a tactic almost like that's the victory. What you can say is that we can try this, other groups have tried this approach and it hasn't worked. We've got A, B, and C. Let's at least try A. If it doesn't work, then we'll go to B and C. It's also important that the organizer should not tie his or her ego to one strategy. We vote here. If the vote is so unbalanced, then we don't do it. The people must make the ultimate decision, so I can't get so invested in my own ideas that I can't hear them.

The organizer must offer concrete suggestions for strategy and tactics for, as a typical leader says, "We know what we need and what we want. It's just that sometimes we don't know how to go about it, so the staff has to help." In assessing strategic options organizers have their own experiences to draw on, knowledge about the activities of other groups, and greater access to information. This technical knowledge makes it logical that the process of examining strategic options begins with the organizer. But neither should the analysis end there. Once organizers have determined ideas that look feasible and effective, they must use their interactional skills to help members understand and assess the options. In the illustration below an organizer for a metropolitan working women's organization explains how she developed a strategy to work on sexual harassment and then worked with members around it.

It was 1977 and our organization had been around about a year. We began by identifying issues and indigenous leadership through a survey of secretaries and women office workers. The survey included questions about their jobs, e.g., child care, family leave, the existence of job descriptions, opportunities for promotions, etc. When we surveyed a woman, especially if she had a grievance, we would try to get her to come to a meeting. We learned from the survey that women office workers were angry about sexual harassment in the workplace and the demeaning things they were asked to do on the job. Other women's organizations had already done things like give "petty office procedure awards." So my antennae about those being good issues were already up when I met Ellen. I approached Ellen in a cafeteria and asked her to take the survey. She did, and then we got to talking. She tearfully told me that she had worked in an office for five years where the boss had constantly harassed her sexually. She was not the only one in the office it had happened to; there were about six women in the office, and all had been approached by this boss. She felt demeaned by it, but also guilty. She needed the job, she said, and couldn't quit. I told her that I knew quite a few women who were in the same boat. Also, the federal courts had found sexual harassment to be discriminatory, and so her situation was against the law. She asked a lot of questions about that. I also said that our survey had found that sexual harassment was the number one problem. We had a group who was meeting about that subject and would she like to come to the meeting and discuss it with them. Ellen felt ashamed about her circumstances, but agreed to come to a meeting. I was thinking that we had our first real issue if I could get the group, and particularly Ellen, to move on it. Whatever we did also had to protect Ellen; we couldn't put her in jeopardy. I began to think that one option would be to file a third-party suit on Ellen's behalf. Quickly, I set up a meeting with some women who had been working on the survey, and I included some of our board members. I talked with Ellen before the meeting, promising that the group would keep her story confidential, and her job would be protected. At the meeting, Sally, the chairperson, reminded everyone about the results of the survey, and the fact that the city, state, and federal government were required to investigate sexual harassment cases, and make amends. Ellen shared her experience, and the women asked a lot of questions. She told us that the boss only hired women who were young, white, single, childless, and attractive. He had made overtures to all the women in the office. Because of his advances there was constant employee turnover. Four women had left this year. Lillian asked Ellen if she thought some of the other women would talk with our group. Ellen said she didn't want to jeopardize herself by talking to the ones still working, but she agreed to call some of the ones who had left. One woman she knew who had just resigned was particularly angry. The committee then discussed what we could do to help Ellen without putting her in jeopardy. I told them that the law allowed for a third-party suit whereby a group could register a claim on behalf of an unidentified party. This sounded good to them, but Ellen still thought her boss would know she was involved. I then said I thought we might be able to "set him up." The women were interested in this idea. I asked whether there were any openings at the company now. Ellen said there were. I asked, "What if we send women to apply for the job, and see if he discriminated around hiring?" Then we would have our own evidence. Everybody liked the idea of this "undercover work." It was a little scary and exciting, and it got Ellen off the hook. We agreed to meet again after Ellen had made her contacts. At the next meeting, Ellen brought two of the company's former employees. They confirmed her story. One had been in charge of personnel, and she told the group that they would find plenty of evidence of discriminatory hiring in the past records. We then discussed our "undercover plan." We agreed that we would send four women to be interviewed: a black woman, an older woman, a woman with children (all who would be qualified for the job), and a young, white, childless, very attractive woman who had none of the job qualifications. The women suggested people they knew who would be willing to act as "plants." The group considered various logistical problems like how would the women know about the job opening, who would be a part of the third party suit, and what would happen if he didn't hire the unqualified woman (and what if he did). Ellen was still a little afraid, but she was game to try this strategy. I think she was buoyed by the group and the surreptitiousness of the plan. We agreed to try it, and see what happened. A few days later I introduced Ellen to a few people who had agreed to be "plants." She agreed they were perfect, and was sure he would hire our unqualified person. We held several more meetings to plan the third-party complaint and the interviewing strategy. I don't think I've ever seen a group more excited. The end of the story is the boss hired our unqualified plant, and she worked in the office for a week. We went public with the third-party complaint while she was working there. Our "plant" collected other damaging personnel data, which we submitted as part of our complaint. At the end of the week fifty women presented the boss with a six-foot doll named "Suzy Sexpot" at his all-male club. We got lots of press, and the government found cause in our case. The boss was forced to resign. He never knew Ellen turned us on to the situation. She felt vindicated by the whole thing, and became one of our most active leaders. And, of course, it launched the organization.

As this illustration shows, although strategic and tactical decisions should be made with members, the critical importance of the organizer's thought process cannot be underestimated.

The process of developing strategy and tactics is comprised of an assessment of goals, targets, and resources for change. As members are engaged in discussions of these areas, as they review alternatives and options, their investment in the organization is strengthened, and they are educated about their potential to make change and assume power.

As we see it, organizers are potentially the biggest obstacle to creative and effective strategy development. When they rigidly adhere to a change orientation, which defines the amenability of targets to change and the role of conflict among alternatives, they unnecessarily restrict what is possible. We encourage organizers to be conscious of their biases and evaluate alternatives as comprehensively and realistically as possible. The kinds of changes they seek demand it.

CHAPTER SEVEN

Implementing Strategy: The Action Phase

In the previous chapter we examined how social action organizations develop strategy. Several writers discuss strategy selection, but they give minimal attention to the details of strategy implementation, essentially assuming that planned strategies are actually implemented (Brager and Specht 1973, Kahn 1970). Pressman and Wildavsky's (1984) analysis of implementation processes suggests the danger in this assumption. It is critical to know whether and how the planned strategies are realized, and how implementors change initial plans as organizations engage with targets. Here the give-and-take of strategy between a social action organization and a target is realized. The strategy plan is, in short, necessary to action, but it is the action itself that truly counts in producing change.

Once an organization elects an issue and a strategy, it must attempt to carry out what has been proposed. The tactics selected by an organization define what work must be done during the action phase. Critical questions for implementation: What types of tactics are actually employed? Who can be expected to implement these tactics—staff or membership? Does the contentiousness of the activity make a difference in who is involved? Finally, how do organizers motivate members to act, especially when asking them to participate in the more contentious tactics like civil disobedience?

A Continuum of Tactics

As we have seen the change orientations organizers support frequently circumscribe the choice of tactics. Rather than a careful calculation of goals, resources, and power, the use of tactics is often guided by the organizers' and members' *perceptions* of themselves in relation to the established system for decision making and decision makers. Consequently, such beliefs and assumptions as the *perceived* legitimacy of the system and decision makers, the *perceived* degree of connection to or alienation from decision makers and systems, and the *perception* of the organization's role relative to those in the system guide the employment of tactics. Thus, tactics can be arrayed according to the way in which the organizer and members perceive themselves in relation to their target system.

Expanding on the work of Brager and Specht (1973) and Delgado (1986), we have identified eleven different tactics employed by social action organizations and placed these tactics into four categories: persuasion activities (letter writing, petitioning, lobbying visits to public officials, and public education), electoral work (campaigning, drafting legislation, referendums, etc.), confrontation (face-to-face meetings with targets, face-to face negotiations around organizational demands), and disruptive action (boycotts, marches, demonstrations, prayer vigils, and civil disobedience). Each category suggests a relative degree of affiliation with or disaffection from the target.

Persuasive tactics are activities in which the social action organization tries to convince decision makers and/or the general public to act, based on the depth of support for an issue and/or the moral imperative to respond to that issue. The use of persuasive tactics expresses a good deal of relatedness to the political system, accepting the power holder as a potentially persuadable actor within a legitimate system and seeking only to influence the outcomes of that system's work. The preferred role of the organization is "persuader," and the preferred goal is to "change minds," thereby influencing actions. Persuasive appeals may be made either indirectly (through letters, petitions, endorsements in newspapers, marches, prayer vigils, demonstrations, dissemination of research reports or analyses, etc.) or directly (through lobbying visits.) Persuasive tactics may be either emotional and angry or calm and low-key.

Electoral tactics are activities in which the social action organization attempts to use the formal structures of representative government to secure desired instrumental goals. Electoral tactics accept a partial relatedness to the political system; they accept the legitimacy of the structures in which that system's actors make decisions while rejecting some actors or the decisions they make. Organizations using electoral tactics see their role in one of two ways: they either demand laws, regulations, or policies that realize the desired goal or they work for the election of people who would promote such legislation. The effort of National People's Action, which organized around the Home Mortgage Disclosure Act and the Community Reinvestment Act, is an example of the first scenario. The organization accepted government's role in relation to banking policy, but drafted and made demands for legislation that circumscribed the lending policy of commercial institutions. Women's organizations that campaign for women candidates who are expected to promote women's issues, believing it less productive to convince male legislators on feminist issues, are examples of the second scenario. Electoral tactics include referendums, candidate endorsements and disendorsements, and drafting laws or regulations.

Confrontation tactics are activities in which the organizer and members attempt to meet directly with the target around the desired instrumental goal. Confrontation tactics imply a greater sense of alienation from the target system and suggest that power holders are not necessarily legitimate decision makers who are easily influenced. The attempt is not to persuade them but to demand changes of them. The role of the organization is to directly confront power holders in a face-to-face encounter, so that the target is forced to negotiate with the organization. Confrontation tactics include mass meetings where the target is present, demands posed at public venues (e.g., city council meetings and legislative hearings) where decision makers are present, and uninvited visits to the target's "turf." For example, a neighborhood group met with the president of a bank, giving him a six-foot "failing report card," and demanded increased mortgage lending and lower home improvement loan rates for the neighborhood. A welfare rights group delivered a casket (symbolizing the infant mortality rates in families living on welfare budgets) to the governor along with their demands for a raise in the basic welfare budget of the state.

Disruptive tactics are activities in which the social action organization attempts to force a response from a target by obstructing its normal operations or the functioning of a system to which the decision maker has some connection. Like confrontation tactics, disruptive activities also suggest a great degree of alienation from the established system. Power holders are not accepted as legitimate decision makers who are easily persuaded. Unlike confrontation tactics, disruption seldom involves face-to-face contact with power holders. Instead, the organization tries to disrupt the target's routine operations, build public sympathy, and communicate its desires through the media so that the target is forced to concede to the organization's instrumental goal. Disruptive tactics include boycotts, pickets, and civil disobedience.

Many or all of these tactics can be used to exercise influence during the course of a strategy, and several tactics can even be used simultaneously. For example, the struggle for the Equal Rights Amendment used persuasion tactics (lobbying visits, letters to congresspersons, petitions), electoral tactics (proposing legislation, campaigning for women candidates) and disruption tactics (protest marches and boycotts).

Sometimes the mere threat of a disruptive tactic is enough to move the target. The classic Alinsky story of the threat to occupy all the toilets at O'Hare airport that forced then Mayor Richard Daley to capitulate to the Woodlawn Organization's demands is an example of such an approach (Alinsky 1971).

In the initial planning stage the use of any tactic should depend on the resources of the organization. Throughout a campaign, however, tactics must constantly be reassessed in light of what is occurring at any moment in time. In the action phase the initial plans selected during strategy development are constantly reformulated, altered, or confirmed. In the example of the campaign to save the Midway theater described in the chapter 6, one can see how strategy was constantly reformulated throughout the two-year campaign.

Future actions are fundamentally influenced by the target's reaction, how members perceive the target's reaction, and what members are prepared to do in view of their perceptions. There is also a question of how the actions of targets affect members' morale. If a target can successfully co-opt members by convincing them of his good intentions or refuting their arguments or defusing their investment, members will be less willing to carry out subsequent actions. On the other hand, as the target openly resists the change and the organization's polite and seemingly conciliatory efforts are rejected by the target, members become angrier. The target's resistance mobilizes people's resolve, and they become more willing to escalate their pressure by using more contentious tactics. Further, the organization's subsequent use of contentious tactics is deemed by the public as acceptable, given the target's intransigence. One organizer tells this story:

> We met first with the housing commissioner and requested low-income loans. We knew he wouldn't give, but we wanted to be po-

lite. Then he couldn't say to the press, "They should have come to me. I always listen to the local people's needs." We met with him, and he said no, and it was reported in the press. And it angered our folks that he didn't agree. He refused a second meeting with us, and this too was reported. Our people got angrier, and they wanted to do more. They had tried the polite American way and it didn't work. By now our complaints couldn't be easily dismissed. Our people were angry. We went to his neighborhood and protested on his street. He told the press that the people were being led astray by "paid professional agitators" who were communists. The people went crazy when he patronized them like that. They were good tax-paying citizens asking for help for their neighborhood. Suddenly, it was war. People wanted to do everything, and our gripes were legitimate, righteous. As an organizer, that's right where you want to be: the public sympathetic and your folks pissed.

In sum, throughout the action phase tactics must be constantly reviewed in the context of the moment. New tactical options, either less or more contentious, arise as the organization's resources increase or abate, as targets resist or accept the organization's goals, and as members' resolve wanes or is strengthened.

Roles in Tactic Implementation

The successful use of any tactic has numerous small tasks embedded in it. A letter writing campaign requires that sample letters be written, and reproduced. People to send the letters must be identified, contacted, and convinced to write. They must be told the names and addresses of those who should be sent letters, receive the sample letters, and, in most cases, be given envelopes and stamps. There must be some way of monitoring how many letters have been sent and from whom, in case the process must be repeated.

The details involved in a demonstration or meeting boggle the mind. People need to be contacted. Flyers must be developed, reproduced, and disseminated. Targets need to be invited to attend. Speakers and chairpeople must be chosen and speeches written. If there is to be negotiation, demands must be formulated, written out, and ready for the target's signature. Buses need to be reserved and paid for, and directions must be given. Signs must be produced, auditoriums reserved, microphones acquired and tested, and chairs set up. Street theater or dramatic tactics require a script, costumes, and actors. Permits must be obtained. Protest songs must be typed and distributed. Press releases must be written and sent to induce the media to cover the event in a positive fashion. Refreshments need to be served. Finally, people need to attend the demonstration or meeting and carry out their responsibilities. Sign up sheets must be drafted, circulated, and filed for subsequent use. Every task takes time, many require skills, and several rely on ingenuity.

A critical question during the implementation phase is who will carry out all the tasks associated with a tactic. The answer will suggest both how much visibility and how much responsibility the organizer assumes during the action phase.

Some organizers argue that staff must both carry major responsibility for tasks and be highly visible during the action phase. They offer several rationales for their position. First, national organizations cite distance as an impediment to involving people. Yet distance need not cripple member involvement during the action phase. Rather, according to their change orientation and practice method, organizers seem predisposed either to encouraging members to carry tasks or to doing the tasks themselves.

A second reason is that organizers feel that staff are paid to carry out these tasks and they feel it is unfair to consume volunteers' time. Piven and Cloward (1977) argue that members who are poor and consumed with the details of survival can only be convinced to take on these action tasks during opportune and historical times. Yet in minority organizations members more often carry out tasks than in white middle-class organizations. Blacks and Hispanics are generally members of local organizations with few staff and lean budgets that may be more reliant on their membership to carry out organizational work. However, minorities are most often members of organizations where issues are directly and immediately related to their self-interest; because of this they may be more invested in putting pressure on power holders, and more willing to accept action tasks. It may be, however, that the difference is once again the function of an organizer's change orientation rather than of the race or class of the constituency. As Brager and Specht (1969) suggest, organizers' pessimism about involving poor people in action may result in a self-fulfilling prophecy.

Third, committees often involve time-consuming debates, and many organizers argue it is easier and faster to do a task themselves than have it done by a committee. As members carry out tasks, they gain input, and consequently the organizer has less control over time lines, the way the task is handled, and the final result.

Fourth, some tasks, such as drafting letters, writing and delivering speeches, negotiating demands, and presenting testimony require a level of competence and expertise that members do not routinely possess. Some organizers argue that when the stakes for change are high competency and expertise are essential. Organizers who support a pluralist pressure orientation and are involved in writing and presenting testimony are more likely to have tasks carried out by staff and a few key leaders because of their respect for the technical skills of these people. Indeed, some authors suggest that power holders are more likely to respond to the arguments of a few influential experts (Dear and Patti 1984).

Finally, some tactics such as sit-ins and directly challenging a target require that people take risks. Organizers may worry that members, especially vulnerable people such as welfare recipients and tenants, may fear retaliation and may not be willing to take such risks. Staff members become organizers knowing they will take risks, while members do not necessarily join with risks in mind. Some organizers argue, therefore, that staff should have the "high profile" in these events, by making speeches and negotiating agreements, actions that would put themselves rather than their members at risk of retaliation. Several authors mention the obstacles organizers face in getting people to take action, suggesting it is easier for people to take less alienated and less aggressive stances (Brager 1963, Haggstrom 1969). We argue, however, that involving members in implementing strategy has little to do with how contentious the tactic is. In fact, the opposite seems to be true: persuasion strategies (lobbying, letter writing) are often carried out by staff and a few key leaders while the more contentious contest strategies such as direct and disruptive actions (with the exception of civil disobedience) are performed by members.

It is probably true that delegating and sharing responsibilities with members requires the organizer to spend more time motivating and coordinating people. Clearly, organizers lose some control over the process and product. These are legitimate concerns. Still, it is curious that social action organizations, which at least in theory rely so heavily on numbers of people pressuring to create change, would not engage as many members as possible in the action phase. In many organizations key decisions around issues, targets, and strategies are made by staff. Similarly, staff often has the primary role in the action phase. If members do not have decision making and implementation roles, how are they involved in the organization?

The obvious consequence of staff planning and implementing all activities is that members, having no work to do, will discontinue their involvement in the organization. There is little motivation for members to become active, to take on responsibilities, to invest in the work. Members are asked merely to pay dues or to "show up," and often begin to wonder why they should participate at all. They learn to depend upon staff to do things for them, to shoulder the burden of work and take the risks they are unwilling to take. They aren't helped to analyze whether a risk is worth taking and why or how they can protect themselves from retaliation. Soon they stop coming at all.

We support a model in which primarily indigenous leaders are visible during the action phase. Staff should never take on such highly visible tasks as speaking to or negotiating with targets. Because of their visibility, these tasks, in particular, offer status and prestige that encourage people to bond with the organization. All tasks should at least be shared but primarily accomplished by members. There are simply too many tasks for the organizing staff to accomplish alone, and an organizer can easily be consumed with details. On the other hand, when members are counted on to carry out a task, their investment is enhanced. When members assume responsibility for tasks, when they take risks on their own behalf, and when they receive the status associated with high visibility, they become further invested in the cause and the organization. Members learn to do the tasks, even the more complicated ones, and take pride in their competence. They see themselves as actors rather than bystanders.

At the other extreme, organizers cannot absolve themselves of responsibility for implementation. When taken to this extreme, organizers can fail to offer members the assistance that would encourage them to do their tasks well and in a timely manner. As members take responsibility, organizers must continue to monitor their work, ensure deadlines are kept, coordinate activities among members, and help members to complete tasks such as writing speeches or drawing up demands that they may feel inadequately prepared to do. Essentially, organizers must work beside members to ensure that tasks are carried out and competently accomplished. Otherwise, members may feel even more incompetent and powerless and embarrassed about their poor performance. Organizers may find that people are angry with them for not providing the assistance that would have made for a better performance.

Motivating and Helping Members to Act

According to Etzioni (1969) people are motivated to join voluntary organizations for moral reasons, and their compliance is gained by invoking norms. In social action organizations, however, even though people may join and pay a small membership fee or make a donation, compliance does not necessarily mean they will engage in the next step of activity, which may call for more time, effort, or risk taking. The action phase requires an additional level of investment.

As any organizer knows, getting people to collect signatures on petitions, write and visit legislators, demonstrate, and confront power holders, is no easy matter. Many people feel they are the only ones experiencing problems; they are loathe to express them, let alone do anything about them. Others feel that the problems are their fault or they have no right to complain. Collecting petitions or writing a postcard to a legislator or taking part in a march challenges such complacency. Many would rather leave it to others to work on the problem; they don't see themselves as "public actors" or they don't want to "stand out" from their friends. They may also feel uncomfortable carrying out new and unfamiliar tasks for which they have little skill or training. They fear failure and embarrassment. For example, people who are afraid to speak in public will be reluctant to visit a legislator or negotiate with a power holder. When people are burdened by work and family responsibilities, they find little time for activism. Tactics take time and energy. Moreover, most people are not accustomed to engaging in pressure tactics; indeed, our society socializes against taking such action. Public displays of anger and distress are frowned upon.

Finally, members may fear that their actions will result in retaliation by the target. This is especially true when members are asked to negotiate with people who hold direct power over their lives (e.g., landlords, directors of welfare offices, etc.) who can (and sometimes do) retaliate. In these cases, members are asked to take real risks that are potentially damaging to them. Even when survival is not at stake, people may worry about their potential loss of benefits, status, or favor, as when tenured professors publicly take an antiadministration stance. There is so much that mitigates against taking action that the question is not why people aren't willing to act but why people agree to take action at all.

If members are to carry out tactics, they must be motivated to act. Some members may be self-motivated, but most will not be. Motivation will depend on their degree of self-interest in the issue and what they are being asked to do. Motivation may also change over time. Life circumstances may change, and people may find themselves with more or less time to pursue their activism. During a struggle a target may respond in a way that fuels people's anger and increases their investment. In contrast, a target's reasonable and approachable demeanor may cause people's anger to diminish. Organizers cannot rely on either self-motivation or serendipitous circumstances, including targets' reactions. They must find ways of motivating people in order for members to sustain their interest and commitment.

Many authors tend to treat the subject of motivation rather abstractly. Although their comments do not specifically address the action phase, Henderson and Thomas (1980b) attempt to be more explicit about motivational methods. They write that "galvanization" involves two processes:

1. Reflection refers to guiding people through an internal reasoning process that helps them articulate the injustice around them, formulate common goals, and decide how to intervene in a way that is planned and predictable. Organizers who develop awareness and agitate about the issue, explore the costs and benefits of collective action, and describe the available power resources are using reflective methods.
2. Vision follows reflection and refers to confidence building. It involves helping people see the world as amenable to change and themselves as people with skills, talents, and knowledge that were previously unimaginable to them.

Haggstrom (1970) also refers to the need for vision techniques,

An organizer must not only perceive how people are, but it is also essential that he be unrealistic in that he perceives people as they can be. Noting what is possible, the organizer projects this possibility and moves people to accept it and to seek to realize it. The organizer helps people to develop and live in an alternative reality in which their image of themselves and their abilities is enhanced. . . . People are moved to accept the new world of which they catch a glimpse because it appears to be attainable in practice and intrinsically superior to the world in which they have been living.   (106)

The ideas of Henderson and Thomas and Haggstrom help us to further scrutinize the methods organizers use to motivate people during the action phase. Motivation is a complex process that requires using several motivational techniques simultaneously. Building on Henderson and Thomas, we have sorted these distinct techniques into three major motivational categories: 1. reflection, 2. vision, and 3. mitigating the fear of risk taking.

Reflection

Henderson and Thomas write, "Reflection enables people to understand the situations that limit them and to attempt to overcome them" (Henderson and Thomas 1980b:116). Similarly, Freire stresses the importance of people seeing the world as a challenge rather than a limitation (Freire 1973). Organizers can be said to use reflective techniques when they help members to better understand the meaning and context of issues, and when they seek to help people see these issues as challenges rather than circumstances that must be tolerated. Techniques that fall within the category of reflection include clarifying and explaining issues and targets to people, agitating, and helping members learn from exposure to targets and the organizing process.

Clarifying and Explaining Making people aware of issues and clarifying the ramifications of decisions is cited by many organizers as a critical motivational technique. Organizers attempt to change members' perceptions about both issues and targets. Often government and media have propagated a version of circumstances that organizers challenge. They consciously work to reinterpret and reframe people's understanding. Bacharach and Baratz (1970) and Freire (1968) argue that the dominant ideology influences the way people perceive issues. Bacharach and Baratz (1970) develop Schattschneider's (1960) concept of mobilization of bias as an instrument of power holders. Freire (1968) calls the resultant inability to articulate issues differently "structural mutism" (97).

In order to clarify issues organizers give information about the subject, explain the causes of the problems and the biases inherent in the current system, and point to contrasts between what should be and what is. In doing so they attempt to show people that the issue is real, can be documented, that there are inherent prejudices, and that the people themselves are not to blame for the problem.

Another important clarifying technique is to educate members about the targets they face, helping people understand that the target is personally responsible for the situation members find themselves in. Organizers personalize the target for people by sharing information about the target's background, views, and life circumstances. People come to understand the reason for the target's opposition. Education about targets also attempts to change people's normal responses to authority figures. Organizers encourage people to see challenges to authorities as acceptable and necessary. By educating members about targets, organizers demystify authority and help members to see the power holder as human, vulnerable, and less potent so that people feel more able to confront them.

Agitation Even though people may know quite a lot about the issue and the target, they may not act. Organizers then agitate around the issue. They personalize it for people, arouse people's indignation, and make clear how intolerable the current situation is. The role of the organizer as rabble rouser and "paid professional agitator" has often been cited in the literature. Grosser (1976) confirms the need for the organizer to take sides, urging people into action. Alinsky (1971), too, stresses the importance of arousing people's anger about a situation, writing that organizers must "rub raw the sores of resentment" (116). Some organizers argue that rage will burn people out or can be harmful in their efforts to persuade potentially helpful governmental actors. An organizer debates this position, saying, "Organizers who deny the correlation between anger and action are living in a dream world. What do they think gets people to act? What motivates *them* to take a risk?" Outrage clearly fuels people's willingness to act.

Many organizers are uncomfortable with the agitator role, and may attempt to redefine it as "building emotion" or "increasing frustration." A political climate that frowns on dissent may encourage organizers to avoid agitation. We think it is also likely that the reluctance to take on this role is related to the fact that organizers are often described as manipulative, tarred as unscrupulously working on others' emotions (*Christian Century* 1961). We agree with Grosser's defense of agitation. "The role of activist is a legitimate one. . . . Passivity and objectivity are, after all, something of a myth in relation to the service professions. People are urged to action of all sorts—to visit a dentist, get a physical examination, contribute to the Red Cross, or register to vote" (Grosser 1976:200–201).

Exposure to Issues and Targets The organizing process itself provides continuing opportunities for people to deepen their understanding about issues and targets. They learn as they act. Members become much more committed to a redefinition of issues and targets when they have direct exposure to situations and targets. These personal experiences will deepen members' commitment and propel them into action.

Even the most informed and incensed person may not know what to do with information or want to take action alone. The issue and target are further clarified as people have the opportunity to act on their knowledge. Their understanding of the issue is deepened, they recognize that others hold the same views, and they have a way of expressing their grievances.

Group discussions create a mutual investment in the actions the members will take. Such discussions can include how serious the problem is and how much a solution is desired, what risks (both real and imaged) exist, and how the risks compare to the potential benefits. As members discuss issues and targets—finally making the decision to take action—they commit not only to the decision but to each other as well.

Even the obstacles normally faced during an organizing drive can be used to make people angry and compel them to act. As people see for themselves how the system operates and as targets subject members to various delaying and co-opting strategies, members' investment is reinforced.

A meeting with the target can often deepen people's sense of outrage, compelling them to further action. As targets resist members' demands, refrain from accepting responsibility, and patronize people, members' sense of outrage is fueled (Alinsky 1971). The contact no longer permits the target to retain a public face. Members now see the target in a clearer, more negative light, realize the confrontation is necessary and appropriate, and act more aggressively. In this technique it is the target, not the organizer, who is provocative.

The practice illustration below shows a committee meeting of a farm workers' organization. The group is planning a meeting with the chief executive of a food manufacturer to push for child care and health benefits for migrant workers. Here the organizer motivates members by using all the techniques of reflection: clarifying the importance of issues, agitating members' emotions, demystifying targets, and helping members learn from their exposure to the target.

PETER: I'm going to call the meeting to order now. We're here tonight to discuss our plan to ask for child care and health benefits from Cannonball Soups. Tony, can you report on the background of this issue?

TONY: Sure. We got started on this about six months ago. Most of you know that we don't have any benefits, and the thing that people want are places to leave their kids when they're out working and health coverage. Our national group is thinking that we have a good chance to get it here in New Jersey because the governor is sympathetic. If we get Cannonball to agree, than the other big ones will follow. Anyway, Bill Stokes is the chief guy here in New Jersey and we sent him a letter asking him about these benefits and told him we wanted to meet. About a month ago we sat down with one of his V.P.s, Blake Yardley, and he said he didn't know nothing, couldn't do anything. He said he would talk to Stokes about us. So now we need to decide what to do next.

PETER: OK, so now what are we going to do?

ORGANIZER: (I wanted them to remember what the meeting with Yardley was like, how humiliated they had been, and how they had been diverted. I wanted them to feel angry about the way they had been treated so I decided to agitate a little here.) Hold on a minute, Peter. Maybe we ought to talk a little bit about that last meeting. How do people think it went?

TONY: I thought it went alright. Yardley was really nice and all. He just couldn't do anything for us. He was the wrong person.

ORGANIZER: Well, if he was the wrong person, why did Stokes send him to meet with us? Do you think they knew he couldn't do anything?

ROSA: That's what I thought. Why am I here wasting my time?

ORGANIZER: Good question, Rosa. Why does Cannonball waste our time like that? They knew what we wanted from our letter. Why did they send that goon? Don't they think we have better things to do?

ROSA: Right. Why did they send him?

ORGANIZER: Why do you think they sent him?

PETER: I think they sent him to try to confuse us. And he was so understanding and all, it did confuse us. He acted like he wanted to help but his hands were tied. It was hard for me to say anything then.

ORGANIZER: (I wanted now to agitate them a little more. I wanted them to feel personally insulted and ready to take on Bill Stokes.) I think that's just what he had in mind, Peter. He came all dressed up in his five hundred-dollar suit and he probably thought, "I'm meeting with a bunch of dumb farm workers. What do they know? I'll just be real nice, promise nothing, and they'll go away."

ROSA: And we fell for it too. We may be farm workers, but we're not dumb. We shouldn't let him do that to us.

ORGANIZER: (Now I wanted to remind them of the importance

of the issue for us. I wanted to point out the contrast between these executives and our people). You know we're just as good as he is. The reason he can afford to buy a five hundred-dollar suit is because of us. You can bet he has childcare and health benefits. He doesn't have to leave his kids for twelve straight hours while he's out breaking his back picking tomatoes. When his kid gets sick he can take him to a doctor. No wonder he can act sweet.

TONY: That's right. He has benefits. And come to think of it, what did he do for us other than promise to talk to Stokes?

ORGANIZER: (Now I had to make the connection between Yardley and Stokes. We had to take Stokes on next, and I wanted them angry at him and ready to handle him differently.) You know, it seems to me that this is all Stokes's fault. He sent Yardley. Yardley is nothing but a dumb flunky. Stokes thought, "Let me send my man, Blake. He can't do anything, and they'll be off my back."

ROSA: Right, it's Stokes's fault. We need to talk to Stokes because he makes the decisions, right? We don't want to have the wrong guy again.

ORGANIZER: That's right, Rosa. He's the head of Cannonball here in New Jersey. He makes the decisions here.

PETER: So let's set up a meeting with Stokes.

ORGANIZER: Okay, but what did we learn from meeting with Blake the Flake that we want to do differently with Wild Bill Stokes? (Here I was making fun of the Cannonball people, I was bringing them down to size. But I also wanted them to remember the lessons of the Yardley meeting.)

PETER: One thing I learned is not to be swayed by how sweet they are to us.

ORGANIZER: If we don't get what we want, then they're not sweet.

ROSA: Right. And don't let them talk down to us.

TONY: It's so hard. We get in the room, and they use all that big language and stuff, and they act like they know everything. I just feel smaller and smaller.

ORGANIZER: That's true, Tony. It's hard to remember that they're no better than you are. Sometimes it helps to remember that they are human just like us. They put on their pants one leg at a time. They sleep, eat, and pee just like us, five

hundred-dollar suits or not. How about if when we plan the
meeting, we role-play it? I'll be Wild Bill Stokes and you'll try
to take me on.

ROSA: That sounds real good. I want to be prepared.

Of course, group discussions and preparation, like the one above,
are not always possible. It is common that people will first attend a
large action, like the meeting planned with Cannonball's chief executive. If these "first timers" are not prepared, they may wonder why
members are so angry and why leaders are behaving impolitely to the
target. There are two approaches to mitigating this problem. People
can be asked to come to the action earlier than the target, so leaders
can explain the history of the situation to the newcomers—the strategy
thus far, how the target has reacted previously, what the risks are, how
the action has been planned, and the intended goals. Many organizers
also use "fact sheets" to bring newcomers on board. For example, an
organization working on environmental hazards was planning a major
meeting with the state commissioner on occupational hazards. The
headline of their fact sheet read *WANTED* in big bold letters, and
underneath there was a picture of the commissioner. The flyer also
gave information on the group's many attempts to meet with him, his
refusal to issue new hazard guidelines, and his record while in office.
It was a quick and dramatic way of informing people who would attend a meeting of the organization for the first time.

We have mentioned several reflection techniques, and essentially all
have a single goal—to help people see their situation as unfair, unjust,
and holding the potential for change. Yet, even if people truly grasp
the injustice of a situation, they may feel incapable of challenging it.
Members' feelings of powerlessness and incompetence make it essential that the organizer work to alter their vision of themselves.

Vision

Henderson and Thomas write,

> Vision follows on from reflection—increased consciousness of me-
> in-this-situation can lead to a vision of me-in-another-situation in
> the future. Effective action is contingent upon local people being
> able to conceive of themselves as "new" people—a conception of
> themselves working at tasks, taking on roles and exercising skills
> and knowledge in ways previously unimaginable to them. . . . The
> worker's task, then, is to develop in people a capacity for visionary

thought, to help them cross what Freire has called "the frontier which separates being from being more."

(Henderson and Thomas 1980b:116)

Whereas reflection techniques focus on helping members *see the situation differently*, vision techniques help people *see themselves differently*—as capable and competent agents for change. Vision techniques include: building confidence, identifying and helping members perform tasks that they can competently handle, and skills training.

Though Henderson and Thomas refer to role modeling as a basic motivational technique, few organizers seem to do it. Clearly, organizers believe that demonstrating tasks has limited effectiveness in motivating members to do them. In fact, when organizers ask people to "do as I do," people may become more inactive. As one leader said, "When I see my organizer do something, it looks so easy, and I could never do it as well. We are better off when he does it. I'll only mess it up." Offering vision requires other techniques.

Confidence Building The most often employed visionary technique is confidence building. Organizers may call this technique "cheerleading," as they remind people what capacities they have and what they have accomplished. Organizers tell members that the talents and skills necessary for organizing already exist within them.

Organizers can help members discover their own talents, skills, and competencies by showing them success rather than telling them about it. They help people experience the successful performance of a task. As a member's confidence grows, the organizer gradually expands the range of opportunities and the level of responsibility in the activities undertaken. People develop a vision of what they can accomplish.

Frequently as members become more involved in organizing, they are interested in education and training for their advocacy roles. When people are ready, interested, and have some experience to reflect on, the organizer can directly teach people the techniques of advocacy. The goal of the training is to help members consciously increase their skills as change agents. Training sessions may be structured as leadership development seminars, but they are equally as effective if done informally throughout the organizing process. As people hold practice sessions, role-play what they will do, and constructively criticize their fellow members, they become conscious about the skills needed to organize. By accepting small parts in an action and practicing them, people are less overwhelmed. Their individual responsibility has been partialized into a small, achievable act. The following illustration shows an organizer for an unemployed workers' group practicing to meet with the president of a development corporation. The group is seeking an agreement that 150 jobs be reserved for unemployed workers. Notice the careful attention to every detail of the meeting, and how the organizer builds the confidence of leaders and rehearses them for their roles as a form of training.

> ORGANIZER: Okay, so let's run through the meeting. We all agreed about who would do what. Tim, you're chairing it. John, you're going to make the demand for the jobs. Judy, you said you would handle his response and make sure he keeps to his time. I'll play Al Silver, and we'll see how it goes. Anytime you want, let's stop and see how we're doing with it. I'll also help when you get stuck. Okay?
>
> TIM: Okay, I'm ready. Is Patrick going to greet Silver and bring him up to the stage?
>
> ORGANIZER: What do you think, Patrick? Do you want to do that?
>
> PATRICK: Okay.
>
> ORGANIZER: You're probably going to have to watch him, Pat. He won't want to come up on the stage, and you'll have to guide him. Do you know what he looks like so you can snag him when he comes in?
>
> PATRICK: Yeah I know him. I'll stand right at the door and wait for him.
>
> TIM: Okay. So, I'll be on the stage and Patrick will sit him down next to me. Then what? Do I start?
>
> ORGANIZER: I think you'll have to watch for a signal from Stan. We want to make sure that our people are here before we start, so it depends when Silver comes.
>
> TIM: Are we all on the stage then?
>
> JUDY: I think we should all be up there then.
>
> ORGANIZER: Okay. So now we're ready to start the meeting. Tim, you go to the mike, and . . .
>
> TIM: So I go up to the mike and I say, "Glad everybody could make it tonight to this meeting of the Unemployed People's Project. UPP has been fighting for jobs for unemployed people and we are meeting tonight with Al Silver to see if we can get some jobs in the Bell's Point Development Project."
>
> ORGANIZER: How does that sound to you folks? Do you know

enough about Silver and enough about UPP from Tim's introduction?

JOHN: I think you should say more, Tim. Tell about the Bell's
Point Project and who Al Silver is, and what we've done to
get him here.

TIM: I think I should, but I don't know enough about it. I didn't
do the research on Bell's Point.

ORGANIZER: Well, Stan knows the Bell's Point stuff inside out.
Do you think he ought to give a "history of Bell's Point" talk?

TIM: Yeah, that would be good. Okay, Stan?

STAN: I could do that. I'll say how the city proposed the idea,
and the bidding process. And I'll say how many jobs are proposed in construction and in the long run.

TIM: Could you also tell about Silver?

STAN: Yeah. I'll tell about Silver's other projects and how many
jobs were produced and who was hired.

TIM: OK. Then I'll introduce Silver.

ORGANIZER: That sounds really good, Stan. We can work on
your speech later to be sure we get all the details down. But,
Tim, I'm not sure you want to introduce Silver right away.
What might happen if he gets the mike right away?

JUDY: He might start talking and never give the mike back.

ORGANIZER: Right. I think we might want to be a little more in
control. How about if John then makes his statement and the
demand for jobs?

JOHN: OK. I think that's better. Then he has to answer us rather
than make his own speech. So I'll read this speech which I
wrote, which is about the loss of jobs in the Bronx and the
unemployment rate and how many jobs are estimated for
Bell's Point and what kind of jobs they are. (John reads the
speech.)

ORGANIZER: That's really great, John. You hit all the points, and
its a pretty emotional speech. That should really be great. Do
you feel comfortable with it?

JOHN: Well, I did it last time.

ORGANIZER: And you were great then. Sounds terrific. So, then,
how will you ask for the jobs?

JOHN: I'll just say, "What do you have to say, Mr. Silver?"

ORGANIZER: Okay, now I'll play Silver. "Thank you all for inviting me here tonight. I grew up in the Bronx and I always like
to come back. I lived around the corner from here and it was

always a great place." (The organizer goes on for awhile and then stops.) What do you think?

JUDY: That's no good at all. He's totally off the subject.

ORGANIZER: Right. If you just ask what I have to say, I can say anything I want. I can talk my way right out of this. What's a better way for John to make the demand?

TIM: How about if John says, What do you have to say to our request?

ORGANIZER: OK, let's try that. Then I'll say, "I think jobs in the Bronx are important, you all need jobs. Everybody should have a job. Jobs are great. But, gee whiz, I don't know about my jobs. People have to be qualified, blah, blah, blah . . . these are hard jobs and I need good workers, and the unions, blah, blah, blah. I'd like to help, but . . .

JUDY: No good again. He's just rambling. So what can we do?

ORGANIZER: Well, what if we make it real simple for Silver? He can just answer "Yes, I'll commit 150 of the construction jobs to the Bronx unemployed." Or he could say "No, I won't do it."

TIM: So if we have a yes or no question, he can't ramble on.

ORGANIZER: Well, it's harder to. Let's play it out.

JOHN: OK, Mr. Silver. Will you reserve 150 construction jobs for the unemployed of the Bronx? Yes or no?

ORGANIZER: Well, that's a hard question to answer. I'd like to but I need to know who these people are, whether they're qualified and licensed, and how the unions feel. My people do the hiring, I don't really get into that. If good people apply, I'm sure they'll be hired . . . blah, blah, blah. Okay, what do you do now? He's still rambling on, he's not committing, and he hasn't really answered your question. Judy, this is your part.

JUDY: I don't know. What should I do?

STAN: Well you have to stop him.

ORGANIZER: One thing you can do, Tim, is to give him a number of minutes for his response. Tell him he has two minutes to answer John's question. That way Judy can interrupt if he goes on too long.

TIM: OK. I'll make myself a note to step in after John's finished and tell Silver he has two minutes to answer.

JUDY: Then I watch my watch, and interrupt when the time's up. Then what?

ORGANIZER: What do you want to say then, Judy?

JUDY: I can say he hasn't answered our question.

ORGANIZER: Yes, that's good, Judy. You can repeat it. "Are you saying yes or no, Mr. Silver?"

JUDY: Okay. You haven't answered our question, Mr. Silver. Yes or no?

ORGANIZER: Well, I'm trying to answer. This job thing is very complicated. It involves . . . .

JUDY: No, it's not complicated Mr. Silver. It requires a simple yes or no answer. We can work out the details later.

ORGANIZER: That's great, Judy! You've really got him now.

OTHERS: That's terrific, Judy! Go get him!

ORGANIZER: Now how about if we have an agreement to sign right then and there. He can sign that he'll do it right away.

JUDY: Yes. We should have the whole thing written up so I can ask him to sign.

STAN: Great, great!

ORGANIZER: Great, so now we know how it goes. Just remember, Tim, Stan, Judy, you've got to help each other. There's only one question: yes or no. OK (all agree)? Now we have some other things to work on, too. We need to decide what we'll do if he doesn't come or if he sends someone else or if he refuses to sign. We have to talk about how to set up the room and who will handle the press. This is going to be great. We're going to be fine!

JUDY: Yeah, this is going to be fun!

Vision techniques complement reflection techniques as they are geared to changing members' perceptions of themselves. Together, they help members reevaluate their world and their place in it. Yet even as members reframe their visions of themselves and their circumstances, they still may not be ready to take the risks associated with action. Consequently organizers need to find ways of reducing members' fears.

Reducing the Fear of Risk Taking Even when there is unlikely to be any danger involved, people are often afraid to act (Gaventa 1980). Much of their fear is related to the fear of embarrassment, of "standing out" in one's group, of seeming "radical." Many people fear the loss of status and prestige that protest may bring. At the base of most people's unwillingness to take action is the fear of social embarrassment.

When people are already nervous all kinds of possible current and future sanctions are imagined. Even the staunchest supporter may be shaken at times. Frequently targets will make implicit threats that will further exacerbate members' fear. For example, a planned student action at a state university was uncovered by the dean, who promptly distributed a university document on the rules of conduct for protest. Despite the fact that the students' plans included nothing prohibited in the document, a wave of fear swept through the group, and several leaders urged a more modest protest.

Finally, some organizations ask members to take positions and be vocal on issues that truly make them vulnerable to possible retaliation. People who perform acts of civil disobedience are in jeopardy of arrest. People who confront their landlords can be evicted. It is not unknown for people who have made demands on city officials to find that their homes are suddenly reassessed. Openly attacking drug dealers in a neighborhood may jeopardize one's physical safety.

Organizers must recognize these fears as normative, and consider their effect when they urge people to action. A number of techniques help to reduce people's fears and counteract people's reticence to action. They are employed to mitigate the uncertainties, passivity, and caution that people normally bring.

Creating an Organizational Culture As we said earlier, most people fear "being different," being embarrassed in front of friends and kin who may frown upon their activism. In order to counteract their fears the organizer works to build an organizational culture with norms and values that support an individual's activism. The organization becomes a new and supportive peer group—a place where people feel liked and respected for their views and actions. As the group coalesces, as people enjoy doing their work together, they find support and encouragement for their individual actions. Their activism no longer seems strange and "radical."

The principle organizers use is a simple one: make the work fun. They find ways of making tedious work pleasurable, and they attempt to provide an informal office ambiance of parties and celebrations where relationships can develop. Parties, singing, and telling "war stories" are all consciously structured into organizational work and events. The tactics themselves should include some humorous aspect that is funny to the people involved. All these methods are seen as ways to build the sense of "we-ness," to encourage participation, and to increase morale, energy, and enthusiasm. One organizer conscious about making events fun for people explains,

> You got to go with a really fun action which people can plan around and do lots of things. For example, they wanted to cut off air conditioning on subways and buses until it got to be 90 degrees outside the bus. So all of us came to the board meetings with fans, and while we discussed it we fanned ourselves. People loved that. We got into the papers and people loved seeing their picture. They really like giving the transit authority a shot back since we get a shot everyday from the transit authority. Once we auctioned off the Exxon building for nonpayment of transit taxes, a big monopoly card. And there's lots of things for people to do through those events—from calling up people to come to preparing banners and materials. You want to provide a lot of different opportunities to do work, to be together, and to have fun.

A sense of comaraderie, fellowship, and shared belief in the cause or issue can be fostered in more serious ways. Organizers consciously try to develop an organizational culture that gives meaning to the work and establishes mutual commitment among those who carry it out. For example, organizers using the parish ministry approach have sometimes held celebrations in churches and synagogues where the liturgy is applied to the work of the organization. Nonsectarian events such as "Nights of Harmony" can also be used. In both instances the organization affords individuals a new frame of reference, a place where their values are nurtured rather than seen as aberrant.

Reducing the Power of Threats Perceived threats frequently scare people into inaction. In fact, most of what people imagine will never occur. One leader tells the story of debating whether or not to join a highly publicized action, one in which she was to have a leading role. She had just accepted a job with an advertising firm, and was worried how she would be viewed by her new employer. She decided to go ahead anyway. The story was widely covered in the press and included her picture. She arrived at her new job to find that her picture was on the company bulletin board, and to her surprise, she was widely lauded for her efforts.

Knowing that people are afraid, organizers should elicit from members all the things they think could happen. As people expose and share their fears with others, the fears cease to have the same strength.

Such discussions are best held in groups so that peers who are less reluctant can counteract their friends' reservations. If the organizer is alone in urging action, fearful individuals will experience that as being "pressured" to do what they don't want to do. When the encouragement comes from others in like situations, it is easier for members to accept their fears as unfounded.

There are times when a target will make an implicit threat. On these occasions the organizer needs to be more active. At the very least, organizers can recognize that people are afraid and may indeed be vulnerable. The organizer can point out the threat, question the target's behavior, suggest that it is once again an indication of the target's intransigence. By reframing the target's action, the organizer creates indignation at the behavior. Again, peer groups can be helpful. One or two members are likely to be outraged, and they are often effective in supporting a more fearful member.

Dealing with Retaliation Even after taking all precautions, retaliation is possible. Police may make arrests and landlords may evict. But when targets do retaliate, they have, in fact, begun to give people more reason for their grievance. Although retaliation frightens people, it can also confirm their initial impressions and harden their resolve.

Nonetheless, as much as possible members should be protected from retaliation. Private acts of defiance—such as writing a letter to or having a discussion with a target—give the target information about who is involved and what they are concerned about. Consequently, the target can respond surreptitiously and punitively to these grievances. On the other hand, when the protest is public and exposed it is more difficult for the target to retaliate because of an individual's involvement in the protest. After all, the right to free speech is respected and respectable, and blatant retaliatory actions will be seen as unjust and vindictive. The media's presence is critical, because it publicly documents the target's behavior and makes it difficult for him or her to do things that would look vindictive. Thus, the public nature of protest protects individual protesters.

It is also easier to retaliate against an individual than a group of people. A landlord will find it easier to evict one family than twenty. There is safety in numbers. As the number of people expands, the target's ability to retaliate individually and quietly decreases. Consequently, as many people should be involved in an action as possible. For example, one person should not be asked to meet with a target and make demands. Instead, a large group of members—preferably at least fifty—should attend the meeting and a number of people should be prepared to speak and handle negotiations. The organizer works with members to enhance peer support, helping members to share the risk and step forward for one another so no one has all the burden. The organizer helps the group recognize verbal and nonverbal clues, which may signify that a fellow member is in trouble or that the group has become divided, and offers ideas (like the use of a caucus) that members can use "on the spot" to prevent problems. One organizer reports this story,

> When we were organizing legal secretaries and paralegals they couldn't come forward about the grievances in their own firm or they would have been fired. We had to figure out a way to make the grievances public without endangering their jobs. What we did was set up a legal committee, and the secretaries would protest at each other's firm. The partners couldn't find the "leak" and they couldn't fire all their help. Yet they had women at their doorstep and quoted in the press telling all their secrets. It worked beautifully and protected the women from losing their jobs.

Meetings and activities, too, can be planned in a way that minimizes the target's power and strengthens the power of members. The goal is to create situations familiar and comfortable for members and uncomfortable for targets. Here organizers talk about holding meetings on the organization's own turf, packing a room with people so the target cannot leave until the meetings is over, and controlling the content and process of agendas—nitty-gritty details that help people feel more confident and make risk taking easier. One organizer says about this approach,

> It makes things a lot easier when the director of economic development came up to our office, where our people had been meeting regularly, rather than for us to go down to the World Trade Center where we can't find them and they can call the police. So we set up a public meeting and the official doesn't get to speak until much later. He has to respond to what we're asking for and he can't leave until we're through. With the cameras rolling, he can't do whatever he wants. He has to be on his best behavior.

We have described numerous techniques organizers use to motivate and help people take action. What we have tried to stress throughout is how organizers need not be visible or responsible for all action tasks. Instead, they can consciously motivate people and help them to take their own action. The organizer must remember that it is very difficult for people to take aggressive stances; they need to be motivated and helped to do things that are so unfamiliar to them. Finally, the motivation and help must be constant. During an organizing campaign members' emotions will fluctuate. They will feel exhilarated and depressed, brave and frightened. The organizer must continually provide the kind of support and assistance people need to act, must make certain that at least some members are enthused at all times, and, finally, must enjoin members to help each other when they feel low and frightened.

CHAPTER EIGHT

Evaluating Outcomes: Victory and Defeat

Throughout the previous two chapters we have documented the process by which members and leaders painstakingly choose issues, select strategy, and carry out activities. The issues of social action organizations vary: utility pay rates, the right to abortion, housing and welfare entitlements, changes in voting regulations, reformulating foreign policy, and disarmament. Each issue can generate competing factions, with very powerful actors in opposition to the organization's goals. Thus, the efforts of these organizers and leaders—which are often carried out over years by people who volunteer time and energy—must always be reviewed in the context of how very difficult it is to make change. At the same time progressive social action organizations must, at least occasionally, succeed in making change and/or be perceived as succeeding in making change. Success is crucial to the health of an organization. Winning or seeming to win breeds confidence and raises morale among members, attracts new adherents, publicity, and funding, and enhances the aura of the organization's power in the eyes of other current or future opponents. Consequently, organizational success is of sufficient importance to an organizing enterprise to warrant detailed attention.

The subject entails a particular dilemma for organizers and leaders. Making instrumental change is a daunting task (Brager and Specht 1969, Haggstrom 1969, Schwartz 1969), difficult to measure (Key, Hudson, and Armstrong 1976). And it is difficult to determine exactly what caused the change (Piven and Cloward 1977). Yet, in order to remain vital in the eyes of members, the public, and power holders, the organization must somehow convince them that it is, indeed, successful. As sportswriters say, "Nothing puts fannies in the seats like winning."

Many authors focus solely on the objective reality of instrumental success. That is, they debate the potential for social action organizations to make change or the relative significance of the victories they do achieve. We believe that while instrumental achievement is important, the subjective nature of success—i.e., how the organizers and leaders of social action organizations define, understand, and manipulate it—is equally so. What interests us is the way in which organizers and leaders redefine success, reframe the meaning of winning, and find ways of convincing others that they have, indeed, succeeded at their efforts. We begin by exploring the various definitions of success, then proceed to describe how the variety of accomplishments are evaluated, how important success is in each area to leaders and organizers, and how leaders and organizers cope with the gap between goals and achievement. We also outline how organizations communicate their accomplishments to members and the public.

The Definition of Success

The question of what constitutes success in social action organizing is one that has plagued social action analysts and practitioners. Some authors have used only environmental change as an indicator of success (Piven and Cloward 1977), some only expressive indicators such as leadership development (Ross 1967), and others have used both instrumental and expressive criteria (Brager and Specht 1973, Warren 1977). We would agree that both instrumental and expressive ends must be achieved.

We posit that there are four types of achievements to which social action organizations aspire: making instrumental environmental changes, developing leadership, developing the organization's resources and capacities, and enhancing the public's awareness of the organization and its issues. For us the accomplishment of instrumental change refers to the ability of the organization to achieve its substantive goals, i.e., to secure the changes on issues the organization pursues. Successful leadership development refers to an ever expanding number of members who are increasingly able to articulate a different vision of the world and themselves, one in which they see themselves as having the right to raise issues and the power to change their situation. Members are also increasingly competent in managing the complex decisions and tasks associated with issue identification, strategy development, and implementation. Effective organizational development refers to an ever expanding number of active members, fiscal solvency, and greater recognition by constituents that the organization does, in fact, represent their views and interests. Effective public awareness refers to increased positive media coverage, increased awareness in the general community of the organization's work, and changed public attitudes that reflect increasingly greater support for the organization's goals.

Organizers consider these accomplishments both separately and together. Each type of accomplishment can and should be monitored and, if possible, measured during every activity the organization undertakes. Yet, while accomplishment is necessary in each area, no one area is sufficient to describe the degree of overall success of an organization. In order to evaluate overall success accomplishment in each area must be examined in relation to all other areas. For example, as an organization develops effectively, as leaders develop, and as public exposure and legitimacy increase, the ability of an organization to effect change on identified issues should also increase. Over time, as instrumental ends are achieved, leadership, the organization's resources, and public awareness should be strengthened. Taken together, achievement in these areas should indicate both the organization's success rate and its ability to keep winning (Boyte 1980, 1989, Boyte, Booth, and Max 1986, Knoepfle 1990). While each goal has its own separate evaluation questions, problems, and measures of effectiveness, all are also interdependent.

Effective Instrumental Change

What most organizers mean by victory is the achievement of the instrumental goals set forth by an organization. This emphasis on instrumental outcomes also appears frequently in the literature, where many analysts are concerned with the degree to which and how often social action organizations meet their change objectives. Change can then be measured by comparing the organization's issue goals with results. Piven and Cloward (1977) rely solely on instrumental indicators. They ask only one question: To what extent was a desired change achieved? For example, a state women's organization that promotes the enactment of the Equal Rights Amendment can be evaluated by whether or not the amendment is ratified by the state legislature. An organization that works on voting registration can evaluate how many states have passed legislation making it easier for people to register to vote.

For a number of reasons achieving instrumental success is of primary importance to most organizers and, to a greater extent, to leaders. First, instrumental success achieves the organization's objectives and attains the individual benefits that members want and need. Not only are people helped through the change, but their self-interest in being members of the organization is reinforced. Accomplishing goals has a special urgency for organizers who work with minority, low-income and working-class constituencies. Such members may have difficulty sustaining their involvement if no results are forthcoming. In these cases the organization's issues are directly related to member needs (e.g., shelter for the homeless, increasing the cash base of welfare grants, redirecting subsidies for public housing), and success will directly and immediately improve the lives of members.

Achieving instrumental results underscores the effectiveness of organizing and working as a group. The victory is an acknowledgment of the efficacy of organizational unity. Beyond confirming individual self-interest, the achievement builds group morale, institutes a sense of pride and confidence in the group that accomplished the change, and reinforces the organization as a positive reference group. Leaders also learn through accomplishment; they gain new skills and new perspectives on change. They realize they are not incompetent or powerless; they can effectively make change happen. Success enhances leadership status, collective self-interest, and enthusiasm for the organization that brought them such good fortune.

Instrumental victories also attract new members, keep current members enthused and motivated, and lift morale. If an organization consistently fails to achieve its agenda, members become demoralized, question the purpose of their involvement, and frequently withdraw their participation. New people are unlikely to respond to the recruiting attempts of an organization that is known for "lost causes," and neither the press nor the public will be much interested in its activities.

Finally, successful instrumental change in one area often breeds change in other areas. The organization gets to be known as "a winner," accruing power and prestige in the eyes of other current or future opponents. Recognizing the organization as tenacious and influential, targets may choose to concede rather than fight. As one organizer told us,

We got to be known as a savvy and relentless organization. We got press, we had friends, we didn't back down, and we won. Got to be that all we had to do was make a phone call and we got what we wanted. A leader would say, "I'm calling from Northwest Bronx, and we want you to fix these potholes," and the city would be out the next day. Now that has its problems because it can make our leaders lazy. But on the whole I'd rather be in that situation than be seen as a losing organization which can be ignored.

Yet, it is not easy for social action organizations to realize instrumental success. Even the best efforts may not counteract other economic and social trends. The effects of an organization's activities may not be immediately recognizable. In the case of community groups that work to stabilize low-income housing or women's groups that try to elect female candidates, data that supports the achievement of their efforts may not become available for years. Moreover, in a formal study the organization's activities may not explain much of the variance. That is, the stability of low-income neighborhood housing and the election of females depend on various factors, many of them beyond the purview of the organization.

Even when success occurs and outcomes are measurable the changes don't always have the desired effect on the organization and its members. Goal achievement doesn't necessarily translate into a change in the lives of people. For example, increased access to voter registration does not necessarily mean that more people will register to vote. Nor does passage of an amendment to protect equal rights for women inevitably mean that women will be treated as equal to men. Consequently, "success" doesn't always correspond with change, and members may not feel the effect of their victory. This, too, may lead to demoralization.

Even when results are achieved, there is always ambiguity about who should "get credit" for the change. The media almost never attributes a victory to the efforts of a social action organization, at least not at the time it is won. Power holders, speaking through the media, will often say that the change was already in the planning stages or was, in fact, made at their initiative. Or they may credit another organization, one more socially acceptable, with influencing their decision. Historians focusing on "change from above" are likely to credit politicians and other public actors with the achievement. For example, many recent books describe the process that culminated in the passage of the civil rights amendment (Branch 1988, Freeman 1983, Garrow

1986). Each has a different perspective on what factors caused the change and the roles various organizations and personalities played in the change. Of course, whether or not an organization receives credit for making a change is critical to its image as a legitimate, powerful, effective group. Though members, leaders, and organizers may share an understanding that the organization is responsible for the change, the lack of public recognition can be demoralizing and harmful to the organization's search for legitimacy.

Despite these difficulties, there is much organizers can do to control, redefine, and manipulate organizational outcomes. To keep the organization strong and its members and leaders enthused they must redefine success, reframe what it is to win, and find ways of convincing members and others that an organization has, indeed, succeeded in its efforts.

One way organizers redefine success is by partializing goals so people get a feeling of accomplishment throughout a campaign. They set out these smaller goals as they plan strategy, point to each small accomplishment, and hold debriefing sessions in which the effect of the tactic and next steps are discussed. Smaller outcomes, such as getting a meeting with the target, are stressed as successes, offsetting the impact the possible lack of progress on instrumental change may have on the morale of members. These small advances keep people motivated and edge the organization closer and closer to its ultimate goal. As one organizer says,

> We try to show that each step is a victory. We wanted jobs committed to the people of the South Bronx by the Port Authority. We say, "See, you got a meeting with the Port Authority personnel. That's a victory. Our big goal is to get the jobs and this is a step." Then we get an assemblyman introducing a bill, and we say, "We're really doing good." Each meeting is a little victory on the way to the big one.

Organizers are careful to point out that these small accomplishments can be seen as harbingers of the future. The small achievement has significance for what it will mean in the next struggle—the next round. People come to expect that there will be another opportunity for change, that they can, in effect, force the opportunity for change, and that their efforts can ultimately be successful. These organizers generally share the view of Brager and Specht, who write, "We believe that modest achievements have, in accumulation, the potential for contributing to larger-scale change. They raise expectations, thus generating pressure for further activity and contributing to a social climate in which alterations in policy and program become possible" (Brager and Specht 1973:59).

Further, as people assess what was gained and what is left to do after each activity, they can correct and reformulate their plans so as to increase the organization's chance for success. In the debriefing sessions organizers help leaders not only to recognize the process that may lead to success but also to calculate and predict what their actions might bring. In the illustration below an organizer for a pro-choice group talks about preparing leaders to target key state legislators who will soon consider a new restrictive abortion bill. In debriefing sessions the organizer stresses the need to look at alternatives, to get a clear sense of the target's reactions, and the importance of planning next steps.

The restrictive abortion legislation was being proposed by State Senator Barnes, a real right-winger. If passed, the legislation would be the most restrictive in the country. And we're a moderate state, so we were worried about what it would mean nationally. So my work with the leadership was to figure out how best to influence those legislators who sat on the fence. First we sat down and made a list of the twenty-three who we thought might be persuaded to vote against the bill. Then we researched each representative. We found out who contributed to their campaigns, who voted for them, what churches they belonged to, who their friends were, what clubs they belonged to. Then for each one we mapped out a plan to influence them. For some we had church women and ministers visit them. For others, we took constituents to their office. For others, we had women in their own party. After every contact, we would have a debriefing session to review their reaction. If they were noncommittal, we asked ourselves what other pressure could be brought to bear. At the same time we were asking ourselves what else we could do. If we didn't have the votes, should we send busloads of women to the capitol? Should we threaten a national boycott of the state's cheese, our largest industry, before or after the vote? Should we start a campaign against the reelection of certain legislators? So we mapped it out, how many legislators, how to best influence them, what type of follow-up we should do with them, and when to use demonstrations and boycotts. With each legislator, we had a plan: if they responded X, we would do Y and Z, and if they responded A, we did B and C. And we had an overall plan. Before the vote, we would announce we would work to defeat Barnes and Zimbast and Henry, our three major opponents in the legislature. Every day for a week before the vote we would take busloads of women from different parts of the state to visit their legislators so they would see it was a statewide effort. Finally, if the vote passed, we would call for the boycott. And we met constantly—every week at least—to see how our plan was going and make the necessary changes. The bill passed the legislature. We met to debrief on the vote, and decided to use our boycott plan. Finally, the governor vetoed the bill. It was the threat of the boycott that did it.

When an organization is successful it is important that the organizations take credit for the achievement, making certain that both members and the general community are aware that the organization is responsible for the change. By communicating the organization's successes, the organization becomes known both within its community and outside it as a "winner."

Organizational success must be identified, discussed, and celebrated within the organization, reinforcing members' enthusiasm for and sense of pride in the organization. Whenever possible organizers should encourage that the organization's successes be discussed at meetings, that "victory parties" celebrating accomplishments be held, and media reports be shared with members. At a minimum, the organization should produce a lively newsletter that announces and celebrates organizational victories and keeps people updated on campaigns in progress. Many organizations keep scrapbooks of their newspaper stories and video tapes of news coverage. These can be displayed and replayed for members' enjoyment, increasing the status of the individual members whose names or pictures appear. At least annually an organizational "scorecard" can be tallied and given to both members and the press.

Externally, the organization must conduct a vigorous and permanent struggle to counter the target's claims and the media's assertions about who is responsible for the change, reaffirming that the organization's efforts were behind the victory. Leaders and organizers should work with members of the media so that their reports also reflect that the organization is responsible for the change. By making activities interesting, writing press releases, following up with telephone contact, and having members make themselves generally available and "quotable" to reporters, the organization can gain media attention and have influence on the slant of stories. All newspaper articles should be compiled and sent regularly to funding sources, politicians, community institutions, and other appropriate individuals. Social action organizations also keep updated "victory lists" that detail all their accomplishments and can also be disseminated regularly. A long victory list that enumerates the successes over years can present impressive data about the organization's effectiveness. By distributing such material the organization's reputation is enhanced among the constituency and in the eyes of power holders.

No matter the skill of the organizer or the competency of the organization and its members, there will always be times when the organization is defeated, when the issue that has prompted so much activity is lost. There are other times when the odds seem insurmountable and the campaign so protracted that members become demoralized. In these cases it may be too costly to continue the organizing campaign. However, such occasional losses need not be devastating to an organization. Morale of current members and reputation in the community will not be destroyed when an organization that succeeds regularly faces the occasional defeat. Such losses can and should be handled within the organization, redefined, and seen in perspective.

The organizer's ability to help people cope with the defeat is critical. In most cases the organization has achieved some small concession in which people can take comfort. By reviewing the struggle with members, reminding them of the intractability of the opposition and the overwhelming economic and political forces that were at odds with the organization's work, members can often come to take pride in the small concession they did win. In the same way, as the organization announces its small victory externally, through the media or in its own newsletters, the public is helped to focus on what the organization did accomplish, rather than what it did not. An organizer working on transportation explains this approach.

> We had been working on the subway fare a long time—over a year—trying to keep the fares stable. Because of the financial crisis it became increasingly clear that the MTA was going to raise the fare. The people were tired; they were beginning to see we couldn't win it. So we started to work on increasing corporate taxes, and were able to win that. The fare went up, but so did corporate taxes. And that's what the press reported, and that's what we talked to our people about. In that situation it was better for us to take half the loaf and declare it a victory. We didn't focus on what we lost. We focused on what we won.

There are rare occasions when organizers and leaders take on what they know to be lost causes, organizing on an issue despite the evident futility of their actions. There are times when members ardently support an issue, and are deeply invested in taking action on it despite knowing they are at a serious disadvantage. To retain the support of its members, to recognize members' rights to determine the organization's agenda, and to remain a legitimate representative of members' interests, the organization needs to take up the struggle. As one organizer says, "You've got to look at the costs on both sides: what it'll cost to be involved in it and what it'll cost in member support and public expectations not to be involved in it."

It is important to note that taking on a losing battle should occur infrequently. The organizer needs to be extremely cautious about asking people to invest their time, energy, and hopes in activities that are unlikely to succeed. Dashed hopes and expectations can easily turn into members' anger at an organizer for misleading them. One organizer tells this story:

> When I think about taking people into a losing fight, I remember Issac Singer's novel *Satan in Goray*. It's the story of an Orthodox Jewish community in Poland during the time of the messianic pretenders. The scriptures say when the Messiah comes all Jews will be magically transported to Jerusalem. So right before Passover, when a messenger comes through town proclaiming that the new messiah is on his way to Jerusalem, all the Jews sell their worldly goods and neglect their religious duties because they believe momentarily they'll be in the Holy City. On the eve of Passover, of course, the messenger returns to the town with the sad news that the pretender has been converted to Islam on his way. And they have destroyed their lives, their culture, for nothing. I've always contended that the real Messiah could go into that town today with a signed statement from God, and not one person would follow him. That's the moral of the story for me: Don't ever lead people blindly down a primrose path.

In cases where victory is unlikely it is incumbent upon the organizer to be extremely frank, sharing fully the improbability of success. The organizer must discuss with members the fact that the organization will be fighting for the principle, that the struggle will be difficult, and that the results will probably be unsatisfactory. People need to decide that organizing is worth their effort despite the poor prospects for instrumental success. While effecting instrumental change is extremely important to social action organizing, it is not the only criteria of success. Indeed, if outcomes are achieved, but there is no corresponding increase in membership or rise in the capacities and sense of potency of members or enhanced public respect, each subsequent organizing effort will be as difficult as the first. Each substantive success will have a greater organizational yield if it is used to enhance other accomplishments.

Effective Leadership Development

Achievement also needs to be viewed as enhanced leadership development. Success in this area is closely associated with the realization of what Brager and Specht (1973) call "sociotherapeutic goals." The term refers to the organization's ability to attract new members, teach them new skills, and give them an increasing sense of competency and power.

The relative success of an organization's leadership development activities also needs to be monitored (Mondros and Wilson 1986). Signs of success in this area include the fact that many members are involved in a particular activity—that significant numbers are new to the organization, are taking on leadership responsibilities, and are members who haven't taken on such responsibilities before. Also important is the organizer's assessment that people are more capable in making decisions and carrying tasks than they were before the campaign—that more people are more able to point to their own progress and competence. By carefully analyzing such data organizers can assess how successful their leadership development activities have been.

There is, of course, a relationship between instrumental outcomes and leadership development activities. Achievement of substantive outcomes has a positive effect on leaders. And, theoretically, as a greater number of people become competent leaders, victories are easier to achieve. Because leadership development and substantive change are related, organizers need to consider them together. That is, the number of people involved, the morale of members, and the degree of competence felt by leaders should suggest whether a "quick victory" is needed or a long difficult struggle can be endured. When people are new to organizing, a protracted struggle may be demoralizing, reinforcing members' beliefs about their own powerlessness. We argue that all new groups will need "quick victories" to increase involvement, prove to people that there is power in numbers, teach skills, and show people that they are competent to make change (Alinsky 1971, Von Hoffman 1966). Only later in its development, when the organization has proven its ability to achieve, can it afford to take on more protracted and difficult battles, in which there is some question about its ability to accomplish desired results. Questions whether or not to take up a campaign, however, last throughout the life of an organization and need careful attention from the organizer.

When organizers consider the pursuit of a particular issue they are essentially evaluating two things: 1. the difficulty of the campaign and 2. the impact a victory or failure will have on their leadership and membership.

As we described in chapter 6, estimating the likelihood of success is a process of examining goals, targets, and resources. Assessing the impact of a potential victory or failure on the membership involves assessing the degree of self-confidence of individual leaders and of the leadership group, the general morale of the membership, and the level of camaraderie in the organization.

In general, success is a boon to leaders and members, necessary when members feel insecure about their competence, doubt their ability to have an influence in changing their situation, or don't trust the potential of the organization to offer them help. In these cases a quick victory enhances self-esteem and confidence and underscores the importance of the organization. Victories are also helpful when group morale is sagging. If an organization has just ended a campaign where the outcome was less than satisfactory, members' enthusiasm may wane unless they succeed again relatively soon. Success is also important when members are engaged in internal conflicts. The existence of an outside opponent—one who can be easily vanquished by a unified organization—can be exploited as a way to mend fences quickly. In all of these instances the organizer will look for a "fixed fight," i.e., an issue that is relatively uncomplicated and easily won. One organizer tells this story:

> I had just taken a new organizing position and it was clear that the organization was in terrible shape. There had been a pretty serious internal struggle, and the last organizer had been fired. They weren't working on any issues, and people were pretty discouraged. I read in the paper that the city had just budgeted a lot of money for street sanitation, and it was fairly easy to go after that money. We started organizing around it, and in three months the city promised to use a good part of that money in the neighborhood. People were rejuvenated; all the old fire was back. We had developed some new leaders to take the place of the old, and new blocks had gotten involved. The importance of that organizing drive was not cleaner streets. It was that the organization was on its way again.

As membership grows and people feel more confident of their abilities, they grow more tolerant of some disappointments. They can tackle issues that are more complex and difficult to resolve. Their sense of power and competence no longer hangs on every issue, and they can accept a defeat every now and again. They have a common history and memory to sustain them.

In fact, when the organization's leadership and membership is strong and confident, it is incumbent on the organizer to encourage people to take on more complicated issues. Leaders can become complacent with the ease of success. They can choose to rest on their laurels, extolling past victories, and supporting only those issues where success is ensured. It is the organizer's responsibility to challenge such complacency, encouraging leaders to tackle bigger issues. An organizer working with a successful ten-year-old organization comments.

> It's easy for leaders to get overly contented. They begin to think they only have to pick up a phone to get things done. Sure, we organized around stop signs in the beginning, but I don't want to be known as the organization which does stop signs. I want people to be thinking about poverty and speculation and the defense budget. I want people to see the picture beyond their front door. I had that in mind when we started on the last big fight. People said, "Let's not do it. We can't win." And I confronted people on it. I said, "What's the good of being the heavyweight champion if you're always fighting bums? It's only good to have muscles if you're going to flex them."

Even when an issue can be easily and quickly won, it isn't always appropriate to take the path of least resistance. Organizational history may not have the same meaning for new members, who themselves haven't had the experience of identifying an issue and pursuing it against a target's resistance. They may refuse leadership roles, opting to rely on the organization's "sophisticated old guard." Or they may compare their fledgling attempts to organize to their more experienced counterparts and find themselves wanting. This only reinforces their own lack of confidence. Instead, it is important for the organizer to help newcomers go through their own process of goal attainment. They then become a new cadre with their own knowledge and history to which they can lay claim. An organizer describes his experience with such a group.

> The coalition has been around ten years, and we have a hell of a lot more influence now than we did then. If a problem comes up most

times we could probably just make a phone call and get it done. That presents a problem, because the organization can get fat and lazy, and we could easily become just a handful of people making phone calls. It would be tempting to cut off some of the leadership development procedures that got us here in the first place. There are some issues that we could win right now with about fifteen people sitting down and negotiating. We purposely avoid winning them like that because there's some new people who haven't had the responsibility, haven't done the learning, haven't felt the power of going through a struggle.

The potential for success and failure, then, needs to be considered in light of the state of the organization's leadership and membership. In order to help people make decisions and successfully experience the organization's accomplishments or lack of them, the organizer needs to be sensitive to members' feelings about themselves, each other, and the organization. Then, as an objective observer, the organizer can skillfully choose when to encourage an easy campaign, when to help people withstand and cope with a protracted one, and when to challenge members to stretch their vision.

Effective Organizational Development

Victory does not just benefit the members but increases the efficacy of the organization as well. Similar to Brager and Specht's (1973) understanding of integrative goals, successes strengthen the organization and make it more capable of pursuing its agenda for change. Accomplishments help the organization grow, increase legitimacy and recognition, spur funding, and convince the opposition of the organization's power. Members increasingly see the organization as the legitimate representative of their needs and as a mechanism for achieving their goals. At the same time, others take note of the organization and are impressed by its achievements. For example, when the nomination of a supreme court justice who was antagonistic to their views was successfully defeated, national women's and abortion rights groups benefitted from a tremendous increase in membership, contributions, and media recognition.

There are a host of indicators that suggest positive organizational development. Numbers of new members, name recognition of the organization within and outside the community, an increase in dues or grants received are all signs of organizational development. Even public attacks by politicians and efforts to jeopardize the organization's funding can actually be indicators of the organization's strength. Power holders are unlikely to direct their attention toward ineffective organizations, and, as one organizer says, "Retaliation is a badge of honor."

One of the most positive signs of an organization's development is that, as an organization's reputation precedes it, the coffers and doors of funders and public officials more speedily open. Funders want to see a track record, and are more willing to give money to organizations that have name recognition, respect, and achievements to show. Politicians—always looking for votes—will seek the endorsement of successful groups. Other groups will seek alliances.

Significantly, power holders, too, begin to recognize the organization as a formidable force, one of the very few groups that cannot be ignored or thwarted. Recognizing the organization's power, targets will often concede to an organization's wishes rather than become embroiled in a damaging public battle. An organizer describes the moment she recognized the level to which her women's office workers' organization had developed:

> We had been around about five years and done a lot of work on job descriptions, office safety, job discrimination, and, especially, sexual harassment. We got a lot of national press on the sexual harassment stuff. We had a victory list about eight pages long, and it seemed like every progressive foundation wanted to fund us. We decided to take on pay equity, and to start with state government because there had been some success in Washington on it. We met with the city commissioner of human rights, and right away she said she'd work with us. She wanted to give us money to study the problem and make recommendations to their department. I mean she had her checkbook open. We'd said we'd do it, but with no promises that we'd back off if they didn't accept the findings. She said that was fine, they just didn't want her department to be humiliated by us the way some others had been. She joked that we struck fear in her heart. But I also knew that things don't come so easily unless it is somewhat true.

Instrumental successes clearly affect organizational development. Organizers must take advantage of this relationship. Every success should be widely publicized and used to raise money, gain members, and enhance the reputation of the organization. An instrumental victory should be "reinvested" in the organization to further strengthen its resources and renown.

Effective Public Awareness

All the work that a successful social action organization does should result in changed public attitudes. Members of the general public should know more about the organization and its issues, be more receptive to and supportive of the organization's views, and demonstrate increasing congruence (in voting behavior or boycotting) with the actions the organization desires.

There are some good indicators that an organization is having the desired effect on public sentiment. Positive media reports, editorials and letters to the editor, invitations to speak at meetings of other organizations or join them in coalition or testify at public hearings are evidence that the group's views are being heard. Public opinion polls, especially those that ask people to name the organizations they perceive as most representative of their views, are another measure. Close examination of election results or consumer reaction to a boycott may, as we have mentioned, yield further evidence.

Influencing public opinion is particularly important when the issue is complex and difficult to resolve and requires a long and protracted struggle. Indeed, by raising public awareness about the issue, bringing attention and focus to it, and sensitizing more people a substantive victory can be achieved. An organizer explains,

> Ideally what you define as a victory for the Environmental Lobby is passing legislation that supports what you think is important. In order to do that you have to raise the issue, create an awareness with legislators and with the public, and force other environmental groups to get involved. Public education is critical. Every time we speak to a group of thirty high school kids or a women's garden club or whatever, and you feel there has been an impact, that could be a little step on your way to victory. And as more and more people jump on the bandwagon, legislators have to take notice. Soon it becomes popular to pass our bill, and politicians can't afford to be on the wrong side.

The work of social action organizations can influence public perceptions. As they propose interpretations and solutions, ideas that once seemed radical become commonplace (Brager and Holloway 1978). Although people may never become active, public support may grease the wheels toward change in ways that are not immediately obvious. While the importance of changing public opinion should not be underestimated, neither should it be enthroned. First, instrumental change doesn't always follow changed attitudes. Indeed, several analysts hypothesize that the reality of the change comes before opinions shift (Burstein and Feudenburg 1978, Freudenburg and Baxter 1985, Hartmann 1977, Snow, Rockford, Worden, and Benford 1986). This research suggests that an organization should go about its business of making change with the assumption that public attitudes will subsequently become supportive. Second, the public is notoriously fickle. Frequently, public opinion supports two contradictory arguments. Perhaps the best an organization can do is attempt, consistently and doggedly, to get on the public agenda through the written media, speaking engagements, presentations on television and radio, so people get exposed to the group's views.

In this chapter we have described the ways in which social action organizations evaluate their accomplishments. We have postulated four areas for evaluation: leadership development, organizational development, public awareness, and instrumental change. We have also suggested that these areas are ineluctably intertwined, that all work together to strengthen and enhance the organization, its members, and its power. As people join an organization and become increasingly active, the organization grows and its power increases. The power of the organization is at least partially dependent on keeping the faithful going and finding new adherents. And the health of the membership is at least partially a function of the organization's success. The relationship between an active membership, victory, and power is a critical one for social action organizations. While we have been emphasizing the membership and organizer, the next chapter focuses on the organization as an entity and other factors critical to its health and survival.

CHAPTER NINE

Social Action Organizations

The main focus of this book is, rightfully, on the actors in social action organizing. There are several facets of the organization, however, that influence and are influenced by the actors and the actions of social action organizing itself. We select six of these aspects of social action organizations: 1. size and type of the membership, 2. nature of the constituency, especially regarding race and class, 3. geographic domain, 4. ideology, 5. goals, and 6. funding. All of these, we argue, become active properties of social action organizations, which, in time, shape the organization and its options. This chapter discusses each of these organizational aspects, the options and opportunities they present, and the ramifications of these choices for the kind of organizing the organizer and members will pursue.

Type and Size of Membership

Membership Type As we have argued earlier, social action organizations rely on a large membership to exert their power. The definition of *member* is somewhat ambiguous in social action organizations. Organizations' definitions of membership vary considerably. The large majority of social action organizations have a formally defined membership, with criteria for joining (e.g., membership applications and dues), rights and requirements, defined roles, and means for terminating a member.

Social action organizations appear to have two types of formal memberships. The first type is individual membership, whereby individuals are contacted by the group, go through at least a minimal process of being accepted into it, and receive some form of certification of membership. The second type is federated membership organizations that are comprised of primary groups (typically churches or synagogues or block clubs), so that the primary group joins the social action organization as an institution or a group. Recruitment and retention of most members occurs through the primary group, and the primary group acts to reinforce and socialize active membership in the federation organization. Although some individuals take active roles in the social action organization, others are members only because they belong to an affiliated group.

In both individual and federated membership structures, membership is formal, reflecting the desire to build a permanent base of active and committed people, as discussed in chapter 3. But not all social action organizations take such formal approaches. Other groups define members as people who are loosely and informally associated with the organization:

- nondues-paying "interested" individuals who are invited to take part in an activity planned by the organization
- an association of social action groups, in which local groups—typically in an urban or metropolitan area—are associated through key contact people who are able to activate their own networks for an action or event

While membership is not formal in these cases, a body of people who can be identified, named, and claimed exists. Though not formally "members," they can be contacted and approached by staff or core members when needed.

Whatever the type of membership, there is always the danger that the membership is only "on paper," i.e., there is merely a list of names and not actual people working for and with the organization. It is, of course, important to have a membership list. First, at least the names of people on it are identifiable as *potential* activists. Second, even "paper members" may convince targets and the media that the organization is credible because of the seemingly widespread support for the organization and its approach to issues. But it is long since passé to claim to "represent the people" or some other amorphous aggregate that cannot be demonstrated on demand.

Organizers should guard against the tendency to rely on paper memberships. Paper members are not activists, and are not likely to demonstrate the organization's strength to a resistant target or an inquiring reporter. In action an organizer or small cadre of active members who cannot produce anything like the numbers of members they claim are easily exposed as the "straw men" they are.

The primary implication of the type of organizational membership selected is the organization's ability to recruit and secure the active involvement of members. Recruiting individual members requires more organizational resources and time than does the recruitment en masse of a preexisting group. Individual memberships require "one by one" contacts, so that the organizer must think of any and every event or activity as an opportunity to recruit more individuals. Organizations that utilize preexisting primary groups allow the organizer to recruit the entire network at once. Recruiting primary groups allows the organizer to concentrate on involving *particular* people—those who provide access to the network or existing membership. For example, it is generally true that when the parish priest "buys into" membership in the social action organization, the entire parish will follow, including the lay leaders who head some of the more active groups within the parish. In this way the organizational "base" can grow quickly. Recruiting in federated systems is like the shampoo commercial, "You tell two friends, and they tell two friends, and so on, and so on, and so on."

There are also recruitment problems associated with federated memberships. First, the organizer may gain access only to those favored in the group and not to the most competent leaders. It behooves the organizer to know the group and its leadership well in order to ensure that she has access to all primary group members. Second, the affiliated primary groups may fix conditions, demands, and obligations that limit the organization's autonomy. These conditions should be established at the point of affiliation, although they may need to be renegotiated throughout the affiliation. Third, individuals recruited from primary groups may feel less personally connected to the social action organization than do those people who were individually recruited, where attention can be given by staff or other members to individual recruits' own concerns and needs. The comments made in chapter 3 on personalizing recruitment messages are especially pertinent to organizers of federated organizations. Finally, one of the most troublesome aspects of the federated system is that, by definition, it is based on primary group membership. If members are only recruited from existing primary groups, the organization may overlook very capable people who are unaffiliated.

Organizers may want to consider the relative benefits of group versus individual memberships. Using a mixture of both types may correct the weaknesses in each and diminish the constant need to recruit members. The choice of membership type can be changed to meet the demands of a campaign or threats of an opponent in the short run. In the long run membership type can be purposefully designed to address past weaknesses in the organization's recruitment and retention of members.

Membership Size There is no consensus about "ideal size" for a social action organization's membership. While "the more the merrier," and "you can never have too many members" are phrases echoed by organizers, others counter with concerns about the staff's ability to organize, coordinate, communicate with, and sustain large numbers of people.

Membership size is a factor affected by many things, only some of which the organizer can influence. Family, job, and other demands of people's lives will almost always take precedence over willingness to join and participate in a social action organization. Work on issues often drags on for months and years, potentially outstripping the interest or motivation or availability of members. Some issues appear to attract followers almost by themselves, depending on such factors as the opponents on an issue, and gut reactions to them; the degree of public understanding of an issue, such that an issue captures people's interest; the degree and nature of threat people feel to something they value. These and other factors can cause organizers to feel powerless about affecting the size of their organization's membership.

We will argue that organizers are not purely pawns in this area. Organizers can choose to neglect membership recruitment by defining themselves as powerless to convince people to join. This, we believe, is merely a justification for not doing the leg work effective recruitment requires. We have argued in chapter 3 that the amount of systematic attention given recruitment and retention by organizers and the degree to which all members carry recruitment responsibilities are two factors controlled by the organization that can influence the size of the organization's membership.

Social action organizations report a wide range of membership sizes, perhaps from a dozen people to hundreds of thousands. The smallest tend to be local grassroots organizations; the largest tend to be national organizations with state and local chapters or affiliates, the national claiming all affiliate members as its own. This is not surprising, given the larger pools of potential members at the state and national domains, and the consequent need to impress governmental and other targets with larger and larger numbers of affiliated people.

Local organizations need not have small memberships, however. A federation of local churches, synagogues, and community groups in a middle-sized city reported five thousand members. This group's membership was structured similarly to the national organization, reporting three hundred thousand members, but aimed at local issues.

Membership figures are difficult to verify. Certainly, there is a potential for overreporting members. Membership size is, after all, a strategic variable. The most effective social action organizations, however, rely on active members to deliver results on their issues and to build and maintain the public perception of the organization as powerful. We argue that organizers can have large memberships—if they actively recruit and involve active members.

Nature of the Constituency and Membership

The nature of the membership of a social action organization is inevitably related to the organization's issues. Organizations attract certain kinds of people because of their issues, and people typically join the organization because the organization's issues reflect their interests, views, and concerns. When people form an organization, organizational issues are generated out of their interests, views, and concerns. Often, though not always, members are drawn from a constituency, i.e., those who affiliate with the organization come from the pool of people who the organization speaks on behalf of. In these cases the members are really "active constituents." Some organizations, however, are comprised of a group of people who speak on behalf of and advocate for some other group of people. In these cases the nature of the membership and the nature of the constituency are not the same, and it is possible that the issues can reflect more of the members' interests than those of the constituency. For example, women's groups composed of middle-class members may choose to focus on issues of reproductive rights, while the poor women who comprise their constituency may be more interested in issues of child care and pay equity.

In any case the organization's issues will attract some people and deter others, and, simultaneously, the issues will be shaped by the organization's membership. To a great extent the nature of the organization's membership predicts the organization's issues. Conversely, the issues an organization chooses will, to a great extent, determine the type of people who will be attracted to the organization.

An organization that generates its issues from members and pursues goals that members want achieved will generally work on issues consistent with members' views and opinions. However, an organization that seeks to reflect the concerns of a constituency without ever involving members of that constituency may find great inconsistencies between what the organization believes are the issues of that constituency and what members of that constituency actually want.

Further, an organization cannot always attract the members or constituency that it wants, given its current issues. Numerous organizations want to reach certain population groups with their standard issues, only to find that they are unable to recruit them and unable to form working relationships with primary associations of people from those groups. Those population groups are simply not interested enough in the organization's issues to become members.

It appears to us that the primary demographic aspects that influence organizational issues are race and socioeconomic status, although certainly gender, sexual orientation, age, or special group status (the physically or psychologically challenged or veterans) will play major roles in many organizations.

Race is a potent factor in differentiating in-group and out- group, or marginal group, status in the United States, now every bit as much as when social theorist Gunnar Myrdal (1944) argued this fact so unremittingly nearly fifty years ago. By extension it is logical to argue that the race of members of social action organizations may well affect what issues organizations pursue, in addition to other aspects of the organizations. Organizations with minority members may have fewer resources and less access to established centers of power, for instance, than organizations with white members.

We find it useful to think of constituencies reflecting a racial continuum from "white" to "minority." Between these poles we find organizations with "mostly white" or "mostly minority" members. We use the term *racially balanced* to describe organizations where neither whites nor people of color predominate. Most social action organizations have racially imbalanced memberships, i.e., the large majority of members come from one racial group. In our experience the more racially balanced an organization's membership, the greater the probability that racial differences are secondary to other common elements in the population, such as a shared physical disability or a common problem with a landlord.

Another category of social action organization membership impossible to fit into this racial continuum we term *split*, because these organizations distinguish between a constituency and a membership. For example, the constituency is predominately people of color while the smaller group of members is made up of white professionals, advocates, or supporters who do not personally share the problems of the larger constituency; this might be an organization that works on behalf of Salvadorans but is comprised of United States citizens who are mostly white: clergy, activists, and professionals.

Like race, social class has major utility in describing differences among Americans. Organizing has mostly been associated with working-class or economically distressed individuals and communities (Alinsky 1974, Fisher 1984). Populist and labor-organizing roots add to this image of class associated with social action organizing (Piven and Cloward 1977). Others suggest middle-class interests have also been, and can be, the focus of organizing (Betten and Austin 1990, Freeman 1983, Knoke and Wood 1981). Some authors argue that the poor are too "fragile," prone to frustration, limited in time and physical energy, and too easily co-opted to be organized (Piven and Cloward 1977), while others rebut this view (Haggstrom 1970). Taken together, these sources underscore the importance of socioeconomic class in the shaping of a social action organization's membership.

We define social class basically as socioeconomic status, including income, wealth, and employment status. We have found a simple continuum of low to high socioeconomic status an effective way to categorize most, but not all, social action organizations. The continuum runs as follows:

> *mostly poor* composed almost entirely of individuals with very low income, mostly not employed, and with low educational levels
>
> *blue collar* composed primarily of working-class individuals with stable but low income and low educational levels
>
> *blue collar-middle income* composed of a mixture of blue-collar and middle-income individuals, with stable incomes and high school degrees

Three additional categories are defined to capture other groups whose constituencies do not fit into this continuum:

professionals composed almost entirely of upper middle-income people with a professional interest in advocating for the issues and interests of others unlike themselves

poor-professionals individuals with personal, poverty-related interests at stake, and professionals without such personal stakes advocating for the interests of the poor

other organizations that could not be given a socioeconomic status designation because the organization's issues were not class-related. Apt to fall in this category are such organizations as a statewide organization working with mostly college students—whose socioeconomic backgrounds vary widely—and a national organization advocating for developmentally disabled individuals—most of whom have no personal income but whose family incomes range from poor to wealthy

A relatively small number of social action organizations may be truly poor people's organizations, focused entirely on interests of the poor and comprised only of low-income members. Far more common are organizations concerned with the issues of poor people but having only or mostly professionals in leadership roles to advocate for these interests. These organizers argue pragmatically for the dichotomy between members and constituents. One result of embracing a poor-professional profile is a greater ability to fund organizers and organizing. An entirely low-income membership generally will have a weak financial base for supporting organizing work, while employed middle-income members can be tapped directly for financial contributions. Second, low-income members may face manifold personal problems and be unable to carry out the organization's work. Many organizers have given up trying to organize the poor, preferring to work with less burdened middle-income individuals whose own survival is not at stake and who are open to and available for the organization's issues and work.

The danger inherent in the "split member/constituency" organization is that professional advocates act in the name of an oppressed constituency. The advocates can easily find themselves working on issues that are, at best, tangential to the concerns of the poor and, at worst, disadvantageous to the poor. Further, while the split model may achieve goals for the poor, it neither empowers nor gives power to the constituency. Even when done with good intentions a different type of organization emerges, one that does not share the goal of empowering and giving power to the people that it purports to help.

Geographic Domain

Geographic domain of an organization defines the geographic area in which it works, the scope of its issues, and the scope of the action the organization pursues. Typically this is the area inhabited by the organization's constituency, and members come from within this geographic scope. The domain can range from a local neighborhood to a city, from the nation to the world.

Geographic domain is an easy way to characterize a social action organization, e.g., a "local group," a "statewide coalition." Groups stake out their "turf," but issues may suggest a change in an organization's domain. Once domain is staked out, however, it may be difficult to change, given the identity established with members and the media and given other groups with competing domains.

We can identify several possible geographic domains organizations can select for their social action organizing:

- *local geographic area*: The constituency and members come from one or more neighborhoods or functional communities within a city; the organization focuses on local issues and targets local institutions as well as citywide institutions that affect the members. These are often called *grassroots organizations*.
- *citywide area*: All people in the neighborhoods or functional communities within city boundaries are considered the constituency; members come from the city and targets and issues are citywide.
- *metropolitan area*: The domain comprises two or more cities in a regional area or a major city plus surrounding communities; constituents and members come from within the area, and issues and targets arise from throughout this area and its manifold governmental units.
- *statewide area*: An entire state, or a major portion of it, is the domain; constituents and members live within the state. Statewide issues are selected and targets arise out of state laws and policies.
- *multistate regional area*: The domain consists of a large region (e.g., New England) or perhaps an area defined by a lake or mountain system (e.g., the four-state region surrounding the Chesapeake Bay); constituents and members come from within the area. Issues arise from commonalities in the region, and targets can be either city, state, or regional actors (e.g., the Port Authority) as well as the federal government when it affects regional concerns.
- *national and/or international areas*: The constituencies and issues are national or multinational, with national and international governmental bodies, organizations, and corporations as targets.

Organizational domain both suggests and reflects the organization's issues, constituency, membership, and targets. On the one hand, domain may be used to define the geographic basis of the organization's constituency and membership and to determine those issues that are appropriate for that domain. Thus, if a statewide domain is selected, the constituency and member pool is determined, issues impacting on the entire state's population are addressed, and targets are state actors. Conversely, if the organization's issues, members, constituency are selected, then its domain may be predetermined by these factors. Consequently, a commitment to work on peace initiative issues would dictate selection of a national domain because actors at more local levels are unable to impact significantly on these issues.

Some issues can be pursued within any domain and thus do not dictate a choice of domain. Women's health issues can be defined in terms of the needs of women in a given neighborhood on up through national legislation affecting all women within the nation's borders. Similarly, targets tied to an issue may exist in different domains. For example, local slum landlords, county-level zoning ordinances, state tax and investment incentive laws, programs, and regulations, and federal tax laws are all involved in issues of low-income housing.

Important differences among social action organizations have been attributed to their geographic domain, so much so that the impact of domain is often accepted as predetermining the kind of organizing that can be done. Arguments are made that local organizers can and must work differently from their statewide or national counterparts. Fisher (1984) accepts vast differences between neighborhood and national social action organizing without stating what those differences are. Based on these differences, he argues for the creation of a national network of local groups that could "work both sides of the street."

We view domain as important in analyzing differences among such organizations, and these differences need to be accommodated in the organizing process. We do not, however, accept vast differences in organizing methods between local organizations and those with national domains. Local issues are inextricably linked to state and national policies, laws, and regulations. The active local organization will almost surely bump up against national issues and targets at some point. National issues are most palpably felt at the local level, and, consequently, national organizations must reach down to the grass roots for members and support. In this sense there are no solely local or national issues.

Yet, geographic domain does have an influence on members. Larger domains include greater distances, so members cannot meet face-to-face on a weekly basis as they can in local organizations. Organizations with large domains must also find a way to interest people in local areas in their issues. Conversely, members of local organizations are likely to experience only those problems at hand as pressing, ignoring the state or national origin of their difficulties.

Most national organizers assume that coalitions will solve these problems. Unable to reach deeper into the grass roots for members, many national organizations form coalitions among several groups interested in the same issue area. This has the advantage of potentially bringing like-minded people together, but it is often the case that the same people are members of the various groups in the coalition, and the coalition does not really reach anyone new. Also, organizers are concerned that their organizations will lose their separate and special identity in the coalition, and consequently only seek out temporary alliances around specific events (e.g., a peace march). The actual ongoing base for change around a common issue is seldom enriched by forming a coalition.

Creating chapters of national organizations has been another common solution to problems of domains. The thinking here is that people can "think globally and act locally" (Dubos 1981:83). To some extent this strategy works. Members are actively engaged in local issues and come together yearly for a national event. Yet most organizations that use this structure admit to tension between local affiliates and the national leadership. Members in the local chapters often feel neglected by the national office, and national leaders complain of having to give time and resources to the interests of local members.

Local organizations, for the most part, have few good ideas about how to involve local members in organizing around national issues when they are mostly motivated to change their immediate environment. Their members' eyes glaze when the organizers talk of national policy. Some organizers have tried to discuss "neighborhood defense budgets," contrasting what is spent on their neighborhood with national defense. Most of these efforts have met with limited success. What has been more effective is the strategy Fisher (1984) supports. National People's Action, ACORN, and the Industrial Areas Foundation are all national organizations comprised of local grassroots organizations that have tackled local issues and the national legislation that is at the source of the problems. For example, the passage of the Community Reinvestment Act in 1976 came out of the efforts of local organizations to influence mortgage lending, and their joint efforts through National People's Action to legislate federal laws of mortgage disclosure.

While the choice of a domain may create problems in the organizing, we also discovered some innovative strategies organizers use to correct for the deficits of their domains.

Consulting Relationships One statewide environmental action organization formed a relationship with a local community group in Harlem. The environmental group (located in rural New York, up the Hudson River) addresses a broad array of environmental issues. It is successful in recruiting members through political activities, celebrations, and Hudson River cruises. Although it defines its domain as the full extent of the Hudson River watershed and its constituency as all people residing in this region, the organization has basically white middle-class members living outside New York City. It has consistently failed to attract poor and minority participants from such areas as Harlem. An African-American organization in Harlem was organizing against the building of a sewage plant on its waterfront. The environmental group began a consulting relationship with the Harlem group, advising them on several campaigns. In this way environmental activism is extended into an area with a population that is not easily reached, while both groups maintain their own identities and issues.

Circuit Riding Organizations with large domains, especially national, regional, or statewide organizations, must work on ways to engage people who live great distances from the group's headquarters. One approach to this problem is a "circuit rider" system, where organizers from the central office travel to local groups rather than expecting members to come to headquarters. In one case a group that advocates on Latin American issues spends a short period of time working with a local chapter, mobilizing them around an issue that has been defined nationally. When the goal has been accomplished, or considerably advanced, the organizer may go on to another city. In this model it is the organizer who bridges physical and interpersonal distance by bringing distant issues to people in local communities.

Lending Staff Another method for bridging a gap between national issues and grassroots membership is exemplified by a national voting rights organization. They solicit the participation of or accept invitations from local grassroots groups working on referendums, election reform, or some other issue that has electoral or legislative features. The national organization sends an organizer to work intensively with the members of the local group to design, plan, and execute a registration campaign. The direction of the campaign, its goals, strategies, and targets, are always decided by people at the local level. The organizer maintains contact with the staff and leadership of these local organizations, and during national elections helps them to coordinate their local registration efforts. In this model people are involved locally, bridges are built around local issues, but the national organization's goals are also achieved. The organizer on loan is the "glue" that, especially at the outset, helps hold the local effort together.

We argue that social action organizations must be creative about solving the weaknesses inherent in their domains. Because few people have the time and resources to travel across the country, national organizations must continue to find ways of relating to and involving people at local levels. The involvement of local people also ensures that headquarters is kept abreast of local issues and attends to local concerns. Because few issues are entirely solved locally, local organizations must continue to find ways to interest local people in national concerns. To the extent that the members of local organizations amass power and become empowered, they will need to work on broader issues that affect them. The strategy of connecting national issues and people living in local communities has not yet been realized, and is a problem that deserves attention from organizers in every domain.

Organizational Ideology

Organizational ideology is another attribute that we believe influences the organizing process. Ideology can be thought of as a set of principles designed to give an organization and its participants an explicit, unified worldview from which to operate. The ideology is shared among members and becomes both the credo and the ethos of the organization. It is a way to declare "which side are you on" (Burghardt 1982). At issue is the utility of an ideology for organizing, and the extent to which ideology guides the social action organization.

Whether ideology plays a useful role in social action organizations and what that role may be are active debates in the literature on organizing. Some authors argue that ideology is the major way organizations define themselves, both to members and in the external environment. Some authors and organizers propose a left-wing political ideology as a guide for organizing efforts (Schurman 1966, Rude 1980). Conservative political movements have used fundamentalist Christian dogma to support a variety of issues that undergird their social action organizing (Liebman 1983).

Some authors are critical of organizing they view as purely pragmatic. They argue that ideology and values are important aspects of social action organizations. Bellah et al. (1985), for example, argue that organizations that pursue "the politics of interest" rather than "the politics of the community" or "the politics of the nation" fail to nurture a form of moral development by providing positive alternatives. Gerlach and Hine (1970) argue, from their analyses of such organizations, that ideology is useful in increasing members' commitment to an organization. Brager and Specht (1973) agree that ideology is important in giving a group a clear sense of itself.

Others argue that ideology severely limits the ability of an organization to reach people with diverse perspectives and values. Saul Alinsky and others trained in his approach regard "rigid political ideology" as inhibiting effective organizing. In this view an organizer who lacks "fixed truths" can act as a "free-society organizer," able to respond "to the realities of the widely different situations our society presents" (Alinsky 1971:11). Alinsky's ideal organizer is guided by one conviction, "a belief that if people have the power to act, in the long run they will, most of the time, reach the right decisions" (Alinsky 1971:11).

We view organizers as having innate values and beliefs. Indeed, as we argue in chapter 2, it is these beliefs that motivate them to organize. Dogmatic ideology may be effective in sustaining members' interest in organizations where interaction with other members and working on organizational tasks seldom occurs. Certainly some degree of ideology is needed to define and maintain the organization's missions and norms.

Yet like most aspects of organizing, values, principles, and beliefs cannot be fixed and immutable. Few organizers and social action organizations find it either necessary or practical to fix their organizing to a dogmatic ideological "wagon" that posits operational requirements. Such a doctrinaire basis for organizing can limit the scope of issues, targets, and strategic responses an organization selects, and can render it unresponsive to the ways current issues and stakes are being defined. Most important, by ignoring or not incorporating the different views and opinions that members necessarily bring, a dogmatic organizational ideology can risk the survival of the organization. At best, the organization's ideology ought to be inclusive enough to attract a broad membership and explicit enough for members to understand why they are joining the organization.

In our experience organizers describe their organizational ideology as composed of several transcendent values that set a general backdrop for why and how they work (e.g., poor people have the right to make their own decisions) or as a set of very general rights or principles that cannot be compromised by the organization or its members. Equal rights for women, gay rights, the principle of a woman controlling decisions about her own body are examples of values and principles around which organizations build their actions. Beliefs help set the organization's goals and issues. Some organizations employ a religious worldview as organizational ideology. This approach is typical of social action organizations that have adopted what has been called the "parish ministry" approach to organizing (Mondros and McGuffin 1992). These federation organizations of local churches and synagogues use religious scriptures calling for fairness and social justice to define the organization's mission and explain the campaigns and even some of the strategies of their organizing efforts.

In other organizations beliefs and principles evolve, are less systematically and clearly articulated, and are yet the rationales for organizing. Warren Haggstrom's (1984) vision of a democratic grassroots revolution, an "idealism rooted in history," reflects this style of organization. These organizations stress populist, democratic beliefs, such as a belief in grassroots democracy, in people making decisions, and in equal distribution of power.

Clearly, a broad organizational ideology has value for educating people and forging a common organizational mission. Ideology also informs the organization's basic orientation, issue selection, strategy selection, and staff-member relations.

Some organizers believe that beliefs must permeate every aspect of their work, that values and day-to-day actions must cohere. Other organizers say that beliefs suggest a way of understanding causation and the origin and meaning of social and economic issues. An organizer with a homeless group says that the organization understands homelessness as a basic societal failure, advocating that the profit motive be taken out of housing, and calling for a radical restructuring of housing policies. That principle keeps this organization looking beyond ameliorative solutions like improving temporary shelters. Another organizer talks of the actions his organization takes being aimed at "creating a deeper political sophistication and fighting repressive attitudes" among members and constituents. An environmental organizer talks of his understanding that conflict over such environmental issues as toxic waste dumping is a reflection of class interests.

Organizers use beliefs and principles to select, define, defend, and present organizational issues. Ideology can determine which issues an organization works on and the positions it takes on its own and other groups' issues.

Ideology can also be used to impact on an organization's strategies and tactics. How an issue is addressed is shaped by preexisting approaches that people understand and accept. New issues do not therefore require a reinvention or rediscussion of tactics and strategies.

The organization's beliefs also influence the way staff interacts with members. Language, for instance, embodies democratic values. For example, calling people *leaders* is done to stress that they make the decisions of the organization.

It is important, however, that ideological rhetoric be matched with reality. Organizers who espouse democratic values but fail to communicate those values in their contacts with members send mixed messages. They run the risk of alienating the people they want to involve and educate around those values. Therefore organizers must constantly look for opportunities to discuss with members the organization's ideology, values, and principles, using whatever information fits a given situation and audience. Protection against empty rhetoric can be built into an organization by regularly scheduling open member meetings where the full expression of views and concerns is supported, creating limits on holding offices within the organization, allowing for new leadership, and providing skill training open to all members interested in assuming leadership roles.

Social action organizing is a mixture of principle and pragmatism. We have argued in chapter 2 that organizers' beliefs and anger at injustice are what bring them initially to this field. We have seen that members' motivations to join combine beliefs and the need to solve problems. It follows that the organizations that evolve to encompass and express the organizing work have to develop and maintain some underlying beliefs about society and people, and the principles for action that express those beliefs. We argue that the most effective social action organizations succeed in using beliefs and principles to inform both major decisions and day-to-day work, not as a straitjacket constraining their resourcefulness.

Organizational Goals

Organizational goals "constitute [an organization's] 'social contract,' binding the participants together in a common endeavor" (Lippit et al. 1958:73–74). These goals remain over time and across campaigns, and come to be known as what the organization "does for a living." Members and organizers select these goals, and modify periodically the sense of "mission" that the combined goals provide.

Organizational goals of community organizations, and human organizations in general, can be highly diverse. Many students of organizing have attempted an overarching categorization. Warren (1977) describes change goals in relation to changes in relationships, behavior, ideas, and the environment.

Other writers suggest somewhat similar categories. Etzioni (1961) suggests there are five goal categories applicable to all human organizations: 1. economic goals (material and monetary gains), 2. cultural-social goals (the advancement of one's own norms and values), 3. order-power goals (gains in power and status relative to others), 4. political goals (changes in the formal political structures and processes), and 5. individual growth goals (changes in people's experiences, capabilities, or positions). Brager and Specht (1973) identify three change goals: 1. integrative (i.e., enhancing the organization, agency, or service), 2. sociotherapuetic (i.e., improved functioning or increased competence of people), or 3. environmental (i.e., improvements in community conditions).

We suggest four types of change goals organizers associate with their organizations:

1. Developing leadership by helping people believe they can make change and developing the skills to make change (this category is related to Brager and Specht's "sociotherapeutic goals").
2. Enhancing the capacity of the organization so it becomes more powerful and better equipped to make substantive changes. (loosely associated with Brager and Specht's "integrative goals," although organizational power rather than services is to be enhanced).
3. Effecting instrumental change in society (akin to Brager and Specht's "environmental goals").
4. Educating the public about an issue, problem, or need of a special population (this category again is loosely associated with the Brager and Specht notion of integrative goals, i.e., making the organization's views on issues more acceptable to the general public).

These discussions suggest that while the goals of social action organizations may be diverse, they can be categorized, and are useful for helping members to see how the various issues they work on relate to a single goal.

The identification and acceptance of goals by an organization is also a commitment to act on those goals. Some of the organization's resources must be dedicated to their furtherance. For instance, if an organization commits itself to develop leadership, then the organizer must spend time developing members' skills, and the organization must offer member training and leadership development activities.

Social action organizations tend to pursue several goals simultaneously. These multiple goals reflect the diverse types of changes desired, and are viewed as highly compatible with and supportive of the ultimate mission of amassing power. Different goal combinations merely reflect the different understandings organizations have about how to attain power. Most common are organizations that want to effect instrumental change, develop leadership, and strengthen the organization. Time, energy, and resources are expended to achieve all three goals. Taken together, these goals are seen as effective ways of achieving the organizations' goals for attaining power and empowering people. Second most common are organizations that want to effect instrumental change, enhance the capacity of the organization, and change public opinion. This combination of goals is also viewed as a way of achieving power, and resources are expended to achieve each of these goals. Whatever the combination, however, social action organizers agree that in order to amass power, they must work on achieving results on a number of fronts.

Organizational Finances

We have chosen not to address the issue of funding the organization up to this point because of the topic's power to draw attention away from the core work of organizing. When funds are short, organizing goals may be displaced by fund-raising goals such that pursuing funding supersedes issue and membership work. Too, organizers may use lack of funds as an excuse for not pursuing necessary organizing tasks, and a negative spiral of self-justification and poor work results.

Yet funding plays an important role in social action organizations. Most social action organizations are labor intensive, i.e., staff constitutes the degree of achievement an organization can expect. Without funding, staff cannot be hired, supplies cannot be purchased, newsletters cannot be produced. All the efforts of social action organizations rely on their ability to pay for them.

As important as it is to have a solid financial base, funding also brings problems with it. The gifts of government, foundations, and corporations may fundamentally constrain and impede an organization's autonomy. Receipt of city funding for housing work, for example, may limit a local organization's ability to target city actors on crime issues. Social action organizations struggle mightily with securing sufficient resources, without restricting their ability to choose issues, targets, and strategies. Of secondary concern to the issue of autonomy is the organization's ability to attract stable funding such that fundraising efforts do not constantly supersede the organizing work. If staff must constantly raise money, they cannot do the kind of issue and member work we suggest. Consequently, social action organizations are constantly faced with the issue of to what degree members and leaders are responsible for raising funds for the organization.

While these are real concerns for organizers, they dislike talking about their actual budgets or specific funding sources. Their reticence comes partly because fund-raising is not what they like or want to concentrate on and partly because of the politically sensitive nature of their work. Revealing a funding source may threaten continued funding ordivulge a source to a competing group. It is possible, though, to discuss general categories of funders, the stability of funding over time, accountability for receipt of funds, and how responsibility for fundraising is distributed in the organization.

Sources of Funds Very few social action organizations can rely on a single source of financial support. Most organizers dream of fully funding their organizations out of member contributions. It is believed that member contributions have fewer "strings" and enhance member's sense of organizational ownership. Yet very few social action organizations can fund their operations totally out of member contributions.

Consequently, most organizations rely on multiple funding sources (Delgado 1986). Even relatively shoestring operations must cover staff salaries, rent, utilities, materials, office equipment, etc., so the level of income needed remains high enough to outweigh the resources one funder can offer. No funding source is completely reliable over time, so using different sources allows the organization to make up for lapses from any one source. Certain projects or types of work may lend themselves to particular funders' concerns (e.g., a foundation funding voter registration projects), allowing allocation of other funds to other types of expenses.

There are many categories of funding sources, and it is incumbent on organizations to consider each as a potential source:

- constituency and membership sources (dues, fund-raisers, bake sales, door-to-door canvassing by members, fund-raising appeals)
- project or product sources (informational materials, T-shirts, calendars, recipe books, newsletters, videos, and books, fees for services such as career or home buyer counseling)
- project or activity grants (from corporations, governments, foundations)
- project funding or outright gifts from supporter organizations (e.g., donations from religious organizations)
- contributions through a United Way or similar campaign

Not one of these sources is, by its character, necessarily incompatible with progressive social action organizing. Some sources have stronger histories of funding social action than others. Almost all social action organizations rely on the contributions of members as a primary, ongoing support. Private philanthropic foundations have a long and rich history of funding some organizing projects, although their tax status limits their involvement with partisan political issues. Religious denominations especially have long been important funders of progressive organizing.

Conversely, corporations, governments, and communitywide united giving campaigns have not typically been major funders of the social action organizing addressed in this book. Each of these sources tends to fund services and will rarely fund organizing directly. The political nature of social action organizing makes the organizations and the funding institutions, to say the least, uncomfortable bedfellows. The challenge to social action organizations is not to dismiss these difficult or low probability sources (which happen to have most of the available funds), but to design an effective approach to them that allows the group to function autonomously.

Insurance companies, for instance, may be very responsive to an anti-arson project that offers the possibility of lower insurance outlays and an image of positive community concern, even though the project is attached to ongoing recruitment and other issue work of a social action organization. Creative design of a government-funded job training program may allow its support of organizing staff along with job trainers. Often these service programs can be established separately from the social action organization, with separate bylaws and tax exemptions. Simultaneously, interlocking boards of directors and staff serve to maintain the relationship between the service project and the social action organization.

We argue that social action organizations should work toward mul-

tiple sources of funding for their work, and should consider it healthy
if these funds come from more than one of the categories of funding
sources or types listed above. Multiple sources means that the organization itself risks no survival-threatening reliance on any one funder,
nor does the organization run a risk of becoming associated in the
public's mind with one funder (and that funder's interests or reputation). With multiple sources of funds an organization is freer to walk
away from one source if unacceptable demands are placed on receipt
of support.

Stability of Funding Sources Once funding is achieved the stability of
these funds becomes a concern. The more long-term and stable these
funds, in general, the better, because less time and energy is demanded
of the organization to service or replace them. But long-term funding commitment to social action organizing is rare. Generally, only
funds raised from individual members or constituents can be relied
upon to continue over a long time span. All other sources may come
and go.

Organizers should plan for the probability of turnover among their
organizations' funding sources. An essentially zero-based budgeting
mentality is needed, with the understanding that each succeeding
year's budget must be built from scratch. Then, potential funders can
be contacted and pursued to fund income needs not covered by firmly
committed funding sources.

Demands Associated with Funding Organizers face a constant tension
around the demands placed on them by financial contributors, and the
need to be free to organize around issues important to members and
constituents. There are several potential tensions:

1. *Explicit or implicit restrictions are placed on the organization by funding source.* Some funding sources, particularly government funders, can easily restrict issues, targets, and strategic
choices, so much so that the organization's activities are fundamentally circumscribed by the receipt of funds. This problem seriously hampers an organization's autonomy and risks the ability
of the organization to pursue power and change. In some cases
the strategy of creating a separately funded service organization
while simultaneously establishing an interlocking board and staff
can allow both the receipt of funds and organizational autonomy. If organizational autonomy, however, is seriously impeded,

the members, leaders, and organizers must evaluate the wisdom of accepting funding.

2. *Funding is received for services or projects (not for the organization's general operating budget).* Even if the service or project is consistent with the organization's mission and change goals, the receipt of funds for the project may require or subtly suggest that the organizer and members place their energies in the project to the detriment of other organizing work. Local organizations find that development activities for which they are well funded, which require much technical work, frequently detract from their organizing efforts on other housing issues. As one organizer says, "It's easier to deal with bricks and mortar than amassing power. It was no surprise that we got interested in the development project and let our organizing slide."

3. *The funding source makes excessive demands for accountability.* The amount or type of information sought, the frequency with which it is demanded, and the time required to remain accountable may limit the desirability of one or another source. Governmental funds are notorious in this respect, and foundations and united giving sources are increasingly asking for more information than the simple project report of the organizer's design. Social action organizations will have secrets they cannot share with funders (e.g., the target of a campaign or how organizing work goes on in service programs). If the funder demands that these "organizational secrets" be exposed, the organization may have to rethink its acceptance of funding.

Organizers should accept that funders do have certain "rights" associated with their contributions. Ideally there is openness and clarity at the outset on what all parties can expect. The organization should be in the position of offering funders some involvement in the organization. Invitations to attend annual conferences or celebrations, copies of clippings and news stories about the organization's work, recognition by the organization for their support, invitations to make "on-site inspections" are possible ways to involve funders without divulging important organizational plans. Involving funders in these ways should connote respect for the funder and a sense of responsibility from the social action organization, yet be minimally burdensome or threatening to the organization and its work.

Assigning Fund-raising Responsibility This issue has received some attention in chapters 3 and 4, in contrasting the roles, duties, and rights of members and staff. Different funding sources may require different skills, therefore precluding who must be involved in the fund-raising. In some organizations, for example, only some staff or members may have the skills to write a government grant application.

On the other hand, everyone in the organization can and should be encouraged to be involved in some aspect of fund-raising. When members are involved in raising funds they come to understand that the organization must have funds to survive, and the various problems associated with different funding sources. They not only gain new skills and knowledge related to the organization but also come to own the responsibility for the organization's survival. As one organizer says, "I can measure people's commitment to the organization by the extent to which they are willing to raise funds."

While members may not have the necessary skills for writing grants, they can be involved in approving the grant application and be instrumental in the site visit the funder makes. Frequently members and leaders are more effective than staff at planning and implementing local fund-raisers like dances, ad books, and membership campaigns.

Fund-raising skills are, therefore, included in member training. Organizations simply cannot afford to maintain a "skills gap" in which staff is always looked to as *the* responsible fund-raisers in the organization. And if members begin to suspect that their role is only to write checks, their sense of involvement with the organization is likely to wane.

We have gathered into this chapter a number of organizational aspects that affect, and are affected by, the organizing, the leaders and members, and the organizer. The organization, in our view, presents more than a given in which members, leaders, and organizers work. The organization can shape, reflect, and reinforce the efforts of those within it.

CHAPTER TEN

The Pursuit of Empowerment: Strengths and Challenges of Practice

Introduction

In this closing chapter we review our understanding of power and empowerment in organizing, place this understanding in the context of three organizing practice methods, and analyze the strengths and weaknesses in current organizing practice. Finally, we suggest the prospects and challenges for the future.

We have defined power as a process of accruing and maintaining influence. It is measured by the extent to which another's activities conform to one's preferences. We have argued that the process of accumulating and possessing power is the primary goal of all social action organizations. In some organizations this goal is explicit; in others it is implicit. For some the goal is the reason to organize; others find they must pursue power in order to achieve desired changes. Nevertheless, power building, in order to influence targets to conform to the organization's preferences, constitutes the work of the organization in its external environment.

The goal to become more powerful than before is pursued through a variety of organizational tasks and activities. Issues, strategies, targets, and tactics are selected with an eye to amassing power. Carrying out pressure activities realizes the aspirations to influence, and evaluating actions are attempts to measure the organization's power. To some extent how the organization is structured and disciplined also reflects how it will pursue power.

Empowerment, we believe, is a psychological state, a sense of competence, control, and entitlement that allows people to pursue concrete activities aimed at becoming powerful. Empowering members constitutes the work of the organization in its internal environment.

The recruitment, maintenance, and development of members, motivating them to act, and helping them assume leadership roles are all part of that work. The methods for selecting issues, strategies, targets, and tactics are also related to goals for empowerment. When members select what they will work on and how they will proceed their control and sense of competence is enhanced. Decisions about organizational structure reflect the nature of the organization's commitment to empowerment by involving people quickly, extensively, and deeply or by keeping them at a respectful distance from the major decisions and activities of the group.

The organization seeks to help members feel powerful, attain influence, and achieve a degree of power. These goals are pursued by and reflected in a variety of tasks. Theoretically, the goals of social action organizations complement one another.

Yet, social action organizations differ materially in the manner in which they carry out these tasks and the relative emphasis they place on them. The ways in which organizations identify issues, select targets, strategies, and tactics, determine the pressure activities employed and how they are evaluated, are substantially different. The way the organizer perceives his or her roles and tasks, and the way members perceive theirs, the efforts to recruit and maintain membership and enhance leadership, and the structures of the organization are distinctive.

Practice Methods and Social Action Organizations

In chapter 2 we attributed many of the differences in social action organizations to the organizers' principles for action, what we have called *practice method*. These principles often grow out of organizers' visions of what the organization is to become (a part of what we have called *change orientation*). Their practice methods suggest roles for staff, leaders, and members, a preferred process and criteria for selecting issues, an understanding of the target, a preference for a particular type of strategy, and an understanding of the role of an organization in building power.

In that earlier discussion we identified and briefly described three prominent practice methods: the grassroots approach, the lobbying approach, and the mobilizing approach. We contend that the application of a particular practice method accounts for many, though not all, the differences in social action organizations. We argue that organizers' practice methods permeate and animate every aspect of their work, from identifying issues to working with members to defining a structure for the organization. Here our task is to describe each of these practice methods more fully and suggest their deficits and strengths.

Grassroots Model

Most organizers who use a grassroots practice method support a countervailing institutional change orientation. That is, they believe that people must be helped to see themselves as powerful, that changes must occur on significant substantive issues, and that power must be redistributed by inducing power holders to bow to pressure on these issues. Targets are power holders, public or private figures who have formal authority and are highly resistant to change. Numbers of people organized into a disciplined organized structure are viewed as the major source of power. Using conflict and confrontation, targets are pressured to conform to and act in accordance with the organization's views.

Grassroots organizers are influenced by the writing of Alinsky, and his successors, including Ed Chambers of the Industrial Areas Foundation and Shel Trapp of National People's Action. Although the thinking has been refined over the years, Alinsky's (1971) description of "have nots" or "have a little want mores" clashing with an entrenched elite still characterizes the strategies of these organizers. Si Kahn (1970, 1992) and Lee Staples (1984) have also written about this type of organizing, and several case studies exist (Bailey 1972, Delgado 1986, Knoepfle 1990, Slayton 1986, Susser 1982). The model is sometimes referred to as the populist approach.

Grassroots organizers invariably organize local groups, defining the constituency either by geographic turf or shared issues. The memberships of the organizations range from the very poor to middle-income people. People of color are most likely to be organized by grassroots organizers.

Grassroots organizations make a clear distinction between the roles and activities of staff, and the roles and activities of members. The organizer is central to the organization; he or she generally conducts a great deal of the issue research and provides opinions about strategy and tactics. The organizer also has an important role in relation to members and leaders. He or she actively recruits and involves new members, works with them to enhance their leadership skills, helps them establish effective decision-making mechanisms, and facilitates and monitors group process. The organizer additionally must keep the organization afloat by monitoring its funding, its staff, and its visibility in the community. For the most part, however, grassroots organizers follow the Alinsky (1971) dictum that organizers work "behind the scenes." That is, the organizer doesn't make decisions on behalf of the organization, doesn't define issues or strategies, doesn't chair meetings, and doesn't speak publicly to the press or power holders. Some grassroots organizers have softened their stance on this principle. Nevertheless, grassroots organizers feel uncomfortable with high profile roles, and assume them only when they determine that leaders need them to step in.

Members and leaders are essential to grassroots organizations. Recruiting and maintaining members is considered critical to the health of the organization, and its ability to make change. Most grassroots organizers believe that members join the organization out of self-interest, and they are recruited on that basis. Members are frequently recruited through a primary network. Recently the parish ministry model of recruiting through religious institutions has been employed with good success (Mondros and McGuffin 1992).

In addition, in grassroots organizing the goal of encouraging people to feel and be more powerful is typically as important as achieving substantive change. Hence, leadership development is crucial. These organizers build "high access" organizations where opportunities for member participation is immediate and extensive. Every member is encouraged to take on leadership roles. Members and leaders make all organizational decisions, from its bylaws to its slogans. Members raise and select organizational issues based on the self-interests of the group, and broad agreement among members is necessary before the organization will pursue an issue. Most grassroots organizations work on many issues at once. Decisions regarding strategy, tactics, and targets are made by leaders and members, using staff consultation. Grassroots organizers believe that if members "own" the strategy, they will be committed to carrying it out. Pressure activities are implemented and evaluated by members. Leaders speak to the press and negotiate with targets. Members and leaders are encouraged to take credit for and celebrate organizational victories. These are envisioned as ways to make members feel and be more powerful.

Grassroots organizers understand individual power holders, both in government and the corporate sector, to be the targets of their change efforts. Grassroots organizers believe that their "have not" members will have to wrest power from these "haves." They pay little attention to public opinion, believing that only a display of power can force power holders to conform to the organization's agenda. Targets shift, depending upon the issue at hand, and are assessed for their formal authority to solve the problem, their vulnerabilities and associations. Targets are often referred to as "enemies" in order to enhance members' sense of victimization and opposition. Collaboration, campaign, and contest strategies may all be employed, depending on the resistance faced, though direct confrontation with targets is the most common approach. Hopefully, targets are pressured to negotiate with the organization. If targets bend to pressure, the organization may seek to make them allies in the next campaign.

Since a formal, disciplined organization is essential to make change, these organizers pay a great deal of attention to organizational maintenance. They are likely to be structured as "organizations of organizations"; the social action group is a coalition of block clubs, churches, senior citizen clubs, home and school associations, and women's groups. Thus, grassroots organizations may claim that all the members of these subgroups are also officially members of the social action organization. Membership is formal and meetings have minutes, agendas, and reports by leaders—all the accoutrements of formality. Informal interaction among members is consciously encouraged before and after meetings to increase the sense of commitment to each other and to the organization itself.

The grassroots model has the advantage of involving people intensely and extensively in the organization and its work, thereby creating a permanent organization that can work consistently on developing power and making change over time. It is not as vulnerable as other organizing methods to the departure of a few key leaders or the organizer. People are recruited and involved in the organization on the basis of their self-interest, and this seems to go a long way to deepen at least their initial investment. Yet, the notion of creating a "people's organization," so basically responsive to members and their immediate needs, creates some tensions in the organizing. The focus on self-interest creates a practical problem of attrition. Members may join out of self-interest, but if they are to stay involved they must move beyond their own individual needs to concern for collective interests. Grassroots organizers and their leaders consistently complain that members drop out when their individual problems are solved.

Some organizers seem resigned to this problem, others try to correct it by creating "exchange mechanisms" so that people with one set of concerns work first with others, knowing that later they will get help on their issue. Other techniques for raising collective consciousness include group problem swapping and problem solving, rewarding participants for extended involvement, enhancing in-group ties, and according status and visibility to seasoned leaders. Because participation is emphasized in grassroots organizations, conflict over leadership roles is frequently a problem. Organizers must pay careful attention to sharing leadership and leadership succession so there is room for and acceptance of new leaders.

Grassroots organizers often work with people with limited means, and that too creates strains. They find themselves making many demands on people with limited resources. Periods of economic decline seem to increase this problem (Mondros and McGuffin 1992). Members who join because of basic needs often have a great deal to lose. Their organizers and they themselves believe they must directly target people with power in order to make change, and yet they are, indeed, vulnerable to retaliation. These organizers train and brief people, help them devise strategy, role-play alternatives, and attempt to mitigate the risks by holding group actions on the organization's terms and turf. All of these techniques are ways of supporting risk taking. While these methods are useful, grassroots organizers need to be constantly aware that they are asking people to do difficult things, and be willing to do a great deal of "hand holding."

It is also constructive to recall that self-interest is not always compatible with the interests of others. Despite Alinsky's defense of the Back of the Yards organization (Saunders 1970), there continue to be ethical questions about working with one group to the detriment of another. Grassroots organizers endeavor to point out common struggles, common issues, and solutions that help all, and to emphasize the "same boat" philosophy. The building of interfaith and interracial organizations helps to counter separatist tendencies. Yet, grassroots leaders and organizers display an awareness that ethnic and racial tensions—reflecting the troubles of the larger society—persist, and must be carefully monitored in the organization before they destroy it from within.

Finally, when members are focused on issues of self-interest and locally organized, it is harder for them to embrace the "bigger picture" and respond to issues of national or international import. Organizers try to educate members about causation, for example, by drawing the connections between drug activity in a neighborhood and national drug enforcement policy. For the most part grassroots organizers remain frustrated in their attempts to have a voice and a role in national policy.

Lobbying Model

We have identified the lobbying approach as another prominent practice method. Most lobbying organizers support a pluralist pressure change orientation. That is, lobbying organizers seek the enactment of laws or regulations related to specific issues. They accept that government and the legal system are the legitimate mechanisms through which social change is negotiated. Political actors are perceived as potentially amenable to influence. Concerned, reasonable people with a good deal of expertise are seen as the major resource for change, and so public education is a major activity of lobbying organizations. The major change strategy is to collect data, develop expertise, formulate solutions, disseminate the information to the public, and use persuasion to convince government officials to conform to the organization's views.

The intellectual roots of the lobbying model come from James Q. Wilson (1973) and Edward Banfield (1961) and writers on interest group lobbying that include Ornstein and Elder (1978) and Berry (1977). The preeminent practitioners include Ralph Nader, whose public interest research groups have achieved national prominence, and other broad-gauge groups, including the American Association of Retired Persons, Children's Defense Fund, and the National Rifle Association.

Lobbying organizers invariably build statewide and national organizations that reflect their preoccupation with the levels of government that make policy. Members of lobbying organizations tend to be white, middle-class people and professionals. They exhibit less self-interest as motivation, and are primarily motivated either by altruism or a professional interest in the issues pursued by the organization (e.g., day care operators working on child care legislation).

The lobbying organizer also has a central role in the organization, albeit generally quite a different one from the grassroots organizer. Frequently, such organizations have substantially greater numbers of staff than other types of social action organizations, generating greater role specialization for the organizer. Most important to these organizers are the goals their organizations set for substantive change on issues. They are hired for their expertise on these issues, they value technical skills, and their jobs are likely to be technical and administrative in nature. They are least likely to describe what they do as organizing. Their primary role is to be knowledgeable about issues, monitoring the issues' progress through the legislative and executive system. They also are responsible for educating and sensitizing the general public about the issue, frequently producing reports on issues and speaking to the press. They also perform the major pressure activities of the organization, i.e., persuading legislators on issues, either alone or with a few leaders.

In lobbying organizations the achievement of instrumental objectives usually takes precedence over goals for empowerment. Thus there are relatively few tasks given to general members who are unlikely to have the same level of expertise as staff members. People join the organization because they are interested in the issues. They are recruited individually through mailings or friends, and are asked to do little more than donate money, write to politicians, or attend a fundraiser. The need for organizational legitimacy and credibility in a political environment requires organizers to attend to the representativeness of their organizations, and they often bemoan the absence of low-income and minority members.

Lobbying organizations have many barriers to member involvement and participation. There is little attention given to leadership development, and lobbying organizers do the least of all three approaches to help people assume leadership roles. While members have few duties, key volunteers, particularly the few committed experts who comprise the board, may have quite significant responsibilities, often doing tasks similar to staff. It is someone's issue expertise that rules the day, and for the few members who are very knowledgeable there is room at the top.

The issues of a lobbying organization are its raison d'être. New issues emerge from the political environment and fall under the umbrella of the organization's mandate. Related issues may be pursued as long as they don't divert the group's attention from its primary agenda. New members are invited to act on the organization's issues, not generate new ones. Decisions on issues, strategy, targets, and tactics are made by the organization's board and staff. The latter are also the people who carry out pressure activities, most often giving testimony at legislative hearings, preparing position papers and model legislation, or meeting individually with legislators.

To lobbying organizers concerned and active individuals are the major change agents. The organization often serves only as a mechanism to coordinate the work of individuals by collecting funds, providing a mailing list and centralized expertise, and, most important, monitoring, communicating, and updating interested people about issues. Most lobbying organizations are comprised of loosely associated individual members who pay dues and receive newsletters and other information. Real authority lies with the board and staff. To build a broader base of support on issues, lobbying organizers occasionally build horizontal relationships with groups working on similar issues.

Lobbying organizations have the advantage of focus. They generally work in a single-issue area, although not on a single issue (e.g., environmental groups, abortion rights groups). They have clear and largely self-apparent targets so that research on the issue and actors involved can accumulate over time. Because the organizations correspond to levels of government (e.g., statewide organizations target state government), they can work on issues of larger import and have access to their governmental targets. Moreover, for the most part they work with members who are not hampered by concrete needs, who are fairly sophisticated and already committed to the issues; there is little need to promote the group's purpose or to provide a great deal of support. Because they ask little of members, people generally do not feel overburdened by their organizational activity. Generally, the organizer can perform her or his work quickly and autonomously, involving the more invested and knowledgeable volunteers when necessary.

Yet the lobbying model also has certain deficits. Organizers consistently complain about their inability to reach and interest poor and minority people. For the most part, the issues of lobbying organizations do not have bread and butter appeal for them, and an organization in which they do not actually participate may feel too abstract and offer few rewards. The poor rarely have resources to regularly attend sessions at the capital or to make long distance phone calls. Poor and minority individuals may have problems trusting that governmental actions can or will help them. Lobbying organizations that work in coalition with minority organizations or lend support to local organizations working on local issues seem to have greater success reaching a more diverse audience.

It is difficult for lobbying organizations to gain grassroots support because people usually live far from organizational headquarters. There is a tendency for members to be engaged episodically, active sometimes, disappearing, and emerging again. It is difficult to count on these members to carry out responsibilities—to be available when needed. The lack of tasks and opportunities for participation may suggest to members that it is only necessary to write an occasional check. Thus, it may be difficult to "get the troops out" on demand and more than occasionally. Some lobbying organizers have corrected for this problem by creating local chapters and working with the local volunteers, at least by telephone, to increase their sense of involvement and participation. Still, lobbying organizers report that local members feel isolated and underutilized. They are often angry at the staff at headquarters, feeling that their ideas and issues are not taken seriously by staff.

Mobilizing Model

The mobilizing model of social action organizing is sometimes called the social movement approach. Mobilizing organizers generally subscribe to a mass education for action change orientation and, occasionally, to a charismatic vision orientation. That is, they want to include the needs and views of the disenfranchised on the national agenda, and achieve instrumental changes that would improve these peoples' lives. The federal government is necessarily viewed as the primary change target. The powerful people who run the government are deemed highly resistant to change, only willing to concede during certain historical moments when economic, social, and political events coincide to make change feasible. Thus two change strategies are required: one for conservative time periods when discontent is muted and another when opportunities for dissent emerge. Mass collective and opportunistic defiance and protest can influence the dominant institutions to alter their agendas. The most notable formulators of this model are Frances Fox Piven and Richard Cloward (1974, 1977). Several studies have described mobilizing in protest movements in the United States and abroad (Boggs 1986, Freeman 1983, Gerlach and Hine 1970, Hertz 1981).

Mobilizing organizers also practice at local, citywide, and statewide levels, although there is a tendency to build national organizations. While members of mobilizing organizations are likely to be white, middle class, and professionals, some local mobilizing organizers build organizations of minorities and low-income people, adding a group of professionals who serve as "supporters."

Mobilizing organizations do not make clear distinctions between the roles and tasks of staff and the roles and tasks of members. Mobilizing organizers think of themselves as "in house" experts who have a great deal of knowledge about the organization's issues, but it is only their commitment as activists that sets them apart from other involved leaders. Because they offer their time and energy, mobilizing organizers feel entitled to greater control of the organization's work and agenda. They, more than their grassroots and lobbying counterparts, describe themselves as "political activists" or "leftists," suggesting their commitment to broad-scale social change, a commitment beyond their organization and its issues. Goals for empowerment and leadership development are secondary. The kind of changes desired and the belief that the environment is not within their control requires marathon endurance on their part. Mobilizing organizers tend to be the least rigid practitioners, perhaps because the environment is seen as beyond their control.

Mobilizing organizers tend to be ambivalent about the importance of recruiting members, probably because they are less certain about the need for people, except during particular historical moments. They are willing to take in anyone who is interested, but prefer people who are veteran activists. They believe people join the organization out of interest in the organization's issues and a shared ideology about social justice. Like lobbying organizers, they would prefer "rainbow memberships" to lend legitimacy to their efforts, and bemoan the absence of low-income and minority involvement.

Mobilizing organizations generally have ambiguous access for new members. While there is seldom training or support for member involvement, there are few barriers to participation. Members can be as active or inactive as they care to be. New recruits are occasionally put to work performing small tasks (e.g., running the copying machine), or are invited to special events like fund-raisers or demonstrations. They are mostly involved during the action implementation phase. Organizers do little to support participants to take leadership roles, but at the same time they don't block people from emerging. People with the energy, time, commitment, and activist credentials can become full participants in the "core" group, who work side by side with staff to make organizational decisions. These core leaders are thought to stay involved because of a common history and ongoing commitment to struggle, and there is a sense of self-sacrifice among these leaders and organizers.

Issues in mobilizing organizations are not often selected, but emerge as a result of an environmental event (e.g., President Bush sending troops to Panama). Issues are evaluated according to the needs of constituents, their intrinsic value, organizational imperatives, and the political environment. Although methods range from involving members to staff making unilateral decisions, there is a tendency for the staff and the core group to formally commit the organization's resources to working on a concern. Mobilizing organizers are wary of new and multiple issues; they want to conserve the energy and resources of their members. They are, however, more likely than other organizers to join in temporary coalitions with groups with similar concerns in order to respond to an event.

Mobilizing organizers generally have two categories of targets. They frequently describe fellow activists as "targets" that can be persuaded to take action or become more active. Thus, mobilizing organizers do a lot of public education. Their other targets, government institutions, are seen as highly resistant to change. Strategy decisions regarding these targets are agreed upon by a few key activists and the organizer, but tactics are carried out by members, staff, and leaders. Pressure activities may be campaign activities or disruption, including marches, boycotts, and civil disobedience. Mobilizing organizers tend to downplay the importance of organizational successes, feeling that it demoralizes people who must be committed for the long haul.

To mobilizing organizers committed activists, not organizations, make change. Indeed, the whole notion of a membership is considered unessential. Mailing lists may suffice. When memberships do exist, they are almost always based on individuals, rarely on federations of other groups. The organization basically serves as a catalyst to bring people, affiliated or not, together to press for issues of importance. It disseminates information and rallies people to action when a cause or an opportunity emerges. Lacking such a clear definition of membership may be helpful; the organizers can claim support without quantifying it. Most meetings (aside from formal, annual conventions) are informal; whoever attends can participate. There is a great deal of camaraderie among members of the inner circle, who have often known each other and worked together for years.

There are several obvious advantages to the mobilizing model. In our view these organizers make good use of ideology and opposition as a way of keeping people motivated. In mobilizing organizations ideology replaces self-interest as the primary method to increase investment of members. Mobilizing organizers clearly articulate the need for broad-scale change, and are not afraid to capitalize on their marginal status and articulate a vision of social justice. These techniques seem to go a long way toward binding middle-class members who are not burdened by concrete needs. Further, they do not ask much of members and have no stringent membership criteria, so that they can involve unaffiliated people at any time, sometimes making good use of "smoke and mirrors" to claim broad-based support. These organizers are not wedded to one particular way of working, so they are able to respond flexibly when situations call for an alteration of plans.

There are also some problems inherent in the mobilizing model. Many mobilizing organizers acknowledge that their organizations are not representative of minority and low-income groups. They don't offer much for members to do, and call on them only occasionally, an approach that may not be responsive to the very concrete and ongoing needs of low-income people. They have a difficult time getting people at a grassroots level to appreciate the importance of their national concerns for social justice.

Most important, with their theory of opening and shrinking opportunities for pressure, mobilizing organizers are not driven to develop broad-based support until the right moment arrives. Members of mobilizing organizations are often minimally involved in the ongoing work of the organization and are suddenly asked to perform disruptive activities. Members are not helped to develop the sense of radicalism necessary to perform such activities. Thus, an opportune environmental moment requires reinventing the organization, recruiting members anew, and making connections with formerly allied supporters. The problems entailed here are an obvious drain on the organizer's time and energy, as she or he must always begin all over again identifying potential members, recruiting, and engaging them.

The mobilizing model clearly relies on veteran activists, and organizers frequently complain about burn-out among them. They note that people with other responsibilities (especially young parents) cannot take on heavy organizational burdens, and, by virtue of circumstance, find themselves quickly outside the inner circle. In this sense the model tends to be insular, and only a few mobilizing organizers search for new activists to join or supplant others. If mobilizing organizers were to consider issues of organization access more seriously, if they were to actively encourage, support, and maintain people during conservative times, groundwork could be laid for those rare but extremely significant moments, and burn-out of core activists might be less of a problem.

Mobilizing organizers sometimes ask members to take risks that could result in retaliation. In many cases organizers want people to ignore these risks and go ahead with the activity anyway, but, realistically, they realize that few people will do so. If they are to continue to use disruptive tactics and want to involve low-income people, they will either have to find ways of protecting people from retaliation or make their issues worth the risks. Figure 10.1 illustrates the differences among practice methods.

The influence of the organizer's practice method is, of course, not

FIGURE 10.1
Differences by Practice Method

	GRASSROOTS	LOBBYING	MOBILIZING
Domain	Local	State/National	Varies
Constituency	Low-Income–Middle-class	Middle-class/Professional	Varies
Change Orientation	Countervailing Institution	Pluralist Pressure	Mass Educating for Action
Staff Role	Strategy/Members/Organization	Expert on Issues	Commitment/Issue Expert
Roles for Members	Many	Few Key Experts	If Motivated to be Active
Recruitment	Self-Interest/Networks	Issue Interest	Ideology
Engagement	High Access	Low Access	Ambiguous Access
Goals	Change/Power/Empowerment	Instrumental Change	Social Justice
Targets	Powerholders	Government Officials	Government Institutions
Power Resources	Numbers/Organization	Information/Public Education	Activists
Selection of Issues	Members/Leaders	Staff/Key Leaders	Varies
Selection of Strategy	Members/Leaders/Staff	Staff/Key Leaders	Staff/Leaders
Preferred Tactics	Contest	Persuasion	Disruption
Implement Tactics	Members/Leaders	Staff/Key Leaders	Members/Leaders/Staff
Organization	Formal	Power at Board Level	Informal

the only factor that affects practice; two other factors also seem to affect social action organizations. The domain of the organization varies from local to national organizing efforts, and influences how change is pursued. Domain suggests how large the potential pool of members is, the degree of access an organizer has to members and leaders, and potential access to funding sources and mainstream media. In local organizations members participate to a greater degree in the everyday work of the organization. National organizations tend to greater numbers of staff and members. The social and ethnic make-up of social action organizations also affects the organizing. Low-income and minority people are most likely to join local grassroots organizations whose issues reflect their self-interest. White middle-class people are more likely to join lobbying and mobilizing organizations whose issues reflect their altruistic concerns.

And, to be sure, every organizer does not fit so neatly within the models we have described above. Some organizers support a combination of change orientations, and the introduction of different views does have an influence on the way they practice.

Occasionally, grassroots organizers describe themselves as supporting both a countervailing institutional orientation to change and another change orientation. Grassroots organizers who combine views tend to deemphasize but don't entirely lose their emphasis on leadership development. They may use other pressure tactics than direct confrontation, most notably disruption and/or persuasion. When lobbying organizers combine pluralist pressure views with other orientations, they are likely to limit staff control and involve members to a greater degree, and use direct confrontation and disruptive tactics in addition to persuasion. Still, they retain their belief in government officials as the sole targets of change. When mobilizing organizers combine mass education for action views with countervailing institution beliefs, they are more likely to involve members beyond core activists and use more directly confrontational tactics. When they support pluralist pressure views, the organizers tend to have greater control over decision making and use more persuasion activities.

Still, organizers who deviate from the "formulas" of the models are in the minority. The models tend to be quite prescriptive for practice and inform almost all the organizer's responses to the important questions that arise in their work. The models prescribe roles for staff and members, define the purpose of the organization and its structure and goals, determine who is to be recruited and how and the level of their participation, suggest how much control the organizer has, what skills are needed, and how the work day is spent. The models inherently have strong biases, and these biases are inculcated into the organization and its work. Most organizers do not seem to fully, rationally, and openly evaluate their issues, targets, members, leaders, and organizations, but rather use the stock responses suggested by their practice model.

Further, organizers are unlikely to compromise their practice model or adapt it when members and leaders see things differently. Instead, they either create the organization in the image of their model, convince members to go along with their views, or restrict decision making to those who have similar views. When organizers are unable to employ their ideas about practice, they leave the organization.

We believe that such predictability unnecessarily hampers organizers and social action organizations in their pursuit of change and empowerment. We conclude by describing the promise and limitations of current social action organizing in today's social climate, and make what we hope are useful suggestions for their sustenance and growth.

Power, Empowerment, and Social Action Organizations

We have come full circle to the questions with which we began this book. How do social action organizations fulfill people's search for collectivity? How do they counter Americans' ambivalence about institutions and engage them in a way that allows them to pursue a common good? How do we enhance these organizations and use them to stimulate the debate about our collective future?

Certainly, the American "free institutions" de Tocqueville observed continue to survive, if not flourish. Progressive social action organizations continue to function today, although they may be less visible in the public debate and receive less attention in the media than they did in their most recent heyday of the 1960s and 1970s. Harry Boyte (1989) argues that in many ways progressive social action organizations are more viable than they once were. He sees them as more connected to their constituencies and members, more interested in their issues, and less dependent on the fickle and self-advancing motives of experts and politicians.

We find Boyte's conclusion to be partially true. Many organizations are composed of white, middle-class professionals, members of "new social movements" (Klandermans 1986, Melucci 1980), but their success is still dependent on the responsiveness of politicians who must be persuaded to their views. Most of these groups, however, at least attempt to recruit people whose views are not represented, or are underrepresented, in the polity. And several other organizations have been particularly successful building organizations of low-income people of color to work on their own issues.

Social action organizations have continued to tackle some of the major social issues in our society and have continued to defend the rights of poor and minority constituencies. They are not merely advocating for stop signs. These organizations have articulated and organized the dissent. Further, the limited successes and frequent losses these organizations experienced in the conservative 1980s have not been as demoralizing as might be expected. Organizers and leaders redefine success by pointing to growth in their membership, the developing skills and confidence of members, and small compromises that can be called victories.

Bellah et al.'s (1985, 1991) discussion focuses on people's search for collectivity—their need to reach out to others and their concerns and to understand their lives in some broader context. Certainly, many leaders and organizers express those sentiments. Low-income leaders, in particular, stress that they participate not only to seek benefits for themselves and their families but to improve the lives of their neighbors and friends. Leaders often describe how their participation enriches their lives. Within the organization there is friendship, solidarity, and good honest work.

Still, there is something in addition to collegiality and a commitment to the common good that overcomes people's skepticism about institutions and encourages them to participate in social action groups. As they see it, they need power, and many see the need for empowerment.

These feelings are relatively easy to understand. Leaders understand that they cannot get their needs met in an increasingly complex, remote, underresourced, and unresponsive society without joining with others. Alone, they cannot achieve their ends; together, it might be possible. As one leader told us,

A good exercise in powerlessness is to go to the gas company and try to get your bill corrected. I assure you, it will take months. You will be sent from one place to another, you will be treated like you are asking for a favor, and you may never get the damn thing done. If you can't even get a correct bill, how the hell can you change energy policy? But if you get all your friends and neighbors together, and they get *their* friends and neighbors together, and they get *their* friends and neighbors together, maybe, just maybe, we can make some change.

These people have no delusions that power is readily amassed or change easily or reliably made. Organizers and leaders hold to a vision of large-scale social change, but are sustained by smaller, more incremental advances that are viewed as the harbingers of things to come. Perhaps such redefinitions may be simply a matter of sustaining morale, but we see them as a more varied and complex definition of power and of change. These views suggest that organizers and leaders have a realistic notion of what can be accomplished by social action organizations, particularly during politically conservative times. But they also have a profound sense of what Alinsky's "have nots" and "have a little want mores" want and need to feel empowered enough to act in their own interests.

People want not only power, but to feel empowered. For the most part, these people feel bypassed in our society. Their opinions aren't heard, their needs aren't recognized, they are made to feel small and insignificant in all their dealings with government and corporate bureaucracies. From welfare mothers, women, gays and lesbians, farm workers, homeless people, blue-collar workers we have heard time and time again how they feel ignored, belittled, and diminished in our society. Social action organizations are places where they feel competent, capable, in charge, and they can act on those feelings.

Thus, there is support for the continued existence of the "free institutions" that de Tocqueville found to promote active citizenship. While many people feel isolated from most collectives, a condition that Bellah et al. (1985, 1991) suggest prevails in America, members of social action organizations join these groups to fight the isolation they feel. This is something new—that in today's social climate people join progressive social action organizations for power and empowerment. While they continue to be wary of most institutions, they see participating in social action organizations as a way of meeting these needs.

The Promise and Limitations of Today's Social Action Organizations

We are at once heartened by the good work we have found among social action organizations, honored to have been able to share time with people so dedicated and passionate in their concerns, and saddened by the difficulties they face and the minimal supports they can count on to offset the known—and certain—pressures of the work. While it is improbable that social action organizers and progressive social action organizations could have stemmed or turned back the conservative tides of the eighties and early nineties, the identification and correction of the practice problems we have addressed in this book may have made them more worthy opponents even during a conservative era.

The major weakness among organizers and organizations is that they do not consciously and adequately recognize the number of options they have available to them. Nor are organizers fully aware that each decision they make has both advantages and attendant costs.

Some organizers are quite thoughtful about these choices and their effects on the organization and members. They make conscious decisions to follow a particular pattern or try an innovation, knowing both the strengths and limitations of their choices. Still, many other organizers seem less aware of options beyond their tried and true patterns, or they simply ignore other approaches. Such myopia threatens to impair the ability of the organization to maximize its potential power and to realize change. We outline four areas where we think the lack of attention to options causes problems for the organizing: 1. the recruitment and maintenance of members, 2. the use of ideology as a force in the organization, 3. the role of opposition in organizing processes, and 4. making connections among issues and alliances among organizations.

Recruitment and Maintenance of Members Large numbers of people are a major resource for power in all social action organizations, although they may be employed differently in different practice models. Numbers lend legitimacy, manifesting that the organization's sentiments are held by many. Large numbers of people permit fund-raising so that staff and expertise can be purchased. Numbers enable the employment of tactics that threaten targets by disrupting their activities or confronting them directly. Though numbers of people are critical, often organizers do not make decisions that would result in the recruitment of new members and maintenance of current ones. In general, they pay less attention to recruitment and maintenance options than is warranted. There are many reasons why organizers tend to do less work with members. Many of them articulate goals for substantive change, not member development, which suggests their priorities. For these organizers recruitment is viewed as a distraction from issue and strategy work. Many organizers primarily value their own expertise;

it is what sets them apart from members. Thus, recruiting new members who may lack skills and yet vie for organization control may be seen as potentially limiting the organizer's control over the organization. Working with members takes time and effort, is never finished, and requires the organizer to have contact with strangers who may not agree with his or her viewpoint. For many organizers there is a sense of fatalism about who can be involved, how deeply, and for how long. Such ambivalence often underlies minimal efforts to involve and sustain members. Yet other organizers are more assertive in their recruitment efforts; they capitalize on the diverse interests and needs that move people to join.

Local, low-income, and minority people tend to join social action organizations out of self-interest. Local organizers have found that recruitment is most effective when friends join together, when they tap primary institutional networks such as churches, and when friends or a respected institutional figure such as a priest encourages their joining. Techniques that encourage people to work in groups, participate, and socialize build both camaraderie and a sense of common fate that augment the initial self-interest. Offering rewards such as media visibility and honors sustains involvement. One organizer promotes the idea of a member benefit package that provides discounts on neighborhood services. Such ideas are helpful to involve and maintain people with concrete and immediate needs.

Middle-income and professional members tend to join statewide and national organizations because of issue interest, but these organizations are sometimes unable to attract local members. Some organizers are trying to develop local networks to counteract the distance among members. Establishing local affiliates that offer members participatory roles, status, and ongoing contact is a way to augment initial motives of low-income members and sustain middle-class members when there is not concrete self-interest at stake. One organization has employed a "circuit rider" approach; an organizer spends extended time working with local organizations on their issues, and the local organization is then asked to work on national concerns. A pro-choice organization is working with local middle-class churches, much as the parish ministry model has done in low-income neighborhoods. These are innovative methods of involving local people in issues of national import, and have the potential of easing the problem of lack of representativeness.

Organizers use relatively few recruitment methods. Recruitment is frequently haphazard and people discover organizations by happenstance. Face-to-face communication along preexisting personal or organizational networks makes for very effective recruitment (Gerlach and Hine 1970). Leaders who were recruited by their priest or rabbi have a sense of being "elected" for the organization. Yet time and distance constraints often mean more impersonal methods such as mail, flyers, and public service announcements must be used. Some organizers reach a wider audience by planting stories in the media, holding press conferences, and taking credit for victories. By using multiple recruitment methods, organizers are reaching out to as many people as possible.

Such innovations are important efforts to correct problems of lack of representativeness, member attrition, and episodic involvement. They are necessary for organizations to reach the number of people needed for change.

The Use of Ideology Organizers apply their beliefs to strategy and dilute their ideology when working with members. The dichotomous way ideology is used in social action organizations has certain limitations.

Organizers' practice methods often determine strategy, targets, and pressure activities. Organizers who support two change orientations, on the other hand, consider more options. These organizers have the flexibility to try different things, to "fill out their strategic hands."

The ideology organizers bring is seldom employed in conversations with members and leaders. Organizers, who define themselves as outside of mainstream thinking, know they must bring their vision and anger to others; they must enjoin others to be marginal as well. Yet most people tend to resist such self-definitions, and organizers seem unwilling to ask people to define themselves as marginal. Perhaps they worry that they will not be accepted by members, and will be marginal even in the systems that they have chosen and created. Thus, organizers tend to limit members to those who share their anger and vision, or conceal their views from members, or drop them altogether, organizing without a broader sense of social change. Yet, for many people, particularly members of the middle-class, ideology is an inducement to join and stay involved. The challenge is to use ideology to recruit and maintain members without being choked by strict adherence to dogma. The most notable innovation in this regard is the parish ministry model, which uses Judeo-Christian values to explain the need for social action. By reinterpreting religious values, these organizers redefine what is marginal and what is mainstream, and they imbue the organization with a redefinition of common traditions, rather than ask people to accept new and alien ones. Such efforts have the potential of solving the organizer's dilemma of being marginal in society but remaining connected to a large number of people.

The Role of Opposition There exist many descriptions of attacks by opponents against social action organizations (Fisher 1984, Glick 1987, Slayton 1986, Wellstone 1978). The organization is assumed to be motivated by this opposition. In fact, organizers and leaders pay little attention to opposition; it plays almost no role in developing strategy or altering members' perceptions. There is a sense, particularly in middle-class organizations, that it is impolite to speak of it, and certainly offensive and hotheaded to retaliate in kind. This politeness, we think, has consequences for the ability of organizers to escalate tactics.

Organizers and leaders tend to make light of opponents' resistance to change or their subtle obstruction of an organization's agenda. Despite the target's response, they are likely to use their standard pressure activities, and do not escalate tactics in response. This high-minded approach is not always effective, and organizations are often frustrated in their attempts to influence a particularly resistant target.

The opposition is also often deemphasized with members. A sense of outrage and self-righteousness at being attacked is missing from many progressive social action organizations. This may be unhelpful in encouraging member support. The refusal to fight back is sometimes perceived as a weakness, and organizers may find it difficult to defend their positions to fence-sitters and even supporters who may begin to wonder if the attack was warranted. Opposition and victimization can be employed to engender emotion and a sense of urgency. This area needs more attention by today's organizers.

Connections Among Issues and Building Alliances Organizers state that drawing connections among issues is the best way to articulate a social change agenda that goes beyond the issues around which they organize. Yet across the board organizers have great difficulty making such linkages, drawing the connections between poor housing and crime, between reproductive rights and pay equity, between drugs in a neighborhood and U.S. foreign policy initiatives. There are some attempts to link issues vertically. A local organization works on a comprehensive housing strategy, including help for the area's homeless. Some statewide and national lobbying and mobilizing organizations have built horizontal relationships with other groups working on similar issues. Yet these efforts to create internal and horizontal connections are infrequent.

What is almost entirely absent are attempts to connect local issues with national issues and vice versa. Local organizations are seldom able to articulate national concerns, and national organizations seldom tackle the self-interested concerns of local people. A few efforts are noteworthy. One local organizer created a "neighborhood defense budget" that contrasted defense spending and spending on neighborhood issues such as housing. An organizer working on voter registration speaks of "loaning" an organizer to work with local groups to register voters during referendum issues, maintaining those connections between campaigns and uniting the efforts of all local groups during presidential election years. But these innovations are rare, and our findings confirm Boyte's point:

> Much of citizen activism of recent years, on both local and national levels, has addressed itself to fairly narrow issues. Activists have not often asked what their work "means" in a larger sense, where they are going in the long run, or how their particular efforts might add up to more that the particular or localized campaigns they engage in . . . like conventional politics, much of grass-roots activism has spoken a thin, sometimes cynical language of narrow interests and protest detached from any enlarged social and political vision.
>
> (Boyte 1989:12)

We also see little evidence of alliances among organizations. Most alliances are short-lived, and form around a particular event. There are several possible explanations for the absence of these coalitions. Organizers often do not know other organizers. Since they are seldom trained or educated in organizing, they do not have long-standing relationships that other professionals often develop in school. There is not much cross-fertilization among organizations either. Organizers are unlikely to have worked together, and are unfamiliar with other organizing networks. For the most part, organizers don't know that organizer training institutes exist.

Organizers are also very aware that they compete for members, funding, and media attention. Their discussions about coalitions are permeated by their fear of the loss of organizational visibility and sovereignty. Coalitions compel organizers, who may have different ideas about change, to work together. The rigidity of practice methods may be a deterrent to collaborative work.

Organizers also work with very different constituencies, around different issues, in organizations with different domains, and according to very different practice models. It is probably true that low-income people will continue to use disruptive and directly confrontation tactics on a local level; they have few resources to do otherwise. It is probably also true that middle-class and professional people will continue to prefer national groups and persuasion tactics. Such different interests and means do not easily coalesce.

We view the absence of new ideas about how to link issues and organizations as particularly troubling. The absence of coalitions hampers the ability to work across issues, to develop local constituencies for national campaigns, and to connect local grievances with the national agenda.

Certain measures might spur thinking in these areas. We see a desperate need for an organizers' network—a way for organizers to share what they are doing, what's working, and what difficulties they face. The demise of the journal *Just Economics*, which reported on diverse organizing efforts across the nation, left a significant gap. There needs to be a mechanism to bring together organizers who subscribe to different practice methods. This is no easy task. There are biases among organizers about who knows the "right way" to organize. For an organizing network to happen organizers of all persuasions will have to recognize that they do different things well, and each model has something to offer the others.

There must be attempts to bring middle-class and low-income organizations together around common cause. There is nothing more innately incompatible about this coalition than there is about upper-class businessmen and working-class fundamentalists being part of the Republican party. Local groups can work on local health concerns, while national groups can argue for issues of health care policy. Citywide organizations can target city administrations around issues of pay equity and housing; national groups can target Congress. Organizers can provide the linkage. Already, local organizers benefit by working through churches. These local organizers can coordinate their efforts by working on national concerns in their local areas. We think that organizers working with the middle class could make similar use of liberal middle-class churches and synagogues, which would enhance their ability to work locally on issue of national import. Indeed, religious institutions may become the mechanism by which these constituencies can be structurally linked. Such a broad-scale coalition would go a long way to solving the need of national organizations for "rainbow coalitions," and help local organizers tackle issues of national import that may not have the same degree of urgency for their local members. Some such linkage is necessary if organizers are to work a broad and inclusive social change agenda.

Progressive social action organizations will continue to exist. Our hope is that this book has suggested questions and ideas for organizers and leaders to analyze and debate as they pursue the power needed to realize their agendas for social change.

APPENDIX: STUDY METHODS

This appendix briefly describes the methods used to design and implement the study of social action organizing that underlies the discussion of organizing in this book.

The aims of the study were to secure very detailed respondent-generated descriptions of community organizing activities and behaviors, to make comparisons across organizations, and to ascertain the "closeness of fit" between these depictions and the models of organizing found in organizing literature. Our study questions encompassed the broad dimensions of organizing framed by organizer attributes (i.e., values, knowledge, interaction skills); and areas of concern in the organizing process—issues, strategy and tactics, targets, victory, member recruitment and maintenance, and organizational development and maintenance.

Limited by financial resources, we selected a study region stretching from Boston to Washington, D.C., a region that includes many varied national, regional, statewide, metropolitan, urban, and local organizing groups. We drew on a variety of printed and personal resources to list over two hundred potential groups. We realized we could not generate a representative sample of groups to study because of indefinite use of the identifying term "organizing," because some groups hide their organizing identity to protect conservative funding; because some groups come into existence and then disappear rather quickly: and because some organizations do organizing work only intermittently.

Study results, therefore, could not be generalized, and the study emphasis was placed on necessarily qualitative understandings of organizing.

To ensure that we approached only organizations actively involved in organizing, we used screening criteria: 1. the organization was in existence for two years or more; 2. had a full-time paid organizer on staff; and 3. had a formal, identifiable membership. Of the number of groups that met all criteria we purposively selected for the study a set of forty-two organizations to represent the geographic diversity of the region, and to represent the diversity of issues around which social action groups organize. Using vignettes, we asked each organizer to identify the organizing approach that most approximated their organization. Fifteen of these groups associated their work with a grassroots model, fourteen with a lobbying model, and thirteen with a mobilizing model.

To reinforce our ability to compare the organizing work done in these organizations we took a number of steps:

1. Based on our set of study questions, we used published studies of organizing, texts, and conversations with organizers to develop lists of variables and how those variables connect with other content. From these variables we evolved specific questions to ask our respondents.

2. The design and substantive concerns of the study required two respondents from each organization—one to be a key informant for the staff perspective, the other a key informant for the member member (non-salaried) perspective. The staff person with the primary responsibility for organizing was selected as the staff informant in all cases. Some of them were called "lead organizer," some "executive director," others "community program director." Our criteria required they spend at least half their time doing organizing work and supervising other organizers (or members) engaged in organizing campaigns, and have been on the job at least a year (long enough to have established themselves).

3. Member respondents were identified by organizers to meet criteria of long-term membership, holding a position of authority within the organization, close involvement with the organizing work, and knowledgeable about different member perspectives. This approach ensured us of getting the views in depth of a well-positioned and well-informed member actor for each group.

4. Our data collection procedures were also designed to both

use systematic procedures across sites and capture the individuality of each site from cooperative respondents.

- A 45-item Pre-Visit Questionnaire was completed by all the organizers, securing parallel information on organizational goals, structure, staffing, activities, roles and responsibilities, funding sources, and membership for each organization.
- A 186-item Organizer Interview Schedule requiring over two hours to complete, was designed to probe all study questions in a similar manner with all respondents.
- A 92-item Member Interview Schedule designed like its organizer-oriented counterpart, taking over an hour to complete, was also designed. All but two items were identical to the other interview schedule to allow comparisons between organizers and members.

An important element in any field research is engaging respondent interest. We emphasized the respondents' expertise and our role as learners, kept to a conversational approach that minimized the formal question-and-answer format, began an area of discussion with open-ended questions and then followed with probes for details and explanations.

5. Through pretesting instruments we discovered the major problem in responses to many of the questions was one of indeterminacy: respondents answered "it depends" and went no further with an explanation. To counter this virtual non-response where we found it most likely to occur we developed fifty-five paired questions. The initial questions were the original open-ended questions. The second question of the pair involved a forced-choice response to a listing of possible options or factors suggested by the literature and our own experience. If the initial response was indeterminate, respondents were handed a card and asked to react to each of the items as applicable to their work or not, to explain the applicability, and to suggest other content not listed. These cards stimulated more substantive and concrete responses than would otherwise have occurred. Conversational flow was interrupted, and interviewer bias was potentially injected through card content, but the substantive value of the approach was judged worth the risk.

The eighty-four interviews were tape recorded, transcribed verbatim, and given minor editing. These transcriptions were the raw data of the study.

Nearly one quarter of the study's variables were quantitative, and coded at nominal or ordinal levels. A second set of 101 variables was scored using "anchoring illustrations" developed for subjective coding of data. Both researchers had to agree on the scoring of a response using the predefined illustrations in order for it to be coded. We attained categorical scales for 171 variables, and ordinal scales for 29 variables. Descriptive analysis of individual variables was followed by cross-tabulations of major study variables by all other variables, looking for patterns in the data to suggest focuses for further qualitative investigation.

We looked to qualitative content to explain why an observed relationship between variables might exist. Multiple steps were used to organize qualitative content for content analysis and interpretation. A logging sheet for each variable was created to cluster all content on that variable in one place to facilitate thematic analysis. We identified themes or points made and merged them into smaller numbers of themes that captured the range of concerns or issues, using respondents' words throughout. These were the terms through which we discuss the content, along with direct quotations on critical points. These analyses were analyzed for what themes were present and how they were presented, what was not being addressed, the most frequent or fervently stated themes, and connections that respondents made between two or more themes. We developed our conclusions about a segment of content with these substantive elements as guides.

The discussion of organizing throughout the book is grounded in the data and interpretations from our study of forty-two social action organizations, even though the results of the study are not a direct and obvious part of the discussion.

REFERENCES

Alinsky, S. 1949. *John L. Lewis: An Unauthorized Biography.* New York: Vintage.
—— 1971. *Rules for Radicals.* New York: Vintage.
—— 1974. *Reveille for Radicals.* New York: Vintage.
Aronovitz, S. 1964. "Poverty, Politics, and Community Organization." *Studies On the Left*, 4(3):102–105.
Bachrach, P. and M. Baratz. 1970. *Power and Poverty: Theory and Practice.* New York: Oxford University Press.
Bailey, K. 1978. *Methods of Social Research.* New York: Free Press.
Bailey, R. 1972. *Radicals in Urban Politics: The Alinsky Approach.* Chicago: University of Chicago Press.
Banfield, E. 1961. *Political Influence.* New York: Free Press.
Bellah, R., R. Madsen, W. Sullivan, A. Swidler, and S. Tipton. 1985. *Habits of the Heart: Individualism and Commitment in American Life.* New York: Harper and Row.
—— 1991. *The Good Society.* New York: Knopf.
Benedek, V., R. Nolan, and T. Thorson. 1980. *CRA: Ten Fights for Reinvestment.* Chicago: National Training and Information Center.
Berelson, B. and G. Steiner. 1964. *Human Behavior: An Inventory of Scientific Findings.* New York: Harcourt, Brace and World.
Berry, J. 1977. *Lobbying for the People: The Political Behavior of Public Interest Groups.* Princeton: Princeton University Press.
Betten, N. and M. Austin. 1990. *The Roots of Community Organizing: 1917–1939.* Philadelphia: Temple University Press.
Biklen, D. 1983. *Community Organizing: Theory and Practice.* Englewood Cliffs, N.J.: Prentice-Hall.
Boggs, C. 1986. *Social Movements and Political Power.* Philadelphia: Temple University Press.

Boyte, H. 1980. *The Backyard Revolution*. Philadelphia: Temple University Press.

—— 1989. *CommonWealth*. Chicago: Free Press.

Boyte, H., H. Booth, and S. Max. 1986. *Citizen Action and the New American Populism*. Philadelphia: Temple University Press.

Boyte, H. and F. Riessman, eds. 1986. *The New Populism: The Politics of Empowerment*. Philadelphia: Temple University Press.

Brager, G. 1963. "Organizing the Unaffiliated in a Low-Income Area." *Social Work*, 8(2):34–40.

Brager, G. and S. Holloway. 1978. *Changing Human Service Organizations: Politics and Practice*. New York: Free Press.

Brager, G. and H. Specht. 1969. "Mobilizing the Poor for Social Action." In R. M. Kramer and H. Specht, eds., *Readings in Community Organization Practice*, pp. 163–173. Englewood Cliffs, N.J.: Prentice-Hall.

—— 1973. *Community Organizing*. New York: Columbia University Press.

Branch, T. 1988. *Parting the Waters: America in the King Years, 1954–1963*. New York: Simon and Schuster.

Burghardt, S. 1982a. *The Other Side of Organizing*. Cambridge, Mass.: Schenkman.

—— 1982b. *Organizing for Community Action*. Beverly Hills: Sage.

—— 1984. "The Strategic Crisis of Grass Roots Organizing." *Against the Current*, 3(1):31–36.

Burstein, P. and W. Freudenburg. 1978. "Changing Public Policy: The Impact of Public Opinion, Antiwar Demonstrations, and War Costs on Senate Voting on Vietnam War Motions." *American Journal of Sociology*, 84(1):99–122.

Carden, M. 1989. "The Institutionalization of Social Movements in Voluntary Organizations." *Research in Social Movements, Conflicts, and Change*, 11:143–161.

Center for Community Organizing. 1989. *Introduction to Organizing*. New York: Community Service Society.

Collette, W. 1984. "Research for Organizing." In L. Staples, ed., *Roots to Power: A Manual for Grassroots Organizing*, pp. 142–151. New York: Praeger.

Cook, T. and D. Campbell. 1979. *Quasi Experimentation: Design and Analysis Issues for Field Settings*. Chicago: Rand, McNally.

Cox, F., J. Erlich, J. Rothman, and J. Tropman, eds. 1970. *Strategies of Community Organization*. 1st ed. Itasca, Ill.: F. E. Peacock.

—— 1977. *Tactics and Techniques of Community Practice*. Itasca, Ill.: F. E. Peacock.

Crenson, M. 1971. *The Un-Politics of Air Pollution: A Study of Non-Decisionmaking in the Cities*. Baltimore: John Hopkins University Press.

Cronbach, L. 1975. "Beyond the Two Disciplines of Scientific Psychology." *American Psychologist*, 30:116–127.

Dahl, R. 1961. *Who Governs?* New Haven: Yale University Press.

Dahrendorf, R. 1959. *Class and Class Conflict in Industrial Society*. Stanford: Stanford University Press.

Dear, R. and R. Patti. 1984. "Legislative Advocacy: Seven Effective Tactics." In F. Cox, J. Erlich, J. Rothman, and J. Tropman, eds., *Tactics and Techniques of Community Practice*, 2d ed., pp. 185–197. Itasca, Ill.: F. E. Peacock.

Delgado, G. 1986. *Organizing the Movement*. Philadelphia: Temple University Press.

De Tocqueville, A. 1969. *Democracy in America*. Trans. George Laurence. New York: Doubleday Anchor.

Douglas, R. 1984. "How to Use and Present Community Data. In F. Cox, J. Erlich, J. Rothman, and J. Tropman, eds., *Tactics and Techniques of Community Practice*, 2d ed., pp. 383–395. Itasca, Ill.: F. E. Peacock.

Dubos, R. 1981. *Celebrations of Life*. New York: McGraw Hill.

Duggan, T. and C. Dean. 1968. "Common Misinterpretations of Significance Levels in Sociological Journals." *American Sociologist*, 3:45–46.

Eaton, S. and K. Scharff. 1979. "Organizing at the Grass Roots." *Dissent*, 26(4):411–413.

Ecklein, J. 1984. *Community Organizers*. New York: Wiley.

Effrat, M. 1974. "Approaches to Community: Conflict and Complementaries." In M. Effrat, ed., *The Community: Approaches and Applications*, pp. 1–32. London: Collier Macmillan.

Etzioni, A. 1961. *A Comparative Analysis of Complex Organizations: On Power, Involvement, and Their Correlates*. New York: Free Press.

—— 1964. *Modern Organizations*. Englewood Cliffs, N.J.: Prentice-Hall.

—— 1969. *Complex Organizations*. New York: Holt, Rinehart, and Winston.

Evans, S. and H. Boyte. 1986. *Free Spaces: The Sources of Democratic Change in America*. New York: Harper and Row.

Fessler, D. 1969. "The Group Process Approach to Community Organizing." In R. Kramer and H. Specht, eds., *Readings in Community Organization Practice*, pp. 251–256. Englewood Cliffs, N.J.: Prentice-Hall.

Finch, S., D. Fanshel, and J. Grundy. 1986. "Factors Associated with the Discharge of Children from Foster Care." *Social Work Research and Abstracts*, 22(1):10–18.

Fink, P. 1984. *The Radical Vision of Saul Alinsky*. New York: Paulist.

Fisher, R. 1984. *Let the People Decide: A History of Neighborhood Organizing in America*. Boston: Hall.

Fisher, R. and J. Kling. 1990. "Leading the People: Two Approaches to the Role of Ideology in Community Organizing." In J. Kling and P. Posner, eds., *Dilemmas of Activism: Class, Community, and the Politics of Local Mobilization*, pp. 71–90. Philadelphia: Temple University Press.

Freeman, J. 1975. *The Politics of Women's Liberation*. New York: David McKay.

Freeman, J., ed. 1983. *Social Movements of the Sixties and Seventies*. New York: Longman.

Freire, P. 1968. *Pedagogy for the Oppressed*. New York: Herder and Herder.

—— 1973. *Education for a Critical Consciousness*. New York: Seabury Press.

French, J. and B. Raven. 1960. "The Bases of Social Power." In D. Cartwright and A. Zander, eds., *Group Dynamics*, pp. 607–623. Evanston: Row and Peterson.

Freudenburg, W. and R. Baxter. 1985. "Nuclear Reactions: Public Attitudes and Policies Toward Nuclear Power." *Policy Studies Review*. 5(1):96–110.

Gaventa, J. 1980. *Power and Powerlessness*. Urbana: University of Illinois Press.

Garrow, D. 1986. *Bearing the Cross: Martin Luther King, Jr., and the Southern Christian Leadership Conference*. New York: William Morrow.

Gerlach, L. and V. Hine. 1970. *People, Power, and Change.* New York: Bobbs-Merrill.

Germain, C. and A. Gitterman. 1980. *The Life Model of Social Work Practice.* New York: Columbia University Press.

Gerth, H. and C. Mills. 1946. *From Max Weber: Essays in Sociology.* New York: Oxford University Press.

Glaser, B. and A. Strauss. 1967. *The Discovery of Grounded Theory.* Chicago: Aldine.

Glick, B. 1987. *War at Home: Covert Actions Against U.S. Activists.* Boston: South End.

Goodwyn, L. 1978. *The Populist Moment.* New York: Oxford University Press.

Gramsci, A. 1971. *Selections from the Prison Notebooks.* Trans. Q. W. Hoare and G. N. Smith. London: Lawrence and Wishart.

Grosser, C. 1976. *New Directions in Community Organization: From Enabling to Advocacy.* New York: Praeger.

Grosser, C. and J. Mondros. 1985. "Pluralism and Participation: The Political Action Approach." In S. Taylor and R. Roberts, eds., *Theory and Practice of Community Social Work,* pp. 154–178. New York: Columbia University Press.

Gurr, T. 1970. *Why Men Rebel.* Princeton: Princeton University Press.

Haggstrom, W. 1969. "Can the Poor Transform the World?" In R. Kramer and H. Specht, eds., *Readings in Community Organization Practice,* pp. 301–314. Englewood Cliffs, N.J.: Prentice-Hall.

—— 1970. "The Psychological Implications of the Community Development Process." In L. Cary, ed., *Community Development as a Process,* pp. 84–112. New York: Columbia University Press.

—— 1984. "For a Democratic Revolution: The Grass-roots Perspective." In F. Cox, J. Erlich, J. Rothman, and J. Tropman, eds., *Tactics and Techniques of Community Practice,* pp. 222–231. Itasca, IL: F. E. Peacock.

Haley, J. 1969. *The Power Tactics of Jesus Christ.* New York: Grossman.

Hartmann, P. 1977. "A Perspective on the Study of Social Attitudes." *Eurpoean Journal of Social Psychology,* 7(1):85–96.

Hearn, G. 1958. *Theory Building in Social Work.* Toronto: University of Toronto Press.

Heifetz, R. and R. Sinder. 1988. "Political Leadership: Managing the Public's Problem Solving." In R. Reich, ed., *The Power of Public Ideas,* pp. 179–203. Cambridge, Mass: Ballinger.

Henderson, P. and D. Thomas. 1980a. *Readings in Community Work.* London: Allen and Unwin.

—— 1980b. *Skills in Neighborhood Work.* London: Allen and Unwin.

Hertz, S. 1981. *The Welfare Mothers Movement: A Decade of Change for Poor Women.* Washington, D.C.: University Press of America.

Holloway, S. and G. Brager. 1989. *Supervising in the Human Services: The Politics of Practice.* New York: Free Press.

Holsti, O. 1969. *Content analysis for the Social Sciences and Humanities.* Reading, Mass.: Addison-Wesley.

Horwitt, S. 1989. *Let Them Call Me Rebel.* New York: Knopf.

House, R. and T. Mitchell. 1976. "Path Goal Theory of Leadership." In G. L. Gibson, J. M. Ivancevich, and J. H. Donnelly, Jr., eds., *Readings in Organizations*, pp. 147–160. Dallas: Business Publications.

Ihilevich, D., G. Gleser, G. Gritter, L. Kroman, and A. Watson. 1981. "Measuring Program Outcome: The Progress Evaluation Scales." *Evaluation Review*, 5(4):451–477.

Joravsky, B. 1990. "Alinsky's Legacy. In P. Knoepfle, ed., *After Alinsky: Community Organizing in Illinois*, pp. 1–10. Springfield: Illinois Issues.

Kahn, S. 1970. *How People Get Power: Organizing Oppressed Communities for Action.* New York: McGraw Hill.

—— 1992. *Organizing: A Guide for Grassroots Leaders.* 2d ed. New York: McGraw Hill.

Kaplan, M. 1986. "Cooperation and Coalition Development Among Neighborhood Organizations: A Case Study." *Journal of Voluntary Action Research*, 15(4):23–34.

Karger, H. and M. Reitmeir. 1983. "Community Organization for the 1980s: Toward Developing a New Skills Base with a Political Framework." *Social Development Issues*, 7(2):50–62.

Kerbo, H. 1982. "Movements of Crisis and Movements of Affluence: A Critique of Deprivation and Resource Mobilization Theories." *Journal of Conflict Resolution*, 26(4):645–663.

Key, M., P. Hudson, and J. Armstrong. 1976. *Evaluation Theory and Community Work.* London: Young Volunteer Force Foundation.

Kiresuk, T. and R. Sherman. 1968. "Goal Attainment Scaling: A General Method for Evaluating Comprehensive Mental Health Programs." *Community Mental Health Journal*, 4:443–453.

Klandermans, B. 1986. "New Social Movements and Resource Mobilization: The European and the American Approach." *Journal of Mass Emergencies and Disasters*, 4:13–37.

Knoke, D. and J. Wood. 1981. *Organized for Action: Commitment in Voluntary Associations.* New Brunswick, N.J.: Rutgers University Press.

Knoepfle, P., ed. 1990. *After Alinsky: Community Organizing in Illinois.* Springfield: Illinois Issues.

Krippendorff, K. 1980. *Content Analysis: An Introduction to Its Methodology.* Beverly Hills: Sage.

Lane, R. 1939. "The Field of Community Organization." In H. R. Knight, ed., *Proceedings of the National Conference of Social Work*, vol. 66. New York: Columbia University Press.

Levy, C. 1973. "The Value Base of Social Work." *Journal of Education for Social Work*, 9:34–42.

Lewis, H. 1982. *The Intellectual Base of Social Work Practice.* New York: Haworth Press.

Liebman, R. 1983. "Mobilizing the Moral Majority." In R. Liebman and R. Wuthnow, eds., *The New Christian Right*, pp. 49–73. New York: Aldine.

Lindeman, E. 1921. *The Community.* New York: Association Press.

Lippit, R., J. Watson, and B. Wesley. 1958. *The Dynamics of Planned Change.* New York: Harcourt, Brace and World.

Lippman, W. 1937. *An Inquiry Into the Principles of the Good Society.* Boston: Little, Brown.

Lofland, J. and L. Lofland. 1984. *Analyzing Social Settings*. Belmont, Cal.: Wadsworth.

McAdam, D., J. McCarthy, and M. Zald. 1988. "Social Movements." In N. Smelser, ed., *Handbook of Sociology*, pp. 695–737. Beverly Hills: Sage.

McCarthy, J. and M. Zald. 1977. "Resource Mobilization and Social Movements." *American Journal of Sociology*, 82(6):1212–1241.

McLuhan, M. 1964. *Understanding Media: The Extensions of Man*. New York: McGraw Hill.

Maluccio, A. and W. Marlow. 1984. "The Case for the Contract." In B. Compton and B. Galaway, eds., *Social Work Processes*, 3d ed., pp. 407–414. Homewood, Ill.: Dorsey.

Mansbridge, J. 1986. *Why We Lost the ERA*. Chicago: University of Chicago Press.

Marable, M. 1986. "Black History and the Vision of Democracy." In H. Boyte and F. Riessman, eds., *The New Populism: The Politics of Empowerment*, pp. 198–206. Philadelphia: Temple University Press.

Marris, P. and M. Rein. 1967. *Dilemmas of Social Reform*. New York: Atherton.

Maslow, A. 1970. *Motivation and Personality*. New York: Harper and Row.

Melucci, A. 1980. "The New Social Movements: A Theoretical Approach." *Social Science Information*, 19:199–226.

Michels, R. 1966. *Political Parties: A Sociological Study of the Oligarchical Tendencies of Modern Democracy*. New York: Free Press.

Miles, M. 1983. "Qualitative Data as an Attractive Nuisance: The Problem of Analysis." In J. Van Maanen, ed., *Qualitative Methodology*, pp. 117–134. Beverly Hills: Sage.

Miles, M. and A. Huberman. 1984. *Qualitative Data Analysis*. Beverly Hills: Sage.

Millikan, M. 1959. "Inquiry and Policy: The Relation of Knowledge to Action." In D. Lerner, ed., *The Human Meaning of the Social Sciences*, pp. 158–180. New York: Meridan Books.

Mills, C. 1959. *The Sociological Imagination*. New York: Oxford Press.

—— 1963. *Power, Politics, and People: The Collected Essays of C. Wright Mills*. New York: Oxford University Press.

Mondros, J. In press. "Thoughts on Power as a Theoretical Construct in Community Organization Practice." *Administration in Social Work*.

Mondros, J. and T. Berman-Rossi. 1991. "The Relevance of Stages of Group Development Theory to Community Organization Practice." *Social Work with Groups*, 14(3/4):203–221.

Mondros, J. and N. McGuffin. 1992. "Yonkers: A New Tale of Two Cities." In C. LeCroy, ed., *Case Studies in Social Work Practice*, pp. 161–169. Belmont, Cal.: Wadsworth.

Mondros, J. and S. Wilson. 1982. "Program Assessment Strategies for Community Organization." *Social Development Issues*, 6(3):25–39.

—— 1986. "Recruitment and Involvement of Community Leaders: What's Happening Out There Now?" *Journal of Sociology and Social Work*, 13(3):507–521.

Mosca, G. 1939. *The Ruling Class*. New York: McGraw Hill.

Mott, A. 1986. "The Decades Ahead for Community Organizations." *Social Policy*, 16(4):11–16.

Myrdal, G. 1944. *An American Dilemma: The Negro Problem and Modern Democracy.* New York: Harper.

O'Brien, D. 1975. *Neighborhood Organization and Interest-group Processes.* Princeton: Princeton University Press.

Olsen, M. 1965. *The Logic of Collective Action: Public Goods and the Theory of Groups.* Cambridge: Harvard University Press.

O'Neill, T., with W. Novak. 1987. *Man of the House: The Life and Political Memoirs of Speaker Tip O'Neill.* New York: Random House.

"Open or Closed Cities?" 1961. *Christian Century,* May, pp. 685–688.

Ornstein, N. and S. Elder. 1978. *Interest Groups, Lobbying, and Policymaking.* Washington, D.C.: Congressional Quarterly Press.

Padgug, R. and G. Oppenheimer. 1992. "Riding the Tiger: AIDS and the Gay Community." In E. Fee and D. M. Fox, eds., *AIDS: The Making of a Chronic Disease,* pp. 229–278. Berkeley: University of California Press.

Panzetta, A. 1975. "The Concept of Community: The Short Circuit of the Mental Health Movement." In R. Kramer and H. Specht, eds., *Readings in Community Organization Practice,* pp. 28–38. Engelwood Cliffs, N.J.: Prentice-Hall.

Patton, M. 1978. *Utilization-focused Evaluation.* Beverly Hills: Sage.

Piven, F. and R. Cloward. 1974. *Politics of Turmoil: Essays on Class, Race, and the Urban Crisis.* New York: Pantheon.

—— 1977. *Poor People's Movements.* New York: Pantheon.

Pressman, J. and A. Wildavsky. 1984. *Implementation.* Los Angeles: University of California Press.

Pray, K. 1948. "When Is Community Organization Social Work Practice?" In *Proceedings of the National Conference of Social Work,* pp. 194–204. New York: Columbia University Press.

Ross, D. 1973. *A Public Citizen's Action Manual.* New York: Grossman.

Ross, M. 1967. *Community Organizing.* New York: Harper and Row.

Rossi, P. 1969. "Theory, Research, and Practice in Community Organization." In R. Kramer and H. Specht, eds., *Readings in Community Organization Practice,* pp. 49–61. Englewood Cliffs, N.J.: Prentice-Hall.

Rothman, J. 1969. "An Analysis of Goals and Roles in Community Organizing Practice." In R. Kramer and H. Specht, eds., *Readings in Community Organization Practice,* pp. 260–268. Englewood Cliffs, N.J.: Prentice-Hall.

—— 1970. "Three Models of Community Organizing Practice." In F. Cox, J. Erlich, and J. Tropman, eds., *Strategies of Community Organization,* pp. 17–36. Itasca, Ill.: F. E. Peacock.

Rothman, J., J. Erlich, and J. Teresa. 1977. "Adding Something New: Innovation." In F. Cox, J. Erlich, J. Rothman, and J. Tropman, eds., *Tactics and Techniques of Community Practice,* pp. 157–165. Itasca, Ill.: F. E. Peacock.

Rothman, J. and J. Tropman. 1969. "An Analysis of Goals and Roles in Community Organization Practice." In R. Kramer and H. Specht, eds., *Readings in Community Organization Practice,* pp. 260–268. Englewood Cliffs, N.J.: Prentice-Hall.

—— 1979. "Three Models of Community Organizations: Their Mixing and Phasing." In F. Cox, J. Erlich, J. Rothman, J. Tropman, eds., *Strategies of Community Organization,* 3d ed., pp. 25–45. Itasca, Ill.: F. E. Peacock.

Rubin, H. and I. Rubin. 1986. *Community Organization and Development.* New York: Macmillan.

Rude, G. 1980. *Ideology and Popular Protest.* New York: Pantheon.

Rule, J. 1988. *Theories of Civil Violence.* Berkeley: University of California Press.

Sale, K. 1974. *SDS.* New York: Vintage.

Saunders, M. 1970. *The Professional Radical: Conversations with Saul Alinsky.* New York: Harper and Row.

Schattschneider, E. 1960. *The Semisovereign People: A Realist's View of Democracy in America.* New York: Holt, Rinehart and Winston.

Schurman, F. 1966. *Ideology and Organization in Communist China.* Berkeley: University of California Press.

Schwartz, W. 1961. "The Social Worker in the Group." *The Social Welfare Forum.* New York: Columbia University Press.

—— 1962. "Toward a Strategy of Group Work Practice." *Social Service Review,* 36(3):268–279.

—— 1969. "Private Troubles and Public Issues: One Job or Two?" *The Social Welfare Forum,* pp. 22–43. New York: Columbia University Press.

Scott, D. and T. Mitchell. 1976. *Organization Theory: A Structural and Behavior Analysis.* Homewood, Ill.: Irwin.

Seabury, B. 1976. "The Contract: Uses, Abuses, and Limitations." *Social Work,* 21:16–21.

Shaffer, A. 1973. "Community Organization and the Oppressed." In J. Goodman, ed., *Dynamics of Racism in Social Work Practice,* pp. 233–246. New York: National Association of Social Workers.

Shilts, R. 1987. *And the Band Played On: Politics, People, and the AIDS Epidemic.* New York: St. Martin's.

Shulman, L. 1991. *Interactional Social Work Practice: Toward an Empirical Theory.* Itasca, Ill.: F. E. Peacock.

Sidel, V. and R. Sidel. 1976. "Beyond Coping." *Social Policy,* 7(2):67–69.

Sieber, S. 1973. "The Integration of Field Work and Survey Methods." *American Journal of Sociology,* 78:1335–1359.

Sieder, V. 1956. "What is Community Organization Practice?" *The Social Welfare Forum, Proceedings, National Conference of Social Work, St. Louis, 1956.* New York: Columbia University Press.

Silberman, C. 1964. *Crisis in Black and White.* New York: Vintage.

Slayton, R. 1986. *Back of the Yards: The Making of a Local Democracy.* Chicago: University of Chicago Press.

Smelser, N. 1969. *Theories of Collective Behavior.* New York: Free Press.

Smith, V. 1979. "How Interest Groups Influence Legislators." *Social Work,* 24(3):234–239.

Snow, D., E. Rockford, Jr., S. Worden, and R. Benford. 1986. "Frame Alignment Processes, Micro-mobilization and Movement Participation." *American Sociological Review,* 51:464–481.

Spiegel, H. and S. Mittenthal. 1968. *Neighborhood Power and Control: Implications for Urban Planning.* New York: Columbia University Press.

Staples, L., ed. 1984. *Roots to Power: A Manual for Grassroots Organizing.* New York: Praeger.

Susser, I. 1982. *Norman Street: Poverty and Politics in an Urban Environment.* New York: Oxford University Press.

Taylor, W. 1986. "Litigation as an Empowering Tool. *Social Policy,* 16(4):31–36.

Tilly, C. 1974. "Do Communities Act? In M. Effrat, ed., *The Community: Approaches and Applications*, pp. 209–240. New York: Macmillan.

Trapp, S. 1979. *Who, Me a Researcher? Yes You*. Chicago: National Training and Information Center.

Tropman, J. 1985. "Societal Values and Social Policy: Implications for Social Work." In G. Martin and M. Zald, eds., *Social Welfare in Society*, pp. 27–46. Englewood Cliffs, N.J.: Prentice-Hall.

Tropman, J. and J. Erlich. 1974. "Introduction." In R. Cox, J. Erlich, J. Rothman, and J. Tropman, eds., *Strategies of Community Organization*, 2d ed., pp. 161–173. Itasca, Ill.: F. E. Peacock.

Twelvetrees, A. 1982. *Community Work*. London: Macmillan.

Van Maanen, J. 1983. "The Fact of Fiction in Organizational Ethnography." In J. Van Maanen, ed., *Qualitative Methodology*, pp. 37–55. Beverly Hills: Sage.

Von Hoffman, N. 1966. "Hard Talk on Organizing the Ghetto." *Renewal* (February), pp. 13–17.

—— 1962. "Reorganization in the Casbah." *Social Progress*, 52(6):33–44.

Vroom, V. 1964. *Work and Motivation*. New York: Wiley.

Walsh, E. 1981. "Resource Mobilization and Citizen Protest in Communities Around Three Mile Island." *Social Problems*, 29:1–21.

Walton, R. 1969. "Two Strategies of Social Change and Their Dilemmas." In R. Kramer and H. Specht, eds., *Readings in Community Organization Practice*, pp. 337–345. Englewood Cliffs, N.J.: Prentice-Hall.

Warren, R. 1969. "A Community Model." In R. Kramer and H. Specht, eds., *Readings in Community Organization Practice*, pp. 40–48. Englewood Cliffs, N.J.: Prentice-Hall.

—— 1977. *Social Change and Human Purposes: Toward Understanding and Action*. Chicago: Rand McNally.

Weisner, S. 1983. "Fighting Back: A Critical Analysis of Coalition Building in the Human Services." *Social Service Review*, 57:295–305.

Wellstone, P. 1978. *How the Rural Poor Got Power*. Amherst: University of Massachusetts Press.

Wenocur, S. and M. Reisch. 1986. "The Future of Community Organization in Social Work: Social Activism and the Politics of Profession Building." *Social Service Review*, 60(1):70–93.

Wilson, J. 1973. *Political Organizations*. New York: Basic Books.

Wilson, K. and A. Orum. 1976. "Mobilizing People for Collective Political Action." *Journal of Political and Military Sociology*, 4:187–202.

Wilson, S. and J. Mondros. 1985. "Organizational Assessment in Power-Transfer Community Organizations." *Social Development Issues*, 9(3):100–107.

Wrong, D. 1980. *Power: Its Forms, Bases, and Uses*. New York: Harper and Row.

Zurcher, L. 1972. "Stages of Development of Neighobrhood Action Groups: The Topeka Example." In H. Spergel, ed., *Community Organization: Studies in Constraint*, pp. 123–147. Beverly Hills: Sage.

INDEX